AF713592

"The joys of reading this volume can only be matched by the personal enthusiasm of its editors: straight out of an extraordinarily imaginative series of film-projection-and-discussion events at Sciences Po and McGill University 'Eating Popcorn Like a Lawyer' (to which I have had the privilege of being invited), this book continues with the same personal freshness, ludic inventiveness, and rigorous analysis of the intersection between juridical thought and moving image. The result is nothing less than astonishing: a panorama of spectacular reconfigurations of what both law and cinema are through a fine balance of personal autoethnographic details, film theory, philosophy, aesthetics, critical legal, and critical socio-legal theory. This is an astutely curated collection, with early career as well as established interdisciplinary thinkers, that pushes the limits of law, image, senses, perceptions, and affects. What unites all chapters is a strong sense of responsibility to open up the law to the revitalising power of films. An extremely fresh and valuable addition to the law and film literature."

Professor Andreas Philippopoulos-Mihalopoulos,
Legal Theorist/Artist/Fiction Author,
University of Westminster, London, UK

Law and Film

This book explores how law can be understood through film by engaging creatively with the intellectual and aesthetic dimensions of both fields.

The contributors to this book consider the need to turn to film and what this means for how we come to understand law and its absences. The chapters explore a variety of narratives, aesthetics, cinematic epistemologies, and legal phenomena, from assessing law in social debates to film as legal critique, from notions of justice to contemplations on evil, and from masculine vigilantism to radical feminism. Taken together, they constitute an inspiring body of work that embodies an urgency for diverse and subversive ways to challenge law's formalism and authority and to think about and respond variously to law's impotence, its disappointment, or its boredom.

This book will appeal to legal scholars and students in law and the humanities, especially those with interests in aesthetics, law and literature, law and culture, law and society, and critical legal theory.

Vittoria Becci is a postdoctoral fellow at the Law Faculty at the European University Institute in Florence, Italy.

Alexia Katsiginis is a doctoral candidate at the Sciences Po Law School in Paris, France.

Edward van Daalen is a socio-legal researcher and postdoctoral fellow at the Labour Law and Development Research Laboratory (LLDRL) at McGill University, Canada.

Discourses of Law
Series editors
Peter Goodrich
Benjamin N. Cardozo School of Law, USA
Michel Rosenfeld
Benjamin N. Cardozo School of Law, USA
Daniela Gandorfer
University of Westminster Law School, UK

The publisher gratefully acknowledges the support of the Jacob Burns Institute for Advanced Legal Studies of the Benjamin N. Cardozo School of Law to the series *Discourses of Law*.

A GlassHouse Book

For information about the series and details of previous and forthcoming titles, see www.routledge.com/Discourses-of-Law/book-series/SE1036.

Law and Film

Critical Reflections on a Field in Motion

Edited by Vittoria Becci,
Alexia Katsiginis and
Edward van Daalen

Routledge
Taylor & Francis Group
a GlassHouse Book

First published 2025
by Routledge
4 Park Square, Milton Park, Abingdon, Oxon OX14 4RN

and by Routledge
605 Third Avenue, New York, NY 10158

Routledge is an imprint of the Taylor & Francis Group, an informa business

A GlassHouse book

© 2025 selection and editorial matter, Vittoria Becci, Alexia Katsiginis and Edward van Daalen; individual chapters, the contributors

The right of Vittoria Becci, Alexia Katsiginis and Edward van Daalen to be identified as the authors of the editorial material, and of the authors for their individual chapters, has been asserted in accordance with sections 77 and 78 of the Copyright, Designs and Patents Act 1988.

All rights reserved. No part of this book may be reprinted or reproduced or utilised in any form or by any electronic, mechanical, or other means, now known or hereafter invented, including photocopying and recording, or in any information storage or retrieval system, without permission in writing from the publishers.

Trademark notice: Product or corporate names may be trademarks or registered trademarks, and are used only for identification and explanation without intent to infringe.

British Library Cataloguing-in-Publication Data
A catalogue record for this book is available from the British Library

Library of Congress Cataloging-in-Publication Data
Names: Becci, Vittoria, editor. | Katsiginis, Alexia, editor. | Daalen, Edward van, editor.
Title: Law and film : critical reflections on a field in motion / edited by Vittoria Becci, Alexia Katsiginis, and Edward van Daalen.
Description: Abingdon, Oxon [UK] ; New York, NY : Routledge, 2025. | Series: Discourses of law | Includes bibliographical references and index.
Identifiers: LCCN 2024040602 (print) | LCCN 2024040603 (ebook)
Subjects: LCSH: Law in motion pictures. | Culture and law.
Classification: LCC K3786 .L35 2025 (print) | LCC K3786 (ebook) | DDC 791.43/6554—dc23/eng/20240905
LC record available at https://lccn.loc.gov/2024040602
LC ebook record available at https://lccn.loc.gov/2024040603

ISBN: 978-1-032-60937-9 (hbk)
ISBN: 978-1-032-60941-6 (pbk)
ISBN: 978-1-003-46118-0 (ebk)

DOI: 10.4324/9781003461180

Typeset in Sabon
by Apex CoVantage, LLC

Contents

Contributors

Elie Aslanoff is a doctoral student at the Sciences Po Law School, France. He is writing his thesis on the socialist origins of economic law.

Vittoria Becci is a postdoctoral fellow at the European University Institute in Florence. Her research interests revolve around the relationship between law, urban spaces, national and international boarders, and property law. She is passionate as well in law and humanities.

Séverine Dusollier is a professor of law at the Sciences Po Law School, France. She specialises in intellectual property, cyber law, and property law.

Günter Frankenberg is professor of public law, the philosophy of law, and comparative law at the Goethe University in Frankfurt/Main, Germany.

Helena Alviar García is a Colombian legal scholar and currently a full professor at Sciences Po Law School, Paris. She is an expert on feminist approaches to law, the relationship between law and development, and law and literature.

Louis Hill is a doctoral student at Sciences Po Law School, France. In his thesis, he studies the evolutionary school of jurisprudence and the original connections it makes between legal adaptation and political self-determination.

Orit Kamir is founder and academic head of the Center for Human Dignity in Israel and has taught law and culture studies at universities in Israel, the United States, and Europe.

Alexia Katsiginis is a doctoral candidate at the Sciences Po Law School, France. Her research fields include human rights, critical legal theory, affect theory, and the links between psychology and justice.

Nathan Moore joined Birkbeck School of Law, UK, in 2004 as a lecturer in law. His research interests include law and literature, law and film, and the impact of statistical thinking on law and power.

Alberto Rinaldi is a postdoctoral fellow at the Lund University Department of Law, Sweden. He holds a PhD in law from Sciences Po Paris, for which he investigated the concept of the foreign fighter in international law.

Geoffrey Samuel is an emeritus professor of law at the University of Kent (UK). His areas of specialisation are the law of obligations, comparative law, and legal reasoning.

Camil Ungureanu is an associate professor of political philosophy and coordinator of the MA in political philosophy at the Universitat Pompeu Fabra (Barcelona, Spain). He teaches cinema and political philosophy.

Edward van Daalen is a socio-legal researcher and postdoctoral fellow at the Labour Law and Development Research Laboratory (LLDRL) at McGill University, Canada. His research interests include international law and policy making, international development, children's rights, and law-and-film studies.

Chapter 1

Eating Popcorn Like a Lawyer

On Fictions, the Senses, and Belonging

Alexia Katsiginis, Vittoria Becci, and Edward van Daalen

Introduction

This edited volume brings together a diverse collection of essays that explore the symbiosis between law and film by engaging creatively with the intellectual and aesthetic dimensions of both fields. The idea and motivation to create this book emerged from our collective experiences and discussions as organisers of the law-and-film seminar series "Eating Popcorn Like a Lawyer". This project began in 2018, at the Science Po Law School in Paris, where we created an informal space for doctoral students to watch and discuss films about the law. The initial title, the "Law and Cinema Club", alluded to its social character. Once every few weeks or so, the revered Room 410T, where most of the school's formal gatherings took place, was reappropriated into a playful and creative space. Cheap wine and beers were smuggled in, accompanied by snacks that were spread across the table. We started off conventionally, watching Sydney Lumet's classic *12 Angry Men* (1957) against the backdrop of Trump's "new" America. But soon we daringly ventured into lesser-known territory as we engaged with Abderrahmane Sissako's conviction of neo-liberal violence in *Bamako* (2006) and Chaitanya Tamhane's damning but purposefully "boring" indictment of India's criminal justice system in his debut film *Court* (2016). Irrespective of the film that played, once the lights were turned off and the projector rolled, the shared intimacy of the cinematic experience was palpable and enhanced by crackling crisps bags, muffled laughter, and whispers in the dark. As one would expect from a group of tipsy critical PhD candidates, as soon as the end credits rolled and light came back into the room in the otherwise dark and abandoned faculty building, debates erupted. The security guards would regularly need to end our meetings because the "working day" had officially ended, and we would continue our discussions at our favourite café across the street. At l'Espérance, €5 pints of beer were served by friendly owners whose names and faces remain dear to us.

But our cycle was violently disrupted when the scale and impact of the COVID-19 pandemic became obvious at the end of 2019, and many of us left

DOI: 10.4324/9781003461180-1

Paris to be with family and friends. Once we understood that this would not be a matter of weeks or months but potentially years, we decided to adapt our format and continue meeting online. Our "club" became a seminar series about law and film, to which we invited scholars to select a film and discuss it from a legal perspective. What had begun as a space to watch films about law together had turned into one in which we talked about the law differently. The pandemic reactivated a dissatisfaction with our discipline that made us ask how films could change the law. We began to build an interdisciplinary project on a site that had brought us pleasure and did so once more. Why had the purpose of the cinema club changed so radically at the moment when we were confined to our homes? The inability to meet in person certainly made watching films together more difficult and less compelling, but perhaps the pandemic also provoked uncomfortable feelings about the law.

The pandemic heightened the effects of the law's formalism because it forced us into a confined space with it. In the absence of shared coffee breaks, harmless gossip, and complaints among colleagues, the law became all the more tiring and boring. We began our academic careers at a moment when the pandemic forced an erasure of the everyday excitements that had given texture to the text. Perhaps the absence of the material everyday, the academy, the library, and our colleagues made it easier to perceive what it was that the law was withholding. We felt its refusals more acutely because we were being deprived of that which had made it bearable. And so, we responded to a deprivation. Our seminars helped keep our collegial community together and added something of the everyday to the law we were studying. However, it was not only human contact that the seminars tried to recover but something of the human in relation to law. We did not meet to discuss our sentimental lives; we met to discuss the law and film, and if our lives entered the discussion, it was because they slipped through while we waited for someone to connect or a flatmate to be caught by the camera. We were trying to recover something in the law that the pandemic had subtracted: we turned to film because we felt that the law alone was not enough.

Our online sessions resembled a more conventional seminar format, yet we remained determined to retain the playfulness and intimacy that had characterised our preceding club. And so, we began each session by asking our respective guests about their relationship to cinema, how it came about, and what role it played in their scholarly work. Throughout these months spent in isolation, we learned about the magic of local cinemas on rainy nights in the England of the 1950s, about how *Mary Poppins* and American Westerns influenced a childhood in Israel, and how cinema played a central role in youthful queer activism. Moreover, these personal accounts did what we hoped they would do: namely, it created a sense of familiarity and ease that allowed these online gatherings to become intellectually stimulating and socially meaningful conversations amongst peers.

To capture the spirit and elan of our transformed endeavour, a new name was queried. With Eating Popcorn Like a Lawyer, we signal and seek to subvert one of the dogmas of legal education, as described in the influential textbook by Frederick Schauers, *Thinking Like a Lawyer: A New Introduction to Legal Reasoning*.[1] By replacing "thinking" with "eating", we aim to suggest a shift from the mind to the body and the personal. Instead of thinking, we offer the intimate activity that nourishes us and is essential for survival and yet, at times, can make us feel overwhelmed, too full, and too sick. The playfulness (and perhaps even blasphemy) of eating popcorn while talking about violence, genocide, subjectivity, and domination can perhaps create a little more space to breathe – an activity as essential as eating for the jurist's own survival and perhaps for the law's too. Once the pandemic ended and new academic affiliations were taken up, we found ourselves reappropriating our seminar to help create physical communities again through an inter-institutional project between the Sciences Po Law School in Paris and the McGill Faculty of Law in Montreal.[2] Our longing for the material and the subversive that grew during lockdowns, curfews, and Zoom meetings was creatively channelled into special "zines" that served as promotion for and souvenirs of each physical session that took place since – a reminder that the norm should never be taken for granted.[3]

Encouraged by Günter Frankenberg after a stimulating session on law as violence (see chapter 4), we created this book with the aim of capturing the creative and intellectual synergy of our club and seminar series, making it available to a wider group of curious individuals and communities. Like Frankenberg, all the other contributing authors have previously presented in our seminar series, and for their written contributions to this volume, we challenged them to consider, in a personal, playful, and experimental manner, why we feel the need to turn to film in the first place and what this means for how we come to understand law and its absence. The resulting chapters explore a variety of narratives, aesthetics, cinematic epistemologies, and legal phenomena, from assessing law in social debates to film as legal critique, from notions of justice to contemplations of evil, and from masculine vigilantism

1 Frederick Schauers, *Thinking Like a Lawyer: A New Introduction to Legal Reasoning* (Harvard UP 2012). The name *Eating Popcorn like a Lawyer*, together with the joy and nostalgia it invokes, was coined by Louis Hill, who was previously part of the organising team behind the seminar series and is one of the contributors to this volume (see chapter 9 for his account on the revitalising function of film).

2 In Montreal, the project found a second home under the auspices of Edward van Daalen and Mathilde Baril-Jannard, while Vittoria Becci and Alexia Katsginis continued in Paris.

3 For a passionate argument on the importance of zines in (academic) life, see, for instance, Alison Piepmeier, 'Why Zines Matter: Materiality and the Creation of Embodied Community' (2008) 18 American Periodicals 213.

to the female gaze. Taken together, they constitute an inspiring body of work that wholly embodies an urgency for diverging and subversive ways to think about and respond to law's impotence, disappointment, or boredom that will appeal to legal scholars and students interested in interdisciplinary methods, aesthetics, arts, culture, and critical legal theory.

While diverse in approach and substance, the chapters share two broad similarities. First, each chapter comments on the law's style and aesthetic devices by bringing it in conversation with cinema. The authors engage with the law through popular visual images and sensorial economies, questioning how aesthetics permit or foreclose certain discursive possibilities. While the formalism of law typically alienates its audiences, the aesthetics of cinema – its combination of words, pictures, and sounds – allows us to sense its objects more viscerally. Cinema privileges an affective exuberance that creates a moment for alienation to turn into an often-overwhelming embodied experience. Second, while each chapter touches on some kind of social violence, the weight of their substantive content has been juxtaposed with a more informal style that draws from the authors' experiences with law, teaching, and their passions. The biographical style of many of the chapters highlights how the law's aesthetics cause the jurist to be affected – to feel paralysed, threatened, or moved to critique.

We hope it has become clear by now that our intention for this book is not to provide a coherent and prescriptive "method" for bringing together law and film, nor a theoretical framework on law and film.[4] Rather, our project is intended as a way of thinking through a shared discomfort about the law and experimenting with sites that bring us joy. In light of this ambition and as a latent framework for reading along and between the different chapters brought together in this volume, we editors like to offer the reader a personal take on what we believe are three imperative and interconnected dimensions embedded in the symbiosis between law and film: fiction, the senses, and belonging.

On Fiction, the Senses, and Belonging

On Fiction

Vittoria Becci

In the final scene of his most iconic film, *The Holy Mountain*,[5] Alejandro Jodorowsky, portraying the Alchemist, reveals the ultimate secret that he had promised to his ten followers:

> I promised you the great secret, and I will not disappoint you. Is this the end of our adventure? Nothing has an end. We came in search of the secret

4 But for reflections and propositions of theoretical framework on law and film, see Orit Kamir, 'Why "Law-and-Film" and What Does It Actually Mean? A Perspective' (2005) 19 Continuum 255, and Louis Hill in this volume (Ch 9).

5 Alejandro Jodorowsky, *The Holy Mountain* (Film, ABKCO 1973).

> of immortality, to be like Gods. And here we are . . . mortals. More human than ever. If we have not obtained immortality, at least we have obtained reality. We began in a fairytale, and we came to life! Is this life reality? No. It is a film. Zoom back camera!"

This last caption is a revelation that simultaneously belongs to the space of the film and to its backstage. It shows the fictionality of cinema with a method that is called "breaking the fourth wall". The first time I saw this scene, I realised the beauty of films. There are many different dimensions embedded in the idea of fictionality and not only in film. Indeed, this idea of fiction is also present in the legal world, where the *fictio legis* has been used since Roman law. But how are law and film related through the concept of fiction? Upon closer observation, we can say that in movies, fiction is a way to access reality, whereas in law, it is a way to escape it. This paradox suggests a flip of places and actions, where lawyers eat popcorn.

Not far from les Jardin du Luxembourg, not far from la Sorbonne lies a street called rue des Écoles. In its extension, it goes from boulevard Saint-Michel until rue Jussieu. Along this street, we find some of the best cinemas in Paris, one after the other: le Champo, Reflet Médicis, la Filmothèque du Quartier Latin, le Grand Action, École Cinema Club. In these cinemas, I watched all kinds of retrospectives and new, bizarre, unknown, never-heard-of films. I have learned over the years that in Paris, going to the cinema is something serious. It is, above all, an action. I never went to the cinema as a lawyer; I go to the cinema because I want to enter other dimensions. Trial films had always bored me, mostly because they tend to push you towards a "right" side, but also because they stage the law in a misleading way. The films I like are those in which you can clearly see that what is happening is fake, either because of the scenography, the acting, or the story itself. These films are, paradoxically, much more interesting to me when it comes to what law is: for example, *Holy Motors* by Leos Carax, *The Addiction* by Abel Ferrara, and *Aurora* by Cristi Puiu, all of which are discussed in this collection.[6] In these films, although there may be crimes, they are not directly linked to the exercise of the law, and yet this is exactly what they are about. Curiously, this says a lot about what the law is. Fiction in films can lead to many more critical interpretations of the law than legal thought itself.

The French literary critic Roland Barthes described cinema as a "cube where one goes as a response to idleness, leisure, free time".[7] There is, as he calls it, a "cinema situation" – a sort of pre-hypnotic moment when the darkness of the theatre is prefigured by the "twilight reverie"[8] that preceded

6 In addition to the films in this collection, guests from our seminars discussed such films as Alfred Hitchcock's *The Birds* (1963), *The Batman Saga*, Alfonso Cuaron's *Roma* (2018), and Kelly Reichardt's *The First Cow* (2020).

7 Roland Barthes, 'Leaving the Movie Theatre' (1975) Communication.

8 Which is a pre-requisite for hypnosis.

it, which leads him from street to street, from poster to poster, finally burying himself in a dim, anonymous, indifferent cube where the "festival of affects" known as a film will be presented. There are different phases in this action of going to the cinema: the "twilight reverie"; the darkness of the room with its screen, a laser beam that projects images; and, from this latter artefact, the taking off.[9] Taking off means leaving the theatre and being transformed. It means taking the distance from the space and from the image. Reflecting or just detaching from what just happened. And "what just happened" was something fictional. The fictional lens in law and film is a way of taking off, as Barthes would say, reflecting on the techniques that one just saw taking place in the movie theatre, both legal and non-legal, balancing, amongst many other things, fiction, illusoriness, truth, and reality.

The semantic field of the term "fiction" opens up vast conceptual ramifications that are cyclically put under tension. The Latin etymology of the term, which alludes to a practice of modelling – shaping, giving form to materials in the *ars fingendi* – already contemplates an abstract meaning in the act of imagination/representation and in its negative reversal of the potential production of deceptive/dissimulating figures. In here, I am dealing with two "expressions: of the *ars fingendi*: the artistic and the juridical. The first, the ancient theoretical reflection on fiction associated with artistic expression (from Aristotelian *mythos* to literature, from figurative arts to abstraction), has absorbed and, over the centuries, returned this original ambiguity between imagination/representation and deceptive/dissimulating, translating it into a fertile philosophical and cultural debate which cinema has intercepted extraordinarily, reasoning directly or indirectly about its essence as *F for Fake*.[10]

While the second is the juridical *modus operandi*, the latter *fictio* is the name of the *modus operandi* specific to law: in other words, the ability of the law to make something that happened be considered as if it had never occurred and vice versa. In law, the procedure is the place and means through which the characteristic of the *fictio* can be negotiated and articulated. Qualification – the imposition of a name, which is a *res iuris* to a thing (*res*) that, otherwise, would not legally exist – is at the heart of every procedure. If one accepts Yan Thomas's argument about the idea of *fictio*[11] – the practice of clothing facts, the technique of producing reality – reality itself will be nothing more than the product of a legal fiction, a provocation of the *ars iuris*.[12]

9 Barthes (n 7).
10 Orson Welles, *F for Fake* (Documentary 1973).
11 Yan Thomas, *Fictio Legis* (Quodlibet [1995] 2016).
12 Giorgio Agamben, 'Tra il diritto e la vita' in Yan Thomas (ed), *Il Valore delle Cose* (Quodlibet 2015).

Therefore, fiction means imagining a reality that represents the truth or a simulation of it. This tension between imagination, reality, truth, and fiction has been captured in films by many directors. We can easily think of Federico Fellini, who marked an imaginary that has been recognised as dreamy and surrealistic, and yet his films are representative of many truthful aspects of life and relationship. On the other hand, we can think of the vivid fake blood staged by Quentin Tarantino as a simulation of violence, revenge, and the criminal world: so fake and so real at the same time!

In this sense, fiction is therefore a *Tέχνη* (*techne*), a way to use a *modus operandi* to achieve a result. Even in this, film and law share a common ground. *Fictio legis* is the juridical escamotage, the everyday operations of the law that are used to imagine reality. Yan Thomas considers *patria potestas* or *confessus pro iudicato*[13] as *fictio legis*, but we can also think of the more contemporary concepts of marriage or property. These "operations" made by the law are abstractions to solve different cases. However, if, in films, fiction is a step towards a truth, in law, *fictio* – the engine of every legal action – designates nothing other than the possibility that things and words do not coincide. It asserts a forced and unreal equivalence between saying and doing. Reality itself could then be considered strictly as the outcome of a performative linguistic act, of a locutionary act, of a *fictio*. Indeed, law is primarily a technique and a technology (an *ars*).[14]

In this *modus operandi*, the director and the lawyer (or the legal scholar) must always be aware of the moves they make in their "fictions". After all, the *modus operandi* is fundamental to the success of the fiction. In cinema, we can think about how suspense is created or about mechanisms that directly address the audience, as we have seen done by Jodorowsky breaking the fourth wall. Or we can also consider specific directing techniques that are used to achieve the desired result: let us take the example of Federico Fellini. In his films, while shooting, he left nothing to chance; the actors were guided even in their gestures and expressions by what the director said. In fact, they did not act; Fellini wanted them to count (literally: one, two, three, four . . .) so they could only listen to him. Not to mention the sounds, colours, costumes, lights, makeup, or camera movements that, if used in a certain way, can convey different things.[15] In the legal world, the lawyer must know how to collect their evidence, have a clear understanding of the laws they will use to build a defence, and follow a narrative line according to certain techniques.

Fiction in cinema fascinates me. It is important to know you are watching something acted and staged. Illusion is a tool that both distracts and reveals

13 Marta Madero, 'Penser la traditio juridique occidentale' (2012) I Annales, Histoire, Sciences Sociales.

14 Agamben (n 12).

15 See chapter 5 by Séverine Dusollier in this volume.

a truth. Even if the blood is clearly fake, it does not mean the scene was poorly done. Even if, in some scene, you can see that the shark is a piece of metal, it does not make me less afraid. Even if the punches do not actually hit any faces, it does not make me think they cannot fight. In this way, fiction is necessary to stimulate emotions that do not make you think about the fact that the shark is fake but make you think about the terror of the unknown, unconscious fears, the relationship with nature, and so on. It is interesting to note that even if *fictio* is the essence of law, the results are the opposite. When reading a paper or a law, it is important that everything is clear, and nothing is left to chance; the message has to be straightforward. As lawyers, we are taught that imagination, or anything that does not fit into a specific category, must first be justified and, in any event, remains very risky. This is why fiction in law or its illusory aspects, like marriage or parental authority, should not "move" us but should, rather, be as abstract as possible, leaving no room for anything other than the search for certainty or the elimination of any reasonable doubt.

Although fiction is present in both law and cinema, it looks like their aims are different. Therefore, while in cinema, fiction remains the foundation for both entertainment and in-depth analysis, propelling the audience towards new narrative paths in search of truth and reality, law, especially jurisprudence, remains, as we will see in what follows, boring. Therefore, law's fictions have made it too illusory and distant. In law, despite always seeking to understand reality, originality is seldom rewarded and rarely viewed positively. When, in 2021, we asked some of the legal scholars who contributed to this collection, "What is cinema's potential for law and legal reasoning?" the responses focused on the image and how it can convey messages. Showing a clip in class can generate a deeper discussion. The amount of work behind a scene – the costumes, the environment, but above all the research into the emotions of a character at a given moment – is, as one of them phrased it, "giving a window into context". This is what fiction does in cinema, reconstructing reality through the meticulous study of the context. In this regard, it is essential for legal researchers to focus on the image created by a specific idea of fictionality. Otherwise, the law will remain boring, with the risk that it will be taken out of context.

On the Senses

Alexia Katsiginis

The first time I wrote about the law, I was ten years old. I had decided to write, very poorly, a poem in the style of a rap about South African constitutional rights. Years later, as a first-year law student, I chose to write my first academic paper on the registration requirements of objects in international space law. While I intentionally wrote in the first person to undermine the objectivity of legal writing, my style was no less anonymous – it could have been written by anyone. Although academically more sophisticated, I had begun experimenting with aesthetics that would create an estrangement. Not only had I erased my voice from the text (a move that no doubt made me feel like I was conducting important work), but I was also alienating myself from my subject. I had gone from writing about humans and deprivation to objects that did not even occupy the same planet as man.

Now, as I consider this change, I wonder how much of it was influenced by the way I was writing, rather than a shift in my thematic interests. I was performing and producing a boredom that distanced me from my work and made my writing far less sufferable to read than the opening line "It bites to have no rights", written by my ten-year-old self. I was learning how to write the dry content that had led Kafka to compare law textbooks to sawdust.[16] (Perhaps, in a way, this collection marks a shift from eating sawdust to eating popcorn.)

If we take boredom seriously as something more than just disinterest, it describes an estrangement from ourselves and our passions; it is the affect that makes us feel heavy; oppressed; and, at times, wishing for death.[17] In law, boredom allows us to become estranged from what is real; the real person who becomes the impartial jurist, the real subject who becomes the reasonable person, and real suffering that is replaced by statistics and legal categories. In other words, the law's form ensures that there is always a big enough gap between the signifier and the signified, which perhaps makes the themes of law (and all its violence) bearable.[18] Perhaps the height of legal estrangement is the obligation to write in a way that erases our own voices from our writing; after all, what's more authoritative than the disembodied, floating voice propped up by the force of law.

For a discourse that structures our most intimate lives (work, marriage, reproduction, cities), the law is remarkably adept at keeping us at a distance. Modernity's obsessive attempts to empty the law of sentiment and impose the discourse of the expert has succeeded in producing a barrier between the law's text and its readers. Indeed, perhaps it's no coincidence that when we discussed this collection with the authors, most indicated that they use cinema to foster an interest in their students;[19] while not everyone is familiar with their country's constitution, they have all likely watched a courtroom drama, a cowboy in a Western, a class action lawsuit. The aesthetics of

16 Kafka 'Letters to Friends, Families and Editors' (1977) as quoted in Costas Douzinas and Adam Gearey, *Critical Jurisprudence* 3.

17 Antonello Correale, 'Boredom: An Uncanny Guide to Something Unknown' (2018) 5 European Journal of Psychoanalysis; Martin Wangh, 'Boredom in Psychoanalytic Perspective' (1975) 42 Social Research.

18 See Alberto Rinaldi in this collection.

19 See, for example, Helena Alviar García and Günter Frankenberg in this collection.

cinema produce a proximity that allows us to feel connected to its subjects and be moved.

However, if the law's boredom keeps us from feeling anything too acutely, it also provokes a pulse to turn elsewhere. When asked why they turned to cinema, most of the contributors expressed that they watched films either when they felt stuck, when the law reached its limit, or when the law moved them not to feeling but to boredom.

The stability and certainty that boredom brings can be necessary qualities for a legal system. But when the law disappoints us, it appears equally stable, and the stability that once reassured us begins to make us feel trapped. Increasingly, legal scholars have lamented that the law is suffering from a crisis of imagination and called for new experiments (turns to interdisciplinarity) to imagine differently and to be radical (to love, hope, and care radically).[20] The ordinary is simply no longer enough.

When we feel stuck in our own discipline, we either give up (leave the law for something that is not hostile to our pleasure), or we look elsewhere. But why do we turn to film (a genre of the senses and the image) to mediate the disappointments we find in law and words? What happens in these moments of interdisciplinary importation, and what is left behind afterwards?[21] Eating popcorn (or cinema) like a lawyer is an embodied experience of consumption which underlines a violence present in interdisciplinary work. Both films and the objects we find in film – concepts, bodies, feelings, etc. – are first eaten by the spectator and then by the law. Whatever is consumed is incorporated into the body of the eater, and, in the process, it is destroyed. It ceases to be what it originally was in film and is transformed, distorted, and mutilated in order to enter the importing discipline and become legible according to the new discipline's rules and constraints.

20 For example, Gerry Simpson, 'Imagination' in Jean d'Aspremont and Sahib Singh (eds), *Concepts of International Law: Contributions to Disciplinary Thought* (Edward Elgar Publishing 2019); Bill Bowring, 'What Is Radical in "Radical International Law"?' (2013) 22 Finnish Yearbook of International Law; Pok Yin S Chow and Stephenson Chow, 'Introduction: Cultural Rights – A Radical Hope?' in *Cultural Rights in International Law and Discourse: Contemporary Challenges and Interdisciplinary Perspectives* (Brill Academic Publication 2018); Kirsi Pauliina Kallio, Isabel Meier and Jouni Häkli, 'Radical Hope in Asylum Seeking: Political Agency Beyond Linear Temporality' (2021) 47 Journal of Ethics and Migration Studies.

21 Rather than merely analytical value (e.g. cinema can foreground the law's background conditions of possibility), I'm interested in how the form and aesthetics of cinema can influence our engagement with law. Nevertheless, I recognise the value of film analysis in a law class. In the first year of my doctorate, I audited one of Helena Alviar García's classes at Sciences Po, for which she had assigned *The Marriage Story* (Noah Baumbach 2019). In determining in which city (Los Angeles or New York) the child, Henry Barber, should live, the court ruled that he was legally domiciled in Los Angeles because it is where he was born. It didn't matter that, in reality, Henry had never lived in Los Angeles or that he had spent most of his life in New York. I was struck by how the facts of the situation were displaced by legal fictions, which, with the help of the law's authority, became facts.

The most glaring difference between law and cinema is that while cinema is concerned with fiction,[22] the law is concerned with fact. One would not be hard pressed to find accounts that describe law as a discourse that sets out to extract and judge truths that are embedded in society.[23] While the law works to persuade us of its rationality and proximity to the truth, cinema proclaims the opposite. It is entangled in passions; it exposes the irrationality of life and human relations; and if some truth leaks through its images and dialogue, it is never fully grasped. Indeed, while law tries to make us certain, cinema understands that one cannot arrive at the truth, only circle around it, approach it, and accept that something will always be a residue that exceeds representation. Although the distinction between reason and passion is rarely a position that is still credible, an anxiety remains about how to manage feelings correctly and about what the "wrong" feelings can produce if they are left unattended.[24] Justice remains frustrated by passions.

It thus seems paradoxical that jurists should turn to film, a genre that aims to make one feel at precisely the moment they should be thinking. However, far from being aesthetically and affectively "neutral", the law's form sustains a foundational fiction of certainty and truth.[25] Boredom helps conceal law's impotence. By suppressing our anxieties and doubts, boredom helps reinforce the law's authority and promotes certainty not only in a legal outcome but also in the law itself. Moreover, as Vittoria Becci argued earlier,

22 Although, like law, cinema is concerned with narrating stories, we have the genre of documentaries to remind us that what we experience when watching a film is art, not truth.

23 HLA Hart, 'Positivism and the Separation of Law and Morals' in Kenneth Einar Himma and Brian Bix (eds), *Law and Morality* (Routledge 2005); Brian Bix, 'Legal Positivism' in Martin Golding and William Edmundson (eds), *The Blackwell Guide to the Philosophy of Law and Legal Theory* (Blackwell Publishing 2005); Stephen Hall, 'The Persistent Spectre: Natural Law, International Order and the Limits of Legal Positivism' (2001) 12 European Journal of International Law.

24 There has been a proliferation of scholarship on law and emotions; however, rather than destabilising law, this move paradoxically seems to strive towards perfecting the law's certainty. See, for example, Anne Saab, 'Emotions and International Law' (2021) 10 ESIL Reflections 1; Richard Rorty, 'Human Rights, Rationality, and Sentimentality' in *Truth and Progress: Philosophical Papers* (CUP 1998). In contrast, see Aristodemou, who describes interdisciplinarity as a kind of hysteria that turns to the Other to perfect the Self, 'A Constant Craving for Fresh Brains and a Taste for Decaffeinated Neighbours' (2014) 25 European Journal of International Law.

25 While the law's content certainly contributes to establishing its authority, its form and aesthetics are equally complicit in stabilising this authority. For a discussion on formalism and critical legal studies, see Mark Tushnett, 'Critical Legal Studies: A Political History' 100 The Yale Law Journal 31; on expertise and authority, see David Kennedy, *A World of Struggle: How Power, Law and Expertise Shape Global Political Economy* (Princeton UP 2016); on Marxism and legal formalism, see Susan Marks, 'Introduction' in Susan Marks (ed), *International Law on the Left: Re-Examining Marxist Legacies* (CUP 2008); on the aesthetics of law, see Desmond Manderson, *Songs Without Music: Aesthetic Dimensions of Law and Justice* (U of California P 2000).

the law imposes on its categories a fictional quality, relying on monolithic and one-dimensional representations of the situations and subjects it regulates. It forces what is real to fit into its own categories and, in the process, erases important chains of responsibility and experiences of suffering.[26] These devices hide the incomprehensiveness embedded in so many of the events the law tries to describe. While cinema can leave us speechless, the law forces words onto us – usually borrowed words that have already alienated us. (I'm always frustrated when I leave the cinema with a friend who refuses to analyse the film with me; perhaps it's my training as a jurist that insists on words.) Any uncertainty is filled with a concept, a rule, a precedent. There's so much to read through that we're constantly moving, never obliged to stop and feel (encounter) reality.

Cinema throws us into an unstable space of haziness, which unsettles us enough to think differently, to make new associations, to find new metaphors. It does not merely bring out the "everyday" of law. It disturbs and challenges the certainty of the law; it saves law from falling into madness. (Certainty is, after all, a symptom of psychosis.) While cinema pulls our passions to the surface, the price we pay is the weight of our senses, an affective unease that de-idealises the law. It exposes the technocratic complexity of legal rules and language as a defence against the complexity of society.

Next, I highlight three similarities between these modes of communication that can perhaps direct an engagement between the two.

First, as in cinema, law narrates the events it addresses; it has the same configurational quality as the arts.[27] Rather than capturing the "real" or "true" event, the law helps constitute the events it describes. When an event is translated into law's language, it is shaped to fit into a particular vocabulary (thus, the event itself is remade) and its importance in society is altered. For example, we take note of hunger not when someone holds their stomach in pain but when it meets the requirements set out in laws, judicial decisions, or international declarations. Moreover, it is only when hunger fits into these categories that it's considered a violence. Similarly, other violence, such as war or forcibly removing someone from their home, is legitimised when it becomes the right to wage war or property, respectively.

Second, cinema and law share the same subjects and audience. Rather than an abstract desire for truth as a value in itself, the law grapples with the messiness of human relations. Both disciplines struggle with what it means to be human and try to communicate to us something about our existence; both are human artefacts directed at man. Indeed, foundational to law is

26 Luis Eslava, 'Istanbul Vignettes: Observing the Everyday Operation of International Law' (2014) 2 London Review of International Law 3, 8.

27 Nicholas Entrikin, *The Betweenness of Place: Towards a Geography of Modernity* (Johns Hopkins UP 1991) 127.

its anxiety about human nature: man desires freedom but is simultaneously too violent to exist in a state of nature without a regime of commands and prohibitions. However, there is also an important difference here that makes a study of the interaction between cinema and law interesting: while cinema expresses man's affective life, the law keeps it in check. It tries to ensure that we are not overwhelmed and destroyed by our desires and drives. The law obsessively tries to suppress affects, fearing the horror of their consequences, whereas cinema introduces us to our affects, often forcing us to identify the most unbearable ones in ourselves. The turn to cinema and the humanities more generally is a turn towards ourselves.

A third similarity is reliance on the image. Although law is a textual discipline that often draws from a technocratic, dry, and clinical vocabulary, the absence of poetry and lyricism has only succeeded in making law boring to read, not in expelling images. Indeed, law's authority is ontologically dependent on the image of the police (how often has "law" become a metonym for the police), the judge, the trial, and justice embodied by a blinded[28] woman. The law is an artefact that both constitutes and is constituted by different images; it has a material effect on our world and provides us founding categories with which to make sense of our society. As with truth, the difference between the two disciplines is not the presence of the image but each discipline's relation to it. The law transforms its images into icons, objects of veneration that reinforce its own authority, while simultaneously disavowing their importance. The law may be predominantly textual; however, its force is derived from devices that cinema openly recognises.

On Belonging

Edward van Daalen

The film *Oeroeg* (1993) by director Hans Hylkema tells the story of Johan, a Dutch army lieutenant sent to colonised Indonesia as part of the government's effort to violently suppress the growing independence movement in the wake of the Second World War. The film's international title, *Going Home*, refers to the fact that Johan was born and raised in the colony as the son of a Dutch plantation owner. On his return as a soldier, some eight years later, he is confronted with his Indonesian childhood friend and "blood brother" Oeroeg, whose father was a foreman on the plantation. In a classic twist of fate, the two find themselves on opposite sides of the war, foreshadowed by a scene in which they find themselves on opposite sides of a cinema screen.

28 I had initially described the corporal figure of justice as blind, however, she could equally be blind*ed*, implying an unwillingness to be blind. Indeed, describing justice as having been blinded reintroduces question of power as it highlights both the actors and social processes that contribute to this blindness. I thank Rashmi Dharia for suggesting a *blinded* figure.

The scene in question is a part of a flashback to their years as graduating high school students, just before Johan left to study in the Netherlands. Instead of revising for their final exams, the two have a night out on the town and spontaneously decide to go see *Tarzan* in the local cinema. The plan is a nostalgic one as they seek to bond over the film, which constitutes a direct reference to the "monkey play" of their childhood and their "forbidden" friendship, in which they were equals despite the structural inequality surrounding them. Yet the power of the scene lies in the fact that quite the opposite occurs when segregation laws force them to reckon with their respective roles as coloniser and colonised. The cinema has two separate entrances: one for white Europeans, which gives access to the regular screening room, and one for "natives", which leads to a space on the other side of the screen from where they are forced to watch the film in mirror image. Still believing that their bond as "blood brothers" allows them to transcend the divisive nature of their political reality, they try to navigate, negotiate, and resist the existent norms and rules. In an incident earlier that evening, Oeroeg got angry with a street vendor who refused to serve Johan when he ordered in Dutch. When they arrive at the cinema, Johan, in turn, haggles with the ticket salesman to let Oeroeg sit on the "white" side. When Johan's efforts are to no avail and he docilly agrees with the salesman that "Yes, rules are rules", Oeroeg suggests they simply take the other entrance. But in the queue amongst the other locals, Johan becomes visibly self-conscious and uncomfortable. With a lame excuse, he tells Oeroeg that he is, on second thought, no longer interested in seeing the film and that he will run some errands instead. Somewhat surprised and disappointed, Oeroeg accepts Johan's suggestion, takes his place in the cinema, and, in anticipation of the film, lights a cigarette he would rather have shared with his friend. When halfway through the film, the projector fails and Oeroeg gets up to see what is going on at the other side of the screen, he sees Johan sitting amongst the other whites. As he stares into his eyes in utter disbelief, Oeroeg seems to internalise the realisation that despite their friendship, Johan is part and parcel of a repressive regime that forces them to be on different sides of a cinema in which, for a moment, they naively believed they could belong together.

Seeing the film for the first time as a young teenager, it deeply affected me, and the cinema scene in particular stayed with me all these years. Being born in the Netherlands as the child of a first-generation "Indo" and a Dutch mother,[29] it is rather obvious why the film's setting and broader themes appealed to me, and the cinema scene will likely resonate with anyone old enough to have experienced the emotions and politics of friendship. Now, a good 25 years later (as researcher at a law faculty and not as a deep-sea

29 In the Netherlands, the term "Indo" is commonly used to refer to people of mixed Dutch-Indonesian heritage.

diver, which I then hoped to become), the scene immediately came to mind when I started thinking about why we turn to film. It helped me realise that an important part of the answer to the question lies in the notion that it helps us meet our need to belong.

I am not talking about "belonging" solely in the sense of access or titular affiliation to an institution,[30] but rather "belonging" in the intuitive sense of the concept. To be able to be "yourself", whether that self is norm defying, confirming, or something in between, and to be accepted, respected, and valued as such, so we can create reciprocal, positive, caring, meaningful, validating, and stimulating interpersonal and collective relationships.[31] As alluded to by Alexia Katsiginis in this chapter and by Louis Hill later on in this collection (see chapter 9), a life that revolves around the law is one that invites and often demands a certain distance and "neutrality". There is something to say for why such a detached and impersonal approach and, by extent, environment are beneficial and, at times, even necessary. Take, for instance, the role of law in the scene from *Oeroeg* I described earlier. How else to relate to a social project that allows and facilitates a system that forces people of different races to sit on opposite sides of a cinema screen? How else to relate to peers, colleagues, and superiors all standing around the table, staring at the blueprint for such an outcome, debating whether it is justified or not, legitimate or not, "right" or not? How to feel you can belong, with all that you are, think, and feel, when what is asked of you is to constantly take a step back, to abstract, to apply a technique and a neutral language?

One poignant, almost satirical anecdote that elucidates this notion is given by Lani Guinier in the book *Becoming Gentlemen: Women, Law School, and Institutional Change*.[32] She describes a male law professor at Yale University who structurally addressed all students in his classroom as "gentlemen", women included. According to Guinier's analysis, he meant it as an asexual term which "evoked the traditional values of legal education: to train detached, 'neutral' problem solvers, unemotional advocates for their clients' interests".[33] It will come as no surprise that when she returned to Yale a decade later, it did not feel like "going home", for she never felt she could belong. Whereas the "gentlemen" account was perplexing even for the times in which it took place (the 1970s), many recent publications and no doubt

30 For a critique of such belonging and the joy of not having to do so, see Martin Benedict Andrew, 'The Great Resignation: The Simple Joys of Not Belonging' (2024) 7 Journal of Applied Learning and Teaching.

31 Roy F Baumeister and Mark R Leary, 'The Need to Belong: Desire for Interpersonal Attachments as a Fundamental Human Motivation' (1995) 117 Psychological Bulletin.

32 Lani Guinier, Michelle Fine and Jane Balin, *Becoming Gentlemen: Women, Law School, and Institutional Change* (Beacon Press 1997).

33 Lani Guinier, Michelle Fine and Jane Balin, *Becoming Gentlemen: Women, Law School, and Institutional Change* (Beacon Press 1997) 85–86.

countless personal accounts suggest that "belonging" in law schools remains a serious problem, especially for racialised, transgender, and gender-diverse students.[34]

Let me be clear: "engaging with film" is no miracle cure to solve all problems of non-belonging, but our experiences with our law and film projects suggest that doing so can contribute in important ways.[35] For clues to why this might be the case, we can go back to *Oeroeg* and ask why the director chose a cinema as the setting for the scene in which Oeroeg comes to terms with the violent and unjust nature of his relationship with Johan and the realisation that, under colonial oppression and segregation, he will never belong in his own country? The scene could have been scripted in many different ways, so why did the director believe this would be the most effective way to portray Oeroeg's transformation? I suggest it is because the cinema is a place of bonding, belonging, and community where, for the duration of a film, all are equal in front of the screen. To be able to share this individual experience and to relay and reflect our thoughts and emotions goes to the heart of any human relationship: namely, connecting over what we feel and think to understand. It is what makes us feel equal in unequal times, what helps us belong. This is why, I would argue, Johan and Oeroeg initially flocked to the cinema, and why Johan's decision to abide by the segregation law in that very space was the ultimate betrayal.

Throughout the course of our project, including the making of this book, we have often witnessed the immediate and lasting ways in which film helps us belong in law. An illustrative example that comes to mind is a special screening for which we invited a newly hired law professor who works and teaches on law and questions of race, inclusion, and diversity. She suggested a documentary recounting the history of a city's black queer community in a neighbourhood in which, she explained, she herself grew up. It was a way for her to show and discuss with students where she came from and where part of her belonging lay. In doing so, she helped others feel that they too could bring the different parts of themselves into the clinical and often hostile environment that is legal academia. In the discussion that followed the screening, one of the students revealed that, besides studying law, they are also a filmmaker, but that they never believed that law school could be a place to show and discuss this part of themself. Their short films had, it turned out, been previously screened and awarded at various film festivals, and we

34 See, for instance, Elizabeth Bodamer, 'Do I Belong Here? Examining Perceived Experiences of Bias, Stereotype Concerns, and Sense of Belonging in US Law Schools' (2020) 69 Journal of Legal Education; Russel A McClain, *The Guide to Belonging in Law School* (West Academic Publishing 2021).

35 Others have had similar experiences. See, for instance, Kate Nace Day and Russell G Murphy, 'Just Trying to Be Human in This Place: Storytelling and Film in the First-Year Law School Classroom' (2009) 39 Stetson Law Review 247.

invited them to present and discuss their films in one of our subsequent special events. During the session, they explained how important their films are for retaining a connection to the arts and to the people, community, and culture featured in the work, to remind them why they are so far from home and to be able to continue believing that pursuing their studies in law will eventually be worth it. One of the shorts they selected for the screening was bought by the faculty library and now constitutes a part of the legal archive, permanently there for others to engage with and be inspired by.

In similar fashion, this volume too is now part of the legal archive. One of the central themes of *Oeroeg* is the ambiguity of "home". While (the) cinema ended up driving the two friends apart, it helped them better understand and relate to a system and a society to which both of them struggled to belong. My hope is that this book and its overall encouragement to turn to film will do the same for those who straddle lines.

Overview of Chapters

As will become clear, the chapters in this book stretch across different legal fields, including legal pedagogy, technology, property law, women's rights, and authoritarianism. Indeed, when organising the structure of this book, we were faced with the challenge that the chapters do not share a uniquifying legal subject that can be traced or progressively developed. Instead, the authors are participating in a conversation revolving around questions such as: How can the two disciplines be put in dialogue with each other? How does film change our engagement with law and scholarship? What can film tell us about the law's as well as our own inadequacies?

We debated two ways of organising the chapters. The first would have structured the book thematically, according to considerations of what cinema can bring to the law. The first group of chapters considers how films can be read to express something the law cannot. In the contributions by Helena Alviar García, Nathan Moore, and Alberto Rinaldi, the reader will find echoes that motivate turning to the law to get closer to reality and to build a more detailed and contextualised picture of the situations that the law regulates. The second group of chapters builds on this question by focusing on failure. Orit Kamir, Günter Frankenberg, and Camil Ungureanu suggest that what is expressed (or exposed) in film is the failure and deterioration of the rule of law. In contrast, Elie Aslanoff rejects the value of this exposure as, for him, both law and film are part of the same failed and alienated reality that destroys authentic communication. Finally, for Geoffrey Samuel, the potential lies in the failure itself – for him, films are valuable not because they expose the law's failure but because they teach us how to fail better. A third group of chapters then turns to epistemological considerations. Séverine Dusollier compares how norms are built in film and law, respectively, by comparing the rhetorical devices of each field, while Louis Hill explores how films can revitalise legal scholarship and the epistemic consequences of giving something (a) "new life".

However, as this project has its roots in our individual relationships with film rather than an academic question, we decided to emulate this biographical quality in our structure. While a thematic grouping like the one provided here would allow the reader to map the chapters academically and intellectually, we propose a second, different map. Rather than creating internal categories, we instead opted for a structure that centres the transformation of the subject into a lawyer, the process of becoming a lawyer, and how that being changes when the law is combined with film. In other words, we suggest an autobiographical reimagining: How would our work have changed if we had become lawyers while watching films and eating popcorn and whether we could have done so without splitting our personalities into lawyer and, separately, cinephile.

This journey starts with the premise that the more familiar we grow with the law and the more we encounter its inherent violence, the more ambivalent we and our work become. Alberto Rinaldi's chapter "Writing about Evil" (chapter 2) explores the ramifications of the relationship between international law and evil. But rather than studying legal categories of evil (slavery, war crimes, genocide, etc.), he turns to secondary sites that are often dismissed as non-legal. He draws on Abel Ferrara's *Addiction* (1995) as an "allegory of academic life" to comment on the psychic function of law's form and to consider how evil leaves its mark on the people who try to bring it into words. How do the devices of legal writing, such as footnotes, citations, and aligned paragraphs, change our relationship to violence? Using his own experiences, he considers how the process of writing a PhD dissertation about evil requires the transformation of the subject while simultaneously allowing the subject to shield herself from the sheer violence that her discipline tries to regulate.

Once we learn how to write and retranslate law and justice into law and violence, Orit Kamir and Günter Frankenberg suggest we turn to film for critical commentary on the force and domination that the law permits, authors, and resists. In chapter 3, "Reading a Law Film in Cinematic Context as a Commentary on the Decline of Liberal Democracy and the Rule of Law: Emin Alper's *Burning Days* (2022) Read Against John Ford's *The Man Who Shot Liberty Valance* (1962)", Kamir is concerned with the crumbling of the rule of law and democratic values under authoritarian leadership in our populist and "post-truth" era. She argues that where the law struggles to take account of its own demise, law films are able to, and Emin Alper's *Burning Days* (2022) does so in a particularly compelling way. Read against John Ford's classic Western *The Man Who Shot Liberty Valence* (1962), she presents the film as a warning of the ease with which legal institutions can slip into the "honour trap" in their well-intentioned fight against populism, corruption, and abuse of power, and the devastating consequences of their failure to refrain from doing so.

Frankenberg's "Violence as Law: Reading *Dirty Harry*, *Unforgiven*, and *Gran Torino* as Comments on Vigilantism" (chapter 4) is a reflection on vigilantism based on a critical reading of the liberal script of rights and law as products of ideological world-making. In this ideology, violence was withdrawn from society, and vigilantism had been drained by the monopoly of legitimate violence of the state executed by legislators, judges, administrative agencies, and the police. However, he argues that the realism of this constitutional script for law rule and its exercise has come under attack. His reading of *Dirty Harry*, *Unforgiven*, and *Gran Torino* presents an illuminating view on the actions of the hero that imply that extra-legal honest revenge or adequate atonement can be justified.

As our questions of the law change, so does the way we orientate ourselves in the discourse. Our own frustration, doubt, boredom, hope, and anguish shape the figure of the law, and disillusionment guides us towards bitter truths. In "The Impossible Truth in Law and Films: The Female Gaze of *Saint Omer* and *Anatomy of a Fall*" (chapter 5), Séverine Dusollier examines how truth and judgment are achieved in law and films through judgment-making operations. In her parallelism between the legal argumentation and filming techniques, she reveals that the choice for objectivity is a gaze that has never been considered in either law or film. She presents two "female-gaze" films – *Saint Omer* (2022) and *Anatomy of a Fall* (2023) – arguing that by refraining from objectivity, the accused women in both films, embracing their unreadable subjectivity, intentionally refuse to tell a definitive story or decisive counternarrative. In doing this, she diverts from most literature on law and film, which tends to guide viewers in forming a judgment. Rather, this chapter points out that movies reveal the very truth of the law: that is, the incapacity to tell the truth.

This apparent dead end is just the occasion to rethink the spaces of the law, most of all law school and the classroom, by asking how films can shake the students and how they can be used in critical legal theories. These questions are explored by Helena Alviar García in "Teaching Law and Feminism Through Cinema: A Proposal" (chapter 6). She depicts the space of the classroom as a politicised place, in which students and professors conceive of legal ideas and passionately explore the limits and possibilities of their content. They seek to link the ideological framework of a legal regime to economic and social particularities while, at the same time, learning to embrace uncertainty and to accept that there is cruelty, irrationality, and pain in the context of the law. Starting from these premises, her chapter provides a specific counterpoint to mainstream legal education by discussing the use of cinema in a course on feminist legal theory.

As we go on, in this transitional phase, we become more mature as well as more disillusioned. Nathan Moore and Camil Ungureanu consider how the law constitutes the (legal) "citizen" in the liberal and post-communist world. In "Holy Motors: Law and Technology" (chapter 7), Moore is interested in the consequences of the technological transition in our society. He considers how the shift from "machine" to "communication and information" supports Deleuze's claim that we are moving from a disciplinary society into a control society. Moore analyses Leos Carax's *Holy Motors* (2002) to consider how the subject responds to and is transformed by this transition. What are the social, economic, and political consequences of living in a society in which the forces that mediate and shape human relations become invisible? Film is used to capture a social movement that the law misses (possibly because it is new, possibly because it is moving) and to consider how we might make, unmake, and organise our images differently.

In "Kafka in the Balkans: *Before the Law*, Nihilism, and Crisis in Cristi Puiu's *Aurora*" (chapter 8), Ungureanu takes the contemporary Romanian film as self-reflective, involving the problematisation of the (directorial) belief in the capacity to represent, criticise, or unveil reality as such. As he explores Puiu's alienated male gaze into a crisis of the individual and societal, he exposes how post-communist reality and its dissolution become a radiography of a society in ruins and all-dissolving nihilism that empties law of any system of belief.

Once we have "become" legal scholars, lawyers, and citizens, we can turn to cinema as a way of undermining law's form, its certainty, and its coherence. While the transition from text to image undoubtable changes the way we think and reason through legal problems, the value of cinema does not lie only in helping us understand or find better answers, as is proposed by the contributions of Louis Hill and Geoffrey Samuel, respectively.

In "Revitalising the Law: An Existentialist Take on Law and Film" (chapter 9), Hill makes a compelling existential argument for why we turn to film – one that foregrounds any of the more instrumental approaches that are commonly listed by legal scholars as "justifications" for turning to film. He observes that law's unequivocal reliance on tradition and technique means it faces the constant threat of being "devitalised", and that cinema's impressive and immersive features provide it with the power to "re-vitalise" or to give "life" to the law in a Nietzschean sense. Once knowledge is revitalised, Hill concludes, it transforms and unveils its critical potential.

In chapter 10, titled "Lost Horizons, or How to Lose More Slowly", Samuel encourages us to turn to Hollywood's film noir genre to learn how to "fail better" as lawyers. He reassuringly proposes that, no matter how great the effort, every serious attempt at truly "knowing" the law is ultimately doomed to fail. Seeking certainty and coherence in the law, he argues, is seeking something fictional and unattainable: an impossible task. Cinema can help us understand how to "lose more slowly", and drawing on the work of Raymond Durgnat, he proposes a "taxonomy of losing", which he explores in three classic crime films – *Out of the Past* (1947), *Kiss Me Deadly* (1955), and *The Killers* (1964) – that all revolve around "losers" from whom we legal losers have much to gain.

But then comes a moment in which all that we believe we understood, learned, and exposed is questioned again. Did we just end up where we started? Elie Aslanoff's closing chapter, "The Legal Spectacle" (chapter 11), introduces a self-reflective scepticism of the law and film genre. He takes aim at the strand of law and film literature which pronounces that cinema provides us with access to the reality that the law disfigures, hides, or misses (or at least to a more complete part). Rather than a critical move that reflects the law's impotence to grasp the conditions of our social world, Aslanoff suggests that the jurist's eagerness to turn to film reflects the success with which the law dominates our imaginations. The law permeates everything; we even find it in film. Inspired by Guy Debord's style in *The Society of the Spectacle*, Aslanoff experiments with 25 hypotheses to suggest that both law and film are relics of capitalism and reflect the reification and alienation of modern life. He considers how the popularisation of images has pulled us into a simulated reality that abolishes authentic communication and renders collective practices outdated.

The chapters in this book should be read as a journey, sometimes personal, some other times objective, but never indifferent. They are, in some way, responding to a dissatisfaction with the law and often implicate it in the production of social injustice. Film becomes a site of experimentation and a response to the law's inadequacies by providing an entry into reality, our passions, and a community. Each author begins not with a traditional legal question but with a personal interest in films that leaks into their work with the law. However, this book remains very much a book about the law and contains an optimism that it can be transformed. Rather than a guide on how to conduct interdisciplinary research, these chapters offer coordinates to map different ways of putting law and film into conversation with each other. For now, we hope that film can create enough room to make the law bearable for a little longer, or, if it must remain unbearable, make it unbearable in a way that gives us energy to keep struggling with it until something changes.

Reference List

Agamben G, 'Tra il diritto e la vita' in Y Thomas (ed), *Il Valore delle Cose* (Quodlibet 2015)

Andrew MB, 'The Great Resignation: The Simple Joys of Not Belonging' (2024) 7 Journal of Applied Learning and Teaching

Aristodemou M, 'A Constant Craving for Fresh Brains and a Taste for Decaffeinated Neighbours' (2014) 25 European Journal of International Law

Barthes R, 'Leaving the Movie Theatre' in Phillip Lopate (ed), *The Art of the Personal Essay* (Anchor Books 1995) [1975]

Baumeister RF and Leary MR, 'The Need to Belong: Desire for Interpersonal Attachments as a Fundamental Human Motivation' (1995) 117 Psychological Bulletin

Bix B, 'Legal Positivism' in M Golding and W Edmundson (eds), *The Blackwell Guide to the Philosophy of Law and Legal Theory* (Blackwell Publishing 2005)

Bodamer E, 'Do I Belong Here? Examining Perceived Experiences of Bias, Stereotype Concerns, and Sense of Belonging in US Law Schools' (2020) 69 Journal of Legal Education 455

Bowring B, 'What Is Radical in "Radical International Law"?' (2013) 22 Finnish Yearbook of International Law

Chow PYS and Chow S, 'Introduction: Cultural Rights – A Radical Hope?' in *Cultural Rights in International Law and Discourse: Contemporary Challenges and Interdisciplinary Perspectives* (Brill Academic Publication 2018)

Correale A, 'Boredom: An Uncanny Guide to Something Unknown' (2018) 5 European Journal of Psychoanalysis

Day KN and Murphy RG, 'Just Trying to Be Human in This Place: Storytelling and Film in the First-Year Law School Classroom' (2009) 39 Stetson Law Review

Douzinas C and Gearey A, *Critical Jurisprudence* (Hart Publishing 2005)

Entrikin N, *The Betweenness of Place: Towards a Geography of Modernity* (Johns Hopkins UP 1991)

Eslava L, 'Istanbul Vignettes: Observing the Everyday Operation of International Law' (2014) 2 London Review of International Law 3

Guinier L, Fine M and Balin J, *Becoming Gentlemen: Women, Law School, and Institutional Change* (Beacon Press 1997)

Hall S, 'The Persistent Spectre: Natural Law, International Order and the Limits of Legal Positivism' (2001) 12 European Journal of International Law

Hart H, 'Positivism and the Separation of Law and Morals' in KE Himma and B Bix (eds), *Law and Morality* (Routledge 2005)

Kallio KP, Meier I and Häkli J, 'Radical Hope in Asylum Seeking: Political Agency Beyond Linear Temporality' (2021) 47 Journal of Ethics and Migration Studies

Kamir O, 'Why "Law-and-Film" and What Does It Actually Mean? A Perspective' (2005) 19 Continuum

Kennedy D, *A World of Struggle: How Power, Law and Expertise Shape Global Political Economy* (Princeton UP 2016)

Madero M, 'Penser la traditio juridique occidentale' (2012) I Annales, Histoire, Sciences Sociales

Manderson D, *Songs without Music: Aesthetic Dimensions of Law and Justice* (U of California P 2000)

Marks S, 'Introduction' in Susan Marks (ed), *International Law on the Left: Re-Examining Marxist Legacies* (CUP 2008)

McClain RA, *The Guide to Belonging in Law School* (West Academic Publishing 2021)

Piepmeier A, 'Why Zines Matter: Materiality and the Creation of Embodied Community' (2008) 18 American Periodicals

Rorty R, 'Human Rights, Rationality, and Sentimentality' in *Truth and Progress: Philosophical Papers* (CUP 1998)

Saab A, 'Emotions and International Law' (2021) 10 ESIL Reflections 1

Simpson G, 'Imagination' in J d'Aspremont and S Singh (eds), *Concepts of International Law: Contributions to Disciplinary Thought* (Edward Elgar Publishing 2019)

Thomas Y, *Fictio Legis* (Quodlibet [1995] 2016)

Tushnett M, 'Critical Legal Studies: A Political History' (1991) 100 The Yale Law Journal 31

Wangh M, 'Boredom in Psychoanalytic Perspective' (1975) 42 Social Research

Chapter 2

Writing About Evil

Alberto Rinaldi

Introduction: A Tale of Academic Vampirism

That law entertains a special relationship with evil and violence has been widely acknowledged and explored.[1] In one of his most famous writings, Walter Benjamin explains, for instance, how law is founded and maintained through violence.[2] The link between sovereignty and forceful authority has been outlined by an entire tradition of thinkers, from Hobbes to Agamben.[3] Scholars like Cover have demonstrated that the act of interpreting legal texts takes place "in the field of pain and death".[4] Moreover, critical thinkers have shown how violence is reproduced, channelled, and maintained through legal categories.[5] Law, one soon realises, is far from a fairy tale. International law is not exempt from the same considerations and critiques. As a bearer of higher ideals such as human dignity and equality, striving for peace and justice, it stands as a champion of universal values. Indeed, its rise after the massacres of World War II makes international law the privileged venue to confront evil. "Never again" was the promise embodied by the Genocide Convention, the first human rights treaty adopted by the United Nations General Assembly in December 1948.[6] The idea of protecting humanity

1 Among the rich literature, see, specifically, Ari Hirvonen and Janne Porttikivi, *Law and Evil: Philosophy, Politics, Psychoanalysis* (Routledge 2010); Austin Sarat and Thomas R Keams, *Law's Violence* (The U of Michigan P 1995); Jacques Derrida, 'Force of Law: The "Mystical Foundation of Authority"' in Drucilla Cornell and others, *Deconstruction and the Possibility of Justice* (Routledge 1992) 3–67.

2 Benjamin distinguishes between law-making and law-preserving violence. See Walter Benjamin, *Toward the Critique of Violence: A Critical Edition* (Stanford UP 2021).

3 See Thomas Hobbes, *Leviathan* (Penguin Classics 2017); Giorgio Agamben, *State of Exception* (The U of Chicago P 2004).

4 Robert M Cover, 'Violence and the Word' (1986) 95 Yale Law Journal 1601.

5 For an example, see Nathaniel Berman, 'Privileging Combat? Contemporary Conflict and the Legal Construction of War' (2004) 43 Columbia Journal of Transnational Law 1.

6 <www.un.org/en/genocideprevention/genocide-convention.shtml>

DOI: 10.4324/9781003461180-2

has since imbued the jargon and practice of international law.[7] Outlawing genocide, prosecuting war crimes, and charging heads of states with crimes against humanity have become common features of post–Cold War politics.[8] Beyond the well-known criticism of invoking humanity to achieve political goals, there seems to be a special bond between international law and these acts of uttermost violence. It is safe to say that confronting evil is part of the agenda of international lawyers, representing their preoccupations and daily bread and butter.

If it is plain that international law finds its rationale in confronting forms of extreme evil, less explored remains the relationship that we legal academics entertain with it during our careers. First as master students, then as doctoral candidates, up to senior researcher positions, we, the writers of international law, constantly deal with violence. However, we tend to remove that discussion from the picture. We distance ourselves from the humanity we describe and from the crimes that are committed against it. As authors, we oddly seem to vanish behind a pile of well-investigated theories, archival work, and case law, proposing this or that reading and offering an explanation of evil. In other words, we detach ourselves from chaos and horror through our dissertations, books, and articles. We find escape routes. Our writing becomes us, and we become our writing.[9] A screen is placed between us and the outside world, between ourselves and the evil we attempt to describe and make sense of. We have learned how banal that evil can ultimately be. We should not worry too much about existential questions but rather produce sound research and drive home our arguments.

My claim is that such an approach often masks a failure to take ownership of what we produce, infer, and ultimately feel as international lawyers. In this chapter, I want to propose another reading of our work and lived experience as students and academics involved in this business called international law. I would like to take the reader through the looking glass of cinema to a less-travelled route. I will use Abel Ferrara's *The Addiction* (1995) as a viaticum for a broader reflection on our dependences as researchers and writers of international law.

Ferrara's cult classic is a powerful allegory of academic life. In this short black-and-white gem, we follow the lives of two female students struggling with the writing of their thesis. The protagonist's descent into the abyss of

7 See, for instance, Ruti Teitel, *Humanity's Law* (OUP 2013); Anne Orford, *International Authority and the Responsibility to Protect* (CUP 2011).

8 On this point, see Kathryn Sikkink, *The Justice Cascade: How Human Rights Prosecutions Are Changing World Politics* (W. W. Norton & Company 2011); Sinja Graf, *The Humanity of Universal Crime: Inclusion, Inequality, and Intervention in International Political Thought* (OUP 2021).

9 For a critique of this position, see Roland Barthes, 'The Death of the Author' in Roland Barthes (ed), *The Rustle of Language* (U of California P 1989) 49–55.

drug addiction can be read as a metaphor for the obstacles of producing any academic work. But Kathleen's story closely mirrors many other aspects of the life and work of international lawyers. In this chapter, I attempt to give the film a personal interpretation centred on the idea of violence and evil inherent in our discipline. Using the structure of storytelling, I step away from traditional film and legal analysis. Rather, I try to mix Kathleen's story with my own. I do this in an attempt to provoke the reader and to bring to light a different tale about international law. By foregrounding the struggles involved in writing a doctoral thesis, I aim to provide a broader reflection on our lives as academics.

On the one hand, adopting this form is an attempt to dismantle the traditional way in which we write about international law. It can be read as a way to confront our idiosyncrasies and inner demons, not to cure or psychoanalyse them but to open a conversation about what we do when we write about our discipline, particularly when we traverse the wastelands of academia. In the words of Gerry Simpson:

> [I]ncreasingly international lawyers are rejecting the surface manifestations of international law . . . in favour of an engagement with its dark heart, its recurring pathologies, its traumatic histories . . . its forbidden material. What can't be done? And why not?[10]

I subscribe to Simpson's plea for sentiment without sentimentality, as he calls it, and I attempt to find my own way of "speaking international law in different sorts of ways".[11]

On the other hand, I have sought to engage with scholarship on law and emotions.[12] The emotional turn is gaining relevance in international academic circles but still remains confined to a reading of traditional material (treaties, practices, speeches, etc.). I would like to push those boundaries here and engage the reader by telling a story about my lived experience. This chapter is "personal" because it is the result of emotions and feelings that have run through me as "the author" and which, I presume, have been experienced, at

10 Gerry Simpson, *The Sentimental Life of International Law: Literature, Language, and Longing in World Politics* (OUP 2021) at 9.

11 Gerry Simpson, *The Sentimental Life of International Law: Literature, Language, and Longing in World Politics* (OUP 2021) at 2.

12 This is a rich and diverse scholarship. For a general overview, see Susan A Bandes and others, *Research Handbook on Law and Emotion* (Edward Elgar Publishing 2021). For a specific account in international law, see Vesselin Popovski, 'Emotions and International Law' in Yohan Ariffin and others (eds), *Emotions in International Politics: Beyond Mainstream International Relations* (CUP 2016) 184–203.

least in some form, by others too.[13] I turn to Ferrara's movie as it lends itself perfectly to the objective.

Shot in murky black and white, with a rap/hip-hop soundtrack that mirrors well the multi-racial urban world of New York, *The Addiction* portrays nightmares that are known, I believe, to anyone who has written a doctoral dissertation. The pressure to perform is enormous, as in today's academic market, you are nobody without a doctorate. At the same time, we also know how difficult, painful, and lonely this process can be People usually sacrifice years, relationships, and parts of their lives during a PhD, only to discover that this is the first step in a long journey through the circles of academic hell. This chapter is structured in six parts, which correspond to six key moments of the movie. Each of the six scenes describes a step in Kathleen's progressive descent into drug addiction, illustrating the consequences of writing her dissertation. As previously explained, I will produce less of an aesthetic or theorical film analysis and focus more on the story itself.[14] The film offers me a lens through which to engage with Kathleen's story while pouring my own into hers. The recounting of her dependence will be extended by way of metaphor to the entire academic enterprise, beyond the writing of a doctoral thesis. So this story of urban vampirism will serve as a sounding board for incidents that will resonate with most students and researchers of international law. One final comment on this introduction. If the reader is averse to meta-analysis and is not comfortable with expounding their feelings, I would suggest reading a different style. To cite Lautréamont:

> There are those who write to gain the applause of men by inventing noble sentiments of the heart. . . . As for me I depict the delights of cruelty! . . . So, timid soul, before penetrating further into such uncharted lands, set your feet the other way.[15]

You have been warned. Let's begin this journey.

Scene One: The Documentary

New York. A renowned academic institution. Doctoral students Kathleen and her friend Jean are attending a documentary screening as part of their

13 This statement is not intended to suggest that other forms of storytelling are less legitimate. Nor should our lived experience and feelings be romanticised, of course.

14 For a different analysis of the movie, see Joan Hawkins, '"No Worse Than You Were Before": Theory, Economy and Power in Abel Ferrara's "The Addiction"' in Xavier Mendik and Steven J Schneider (eds), *Underground USA Filmmaking Beyond the Hollywood Canon* (Wallflower Press 2002) 13–25.

15 Comte de Lautréamont, *Maldoror: Les Chants de Maldoror* (Peter Owen Publisher 1943) at 12–14.

philosophy course. The movie portrays the My Lai massacre, one of the most shocking mass slaughters of the Vietnam War at the hands of the US Army. The two are visibly troubled, but it is Kathleen who seems most affected by the images as she shakes her head and sighs: "The whole country, they were all guilty, how can you single out one man? . . . If you want to prosecute war crimes, you want to make sure more than one man takes the blame for it".

This will sound familiar to many international law students. You are a young, idealistic graduate. You are part of a renowned programme in human rights or in international criminal law. You believe that change is possible. Certain crimes cannot go unpunished. Many of us have sat in that classroom and watched a documentary on the Holocaust or other crimes against humanity. Countless research projects have been started from that emotional reaction to absolute evil. We have been there. We remember that hunch that once whispered to us: "never again". And a moment later, "I will do something about it".

In contrast, Jean seems more rational about the whole thing. Jean is our sceptical friend, perhaps less prey to emotion, perhaps already strategic about the thesis she will write, which will be functional in landing her an internship at the ICC: "What do you want me to say, the system is not perfect? . . . You can't jail a whole country, they needed a scapegoat". And Jean is probably right. But, like Kathleen, we will only realise that later.

Once outside the university perimeter, the two friends say goodbye to each other. They take different directions. Kathleen goes home, crossing a run-down part of the city. She is still very much absorbed in her thoughts. The camera follows her closely while she crosses the multi-ethnic streets of New York. But something has changed in her. Something has clicked.

At a crossroad, Kathleen is approached by a beautiful woman dressed in an elegant evening dress. "Nice night", she utters, before grabbing Kathleen by the wrist and pushing her into a dark cul-de-sac. It is here that Kathleen comes face to face with the vampire Casanova and her thirst for blood. "Look at me and tell me to go away", she enjoins Kathleen. "Don't ask, tell me". But our young student is paralysed by fear. She could have fought back. Instead, she is only able to mutter: "Please, don't hurt me". "You think this is going to stop me?" Casanova asks rhetorically. Then she bites Kathleen on the neck. She starts sucking her blood.

All of a sudden, Kathleen is experiencing what the civilians of the Tai Li massacre, as well as those of many other massacres in history, have deplorably suffered. She has become the perfect victim, begging not to be hurt by her perpetrator. Yet this bond, we discover, is not as simple as it looks. The relation between us and evil, between Kathleen and Casanova, is not a plain one. Something happened to Kathleen while watching that documentary: hunch, discomfort, willingness to make things better. The writing mechanism was triggered. We have been there, both as students and scholars. But we do not often confront our initial bite. Our texts, books, and articles depend on the evil which we strive to describe. "Collaborator", whispers the vampire to Kathleen before leaving her bleeding in the dark tunnel.

Scene Two: The Exhibition

Back home, Kathleen finds herself in a state of distress. She experiences pain and sadness as she looks at herself in the bathroom mirror. She gazes at her wound, crying. She turns in to her bed. Her night is full of nightmares. She has been visited by her own demons. She has experienced evil. No one told her that writing a thesis would be such hard work. A job that would take away her sleep, her strength, her appetite. She should have chosen a simpler, perhaps less controversial subject. She should have followed Jean's approach. Write about the application of a certain rule. Solve a legal technicality. Analyse some case law and compile neat footnotes. Be strategic so as not to be consumed by existential questions. We have been Kathleen and will be for years to come. We refuse to compromise. We do not settle for simple things, nor are we strategic. And so we continue to be accompanied by the demons of writing.

As part of her doctoral course, Kathleen has to attend methodology lectures. Her thesis advisor is giving a class on evil, determinism, and salvation. "Suffering is a good thing . . . guilt is a sign of God". No pain, no gain – that is the trope of the academic profession, after all. Suffering and sweat will be part of our lives, something to cherish, not to avoid. But Kathleen lives the class. She is sick. She has to go to the hospital. Something has definitely changed in her. She can feel it. At home, she lies in bed. Or rather, she hides in a corner of her room.

The next day, at the cafeteria, Kathleen is unable to eat her lunch. She stares at Jean and the other students around her. But her mind is far away. "They are all liars", she says about the philosophers she had to read for the class. She starts to question the whole academic business and the dissertation she is writing. We have felt that far too many times. We went through ups and downs. Afternoons spent in the faculty cafeteria, watching the raindrops, fantasising about other places, other lives.

Jean glances at her (at us) without comprehending. She is absorbed in the pages she is reading as she bites into her sandwich. "How can you eat and read at the same time?" Kathleen asks her in disgust. We have frequently met those who do not question themselves. Academics who just go on, as if nothing mattered, as if everything was normal. But for us, bitten by anxiety and existential doubts, the stakes are very different. Writing has changed us. It has made us aware of feelings and emotions we did not know beforehand. Jean's dumbfounded look suggests that "a good thesis is a finished thesis"; we will get there in due course. But in the meantime, there is the vast and relentless sea of writing, our awkward bond with it, our sense of sin.

So when you are frustrated, you do something else. You entertain yourself with activities somewhat related to your thesis. You visit an exhibition. Art and the law – who knows? Maybe you will get some inspiration. And so does Kathleen. An exhibition on genocide: other bodies, other crimes. Somehow, a Nietzschean echo pops in her head: "There is no history. Everything we are, is eternally with us". Time is an eternal return of the same; there is no moral. If no ethics can be inferred from historical atrocities, why keep setting up more tribunals? We seek through other forms what the law cannot offer to us. We cannot get enough because we have realised that there is no salvation. The addiction has taken over. "That those who do not learn from history are doomed to repeat history. It is a lie", Kathleen ponders. And yet we ought to write in a detached, objective, rational way.

A German-speaking voice in the background. Sounds of war, images of massacres. More bodies, more death. "What can save us from this crazy existence?" Kathleen murmurs to herself. She starts to see time floating in front of her eyes. Images of the past and the present mix. Then she walks home at night. And now, for the first time, she starts to hunt. She has embraced life without ethics. "It makes no difference what I do. It's the violence of my willingness against theirs". In this business, it is a war of all against all. This is academia, whether you like it or not. From thesis writing to the job hunting, an endless spiral of violence. And we, as junkies, embrace it all.

Scene Three: The Library

Kathleen is back in class. Another lecture, more readings to cover. Kierkegaard, Sartre, Heidegger. We need theory to satisfy our hunger. We have to fill out those footnotes, comply with the canons of the struggle. After class, Kathleen joins her professor to discuss the progress of her thesis. They attend a concert. Crossing lines? We all know that the relationship between a supervisor and their pupil is a tricky one. Sleepless hours thinking that we are not good enough, that what we write will not be received well. We have replaced our parents with a different totemic figure. We have traded authority for authority. Then one day, a terrifying doubt hits: What if Jean's research is more in line with our supervisor's? What if she gets ahead of us? The dreadful feeling of being downgraded. Banished from the graces of our mentor, we feel orphaned. And suddenly, we discover that writing a thesis is a bloodshed to flatter the ego. "It makes no difference what I do. It is the violence of my will against theirs".

A small, bohemian café. Sad, classical music. The supervisor presses Kathleen: "you haven't said a word all night long". She keeps staring into the void, then starts quoting her mentor's favourite authors. Kathleen has a plan. She has been bitten, and she has learned the lesson. She takes the supervisor home. They kiss. They are addicted to the same habit. But she has overcome his ego. All the mirrors in her apartment are now covered by heavy drapery. It is wise not to stare at yourself when you have gone down that path.

Yet there is a capital moment in the writing of any thesis: the decision on your material. What is your archive? supervisors and colleagues ask. What is your research object? How will you justify your theoretical method? What are your case studies? Those voices will reverberate in your head for weeks and months. Maybe you do not want any practical counterevidence. But in this business, it is the fight of their will against yours. After infecting her supervisor, Kathleen pays a visit to the university's library, the pagan temple so dear to researchers. Months spent sitting among its shelves, immersing oneself in the thoughts of great thinkers, only to grasp their quirks, their compulsions, their madness. "This is a graveyard", Kathleen murmurs. "Rose and crumbling tombstones, vicious, lifeless epitaphs, and we are all drawn here like flies". There comes a time when international lawyers seek a breath of fresh air. Dissatisfied with theories, disgusted by the stench of rotten pages, they seek an answer out there, in "real" life.

And so does Kathleen. She wanders the corridors of the library, looking for her new victim. She approaches a nice-looking girl, who is flicking through a pile of books. She sits next to her. Then she gently asks what her major is. "Anthropology", the student answers. Something clicks in Kathleen, like a revelation. When asked if she enjoys working in her field, the student adds with confidence, "What else is there? Man is the measure of all things". Kathleen seems fascinated by this answer. Perhaps she found an escape route from that eternal piling of footnotes, a way to support the theories of evil she has been feeding herself over the past months. Kathleen's thirst for an object of study is insatiable. This is what academic research makes you become. A slave to your cravings, a vampire in search of other disciplines to bleed out. After leading the anthropologist to her lair, she performs the usual ritual. "This does not affect you at all?" asks the student in tears. "No", Kathleen replies, "it was your decision".

When you have spent enough time in international law, moving towards other disciplines is no longer an oddity. In fact, it becomes quite a natural move. International legal researchers are constantly searching for a new "fix", for the next big thing, in order to perpetuate their existence and to differ meaning. All that talk about humanity, uttermost violence, human dignity. All these ideas have gone into their heads; they have bewitched and drained them. International lawyers know too well that their discipline is not enough. They jump into history, political philosophy, anthropology, sociology, cinema, etc. Like bloodthirsty vandals, they plunder other fields with no remorse, only to casually wink and say, "It was your decision".

Once you have taken the step of interdisciplinarity, there is no way back. Kathleen has undergone a path that will take her again through the streets of New York in search of more blood. Meanwhile, Jean senses that something is off with her friend. Back at the university, the two meet again. Jean confronts Kathleen: "You are halfway through your dissertation. You don't go to class; you don't do conferences. I don't know what you are doing". Jean is right. She represents the voice of reason. Instead of indulging in other disciplines, one should stick to the letter of the law. Play the academic gig. Do things; promote oneself; be on social media. "You are acting like a lunatic", she reprehends Kathleen. But the latter is no longer easily impressed. She has already gone deep enough into her fears, confronted the demons of her writing, banged on the door of other disciplines. "The appetite is insatiable; this is what I have learnt in the last couple of weeks". Jean somehow tries to shield herself from those attacks: "Do you want an apology for ethical relativism or something?" she replies, irritated. "No", says Kathleen. "Prove there is no evil, and you can go". Then Jean's paper castle starts to crumble. Egged on by Kathleen's words, her confidence falters. "You are addicted as much as I am. It is the nature of the organism". Kathleen has put her up against the wall. Those who are engaged in seemingly rational and scientific research are no different from others. They too are part of the collective academic addiction. They only disguise it better, masking it behind piles of footnotes, case law, and legal technicalities. But their hunger is the same as that of their colleagues, if not worse.

Scene Four: The Mansion

Kathleen's journey through this particular kind of self-revelation is fully underway. She knows there is no turning back now. She has realised that everything she is producing is a lie, that the prepositions she writes are false, that they do not correspond to any external reality. Above all, they have no value to the world. They will have no ethical consequence. It is just a flattering of the ego. A disposing of the pain and suffering of others to obtain a degree and later, perhaps, an academic position in some fancy university. Carry on the model; reproduce it for future generations; stay addicted. After the doctoral thesis, there are articles, books, and papers to present. And hovering over all this, the process of writing: draining, antisocial, egoistic. A disposing of the body and soul of people of whom we really know nothing, whom we use for our own purpose and pleasure. But others, just like her, had to traverse those wastelands. How did they survive? What was their strategy? And here comes another core moment of every PhD: the encounter with a senior academic. Someone who has already gone through that pain and has learnt how to endure. It might be during a visiting abroad, at a conference, or in a symposium.

Kathleen wanders the streets, looking for a new fix. Until she meets *him*. When she tries to grab him by the wrist, he does nothing to put her off. "Why don't you just tell me to leave you alone? You wanna go someplace dark?" he asks ironically. Immediately, Kathleen recognises his strengths: he is well versed; his words are perfect; his style is dry but self-explanatory; his voice is controlled and persuasive. He is that great academic we've always longed to meet. We have read all his works. Now we finally get a chance to be in his presence. Peina. The vampire master. He has been roaming the streets for decades. He takes Kathleen to his mansion, and he wastes no time: "You can never get enough. But you learn, like the Tibetans, to survive on a little".

It sounds as if he knows us intimately. Peina is well aware of the risks of our profession. "You are like all the rest", he says. The constant ups and downs, the frustration, the spasmodic search for a method to momentarily quell the addiction. Yet he seems to have found his own strategy. In his presence, Kathleen is baffled. Peina speaks from sidereal distances, with words carved in stone: "The entire world is a graveyard. Mankind is thrived to exist beyond good and evil". Yes, he is the great inquisitor of international law. The revolutionary academic. The brilliant critical scholar. You have been given that one chance to meet him. You do not want to waste it.

Kathleen walks through his mansion. Massive paintings on the walls, books scattered on the floor. Knowledge swirls in the air. But it is a crisp, stimulating sensation. Far away from the morbid smell of libraries, with their piles of dead authors. This is what we were looking for. And it is a privilege to be there in the presence of that virtuoso. "You want tea?" Peina asks kindly. He seems approachable. Like Kathleen, we would like to pose him endless questions. How did he survive the addiction? What was his method? Above all, what should we make of our research project? How do we put into words that evil that has been staring at us? We are young vampires. We do not fully comprehend the mechanisms of academia. Like Kathleen, we are still looking for answers.

"Have you read *Naked Lunch*?" Peina asks Kathleen. "Burroughs describes perfectly what it is to go without a fix", he explains. The virtuoso knows how to charm us. He does not preach about the principles of international law. His is a wide-ranging reflection. He refers to unorthodox authors; he introduces uncanny perspectives into the story. For a moment, we think we have found an ally. Just like Kathleen, we believe we have uncovered the missing piece in our quest. We are prone to pander. To enslave ourselves to his art. Kathleen is truly fascinated by him. But she also feels the power Peina is exerting over her. "What do you want?" she asks. "What do I want?" he promptly replies. "No!" he screams. "What do *you* want from *me*?" Peina rectifies. "You came after me, you took my hand, you tried to force me. You think you understand? You know nothing, you understand nothing. I will show you what you are".

Now the house is infused with classical music. In a cozy robe, Peina proceeds with his gargling. In the other room, Kathleen is left bleeding on the floor. He used her body, as he did with all the others who came before him. Peina approaches and takes the time to elucidate the addiction: "You think you know who we are. . . . The point is to blend in". Is this the much-sought-after method? Find a way to infiltrate. Critiquing international law from within.

Know how to read its technicalities in order to deconstruct them. Learning the gospel of power to fight it from the inside. Become an expert in the art of vampirism. "My habit is controlled by my will. My will was initially formed by my addiction, but now I am strong enough to dictate it. . . . [I]s that too abstract?" Peina asks Kathleen. But she is crawling on the floor. The encounter was devastating to her. Getting to know a genius and feeling his influence and power over you is not an easy task. And Peina is restless. "Whatever good is in you I will use for my sustenance". He is like everyone else. A bloodthirsty academic. "Pain is something we all know, but it takes a special person to see it". After all, we got what we wanted. Peina showed us what lies at the bottom of that special kind of hell. Forever chained, like everyone else in this business. It takes someone special to describe that suffering. To such a task we will devote our days. "Read the books", Peina urges Kathleen. "Sartre, Beckett, Baudelaire". Pufendorf, Clausewitz, Grotius. Hobbes, Machiavelli, Schmitt. The list grows longer. "Anything for a fix". There is no escape. "Eternity is a long time. Get used to it", utters Peina before leaving Kathleen alone.

Scene Five: The Thesis Discussion

Kathleen wanders back on the streets. Her conversion to evil is now complete. She has assimilated the lesson. She understands how to hunt and procure her game. She is no longer lost in the writing of her dissertation. On the contrary, she knows the method to satisfy her addiction. So as the virtuoso taught her, others become disposable to her. Kathleen falters in the street, calling for help. A young man stops to rescue her. She attacks him mercilessly. She takes from him what she needs for her survival, to go on for another month, another chapter, a few more pages. The clarity of her addiction opens wide before her eyes:

> I finally understand what all this is. Our addiction is evil. . . . [T]he propensity for this evil lies in our weaknesses before it. You reach a point where you are forced to face your own needs. And the fact that you can't terminate the situation sets on you with full force. . . . It is not *cogito ergo sum*, but *dedita, ergo sum. Pecco, ergo sum*".

This particular twist to the Cartesian formula reveals to her the essence of that journey. Her turning into a professional academic is now complete. She is back on track. She works hard to finish her dissertation. She spends her days at the table writing, footnoting, paragraphing as if caught in a trance. The aches of the last few months seem to have disappeared. She is able to move forward at a pace she has never experienced before. She got the gist of the game. From the documentary to the lectures, through the libraries and the visiting stays, her season in hell finally makes sense: "Philosophy is propaganda", Kathleen reflects. "There is always an attempt to influence the object".

Il n'y a pas de hors-texte. The vampire Casanova was right. "Collaborator", she had called Kathleen. We philosophise about genocides, war crimes, crimes against humanity. We seek solutions for environmental disasters; we spot human rights abuses; we criticise structural economic injustices. We do so in a detached and neutral tone, not realising there is no such thing as a neutral space. We use other people's stories for our own purpose and pleasure. We throw our caprices, desires, and idiosyncrasies into what we write. Then, like Pontius Pilate, we wash our hands. Why is it so hard to admit it? Perhaps that realisation invalidates the scientific claim of our research. Or does it reveal something too uncomfortable about us?

"The real question is what the philosophers' impact on other egos is. . . . That's what it comes down to. Our impacts on other egos". Kathleen guessed it right. That is what we do. We produce arguments to convince others. To bend them to our logic. And thus, to publish and advance in the struggle. The more convincing we are, the more other egos will be subjugated. Never mind the method or the resources. What matters is the results. That is why we have to devote ourselves to hunting. Spending days and years to win an argument. Use the resources around us. Critique the system by staying in the system. Sitting in comfortable chairs and pontificating about the world. Feeling like the masters of our sentences and, from our offices, shooting arrows at our enemies. Bringing our work to completion, whatever it takes. Because, in this business, that is the only thing that matters. Publishing, moving forward, getting ahead, finding a space for oneself, killing others.

Kathleen discusses her thesis successfully. The jury is impressed with her work. She is finally a doctor. Professors and colleagues praise her. They wish her all the best in her future academic career. She made it. The end of a PhD is such a relief. You have shown that you can get the job done. You are officially part of the clique. No more sleepless nights, no more having to prove yourself to your supervisor. Anger, frustration, anxiety, everything is behind you. Or so you think.

Kathleen is on her way to her dissertation party. In the taxi, she ponders:

> There is a dual nature to the addition. It satisfies the hunger. But it also works to make us forget who we really are. . . . We drink to escape the fact that we are alcoholics. Existence is the search for relief from our habit, and our habit is the only relief we can find.

This is how we work as academics. For eternity. The thesis is only the first step in the long spiral of our job. The discussion of a doctorate is a momentary relief. Habit will take over again. Find a post doc, think about another project, assess the best publisher for your dissertation, struggle to secure a position. In this endless descent, rare are the opportunities to stop and reflect.

Just before the party starts, Kathleen crosses a man on the stairs of the faculty. A young man who is distributing flyers for a voluntary organisation. Kathleen invites him inside; she would like him to be her next victim. But the young man politely refuses: "I cannot, thank you. I appreciate the offer. Perhaps another time". As in Bartleby's famous formula, the young man "prefers not to" participate. He declines to be part of the circle. He will devote his life to some other activity. He has had the courage to give up the addiction. That thought crossed our minds. Barter everything for nothing. Bet on yourself and your strengths; no longer be part of that dreadful mechanism. Be truly free at last.

But Kathleen is outraged by this encounter. In the dressing room, she screams and kicks. How is it possible to withdraw like that? The logic of academic addiction is ingrained in her. She is a doctor now. And she is furious. She needs new victims. Soon after, the party starts.

Scene Six: The Graveyard

Kathleen is covered in blood. Her party has become a banquet of evil and violence. The academic ritual has been performed. Now she fully belongs to that world. She staggers through the streets. Some bystanders notice her tortured body. They call an ambulance. She is taken to the hospital. This time, she does not escape.

A children's lullaby is playing in the background. A restful, soft atmosphere. In her bed, Kathleen looks docile and peaceful. She gently asks the nurse to open the blinds. We understand her intent: vampires cannot tolerate light. She wants to relinquish her pain. Leave everything behind with a clean break. Somehow, we feel for her. We understand her suffering. We have experienced it firsthand. One simple blow would erase it all.

"It is not that easy, Doctor". Casanova suddenly appears at the side of her bed. Once an accomplice, forever an accomplice. You are not outside the text. The addiction is bound to continue. "To find rest it takes a real genius", utters Casanova as she shuts the room's curtains. In this business, we are all sinners. We are all part of that evil we keep describing so clinically and neutrally. Our options are reduced to the content of our sentences, the style of our footnotes. We have embarked on a journey with no return.

A priest enters the room. He reaches Kathleen's bed. She wants to confess, to ask for forgiveness. The priest proceeds. This is not a story of redemption, however. Salvation is not an option for international lawyers, but a further illusion. Perhaps the ultimate form of delusional violence: the endless swinging between apologetic and utopian claims.

The final shot of the movie takes place in a cemetery. Kathleen puts a rose on what seems to be her own grave. "To face what we are in the end. Self-revelation is an annihilation of self", she mutters.

Yes, she has buried herself. All her other selves. Immolated on the altar of the academic abattoir, from which there is no escape. Embrace the contest, its uttermost violence, the constant pressure. Embrace the logic of publishing or perishing. Learn to backstab, the power games, the secret alliances. Show no remorse; feel no compassion. Disguise yourself with good feelings. Learn the jargon; advance human rights arguments; sprinkle it all with a touch of ethics. Tell them you are doing it for others. You are an international lawyer; humanity is dear to you.

Kill; kill again; kill better.

Reference List

Agamben G, *State of Exception* (U of Chicago P 2004)

Bandes SA and others, *Research Handbook on Law and Emotion* (Edward Elgar Publishing 2021)

Barthes R, 'The Death of the Author' in R Barthes (ed), *The Rustle of Language* (U of California P 1989) 49–55

Benjamin W, *Toward the Critique of Violence: A Critical Edition* (Stanford UP 2021)

Berman N, 'Privileging Combat? Contemporary Conflict and the Legal Construction of War' (2004) 43 Columbia Journal of Transnational Law 1

Cover R, 'Violence and the Word' (1986) 95 Yale Law Journal 1601

Derrida J, 'Force of Law: The "Mystical Foundation of Authority"' in D Cornell and others (eds), *Deconstruction and the Possibility of Justice* (Routledge 1992) 3–67

Graf S, *The Humanity of Universal Crime: Inclusion, Inequality, and Intervention in International Political Thought* (OUP 2021)

Hawkins J, '"No Worse Than You Were Before": Theory, Economy and Power in Abel Ferrara's "The Addiction"' in X Mendik and SJ Schneider (eds), *Underground U.S.A. Filmmaking Beyond the Hollywood Canon* (Wallflower Press 2002) 13–25

Hirvonen A and Porttikivi J, *Law and Evil: Philosophy, Politics, Psychoanalysis* (Routledge 2010)

Hobbes T, *Leviathan* (Penguin Classics 2017)

Lautréamont, *Maldoror: Les Chants de Maldoror* (Peter Owen Publisher 1943)

Orford A, *International Authority and the Responsibility to Protect* (CUP 2011)

Popovski V, 'Emotions and International Law' in Y Ariffin and others (eds), *Emotions in International Politics: Beyond Mainstream International Relations* (CUP 2016) 184–203

Sarat A and Keams TR, *Law's Violence* (The U of Michigan P 1995)

Sikkink K, *The Justice Cascade: How Human Rights Prosecutions Are Changing World Politics* (W. W. Norton & Company 2011)

Simpson G, *The Sentimental Life of International Law: Literature, Language, and Longing in World Politics* (OUP 2021)

Teitel R, *Humanity's Law* (OUP 2013)

Chapter 3

Reading a Law Film in Cinematic Context as a Commentary on the Decline of Liberal Democracy and the Rule of Law

Emin Alper's *Burning Days* (2022) Read Against John Ford's *The Man Who Shot Liberty Valance* (1962)

Orit Kamir

Introduction

I first saw Emin Alper's *Burning Days* at the Jerusalem Cinematheque during the Jerusalem Film Festival in the summer of 2022. The film offers powerful visual imagery of massive sinkholes that pop up in and around Yaniklar, a small town in the middle of arid nowhere, Turkey. Emre (Selahattin Paşali), a young and inexperienced prosecutor sent from the big city, sets out to inquire into the phenomenon. Murat (Ekin Koç), Yaniklar's independent journalist and owner of the local opposition newspaper, provides him with documentation indicating that the sinkholes were caused by municipal greed and corruption. The powerful local mayor, owner and operator of the town's water pumps, has been overexploiting the groundwater, thus causing the appearance of the hazardous sinkholes. The uneducated local population treats him as a local hero: he is their all-powerful patriarch; the provider of precious water; their most celebrated boar hunter, oozing with manly prowess. As the owner of a local newspaper, he is also their main source of information and its interpretation. When Emre attempts to apply the rule of law even to the powerful mayor and his son, he is undermined and vilified as the enemy of the people. On the night of the mayor's reelection, as the townsmen joyously celebrate his overwhelming victory, Emre, embodying the rule of law, and Murat, free media, run for their lives, trying to flee the town. The townsmen ominously chant "This is Yaniklar; there is no way out". The film ends as it opens, with an image of a sinkhole: a kind of dramatic, sinister, inverted version of John Ford's Monument Valley.

Six months after my first encounter with the film, I was reminded of it when Turkey's neglected southeast was hit by a powerful earthquake, causing the deaths of 60,000 people and leaving hundreds of thousands homeless.

DOI: 10.4324/9781003461180-3

Much of the damage was due to widespread corruption: building projects were not properly supervised by local municipalities. Three months later, Turkey's president, Recep Tayyip Erdoğan – who has steadily transformed the country from a semi-liberal democracy into a corrupt, regressive, totalitarian autocracy – was reelected by his conservative supporters, who continue to view him as their all-powerful patriarch and saviour. Emin Alper's Yaniklar was playing itself out in Turkey's national politics.

That same winter, images from *Burning Days* resurfaced again in my mind when a populist, extreme right-wing government took power in my own country, Israel. In January 2023, determined to rescue prime minister Benjamin Netanyahu from his ongoing trial on many counts of corruption, his new government announced its all-out attack on Israel's rule of law and, with it, on its liberal democracy. The attorney general and the Supreme Court were vilified by Netanyahu and his ministers as enemies both of the wronged, victimised patriarch portrayed by them as "a strong leader" and of the entire country. The vision of vilified Emre and Murat chased as they attempted to flee the crazed Yaniklar now seemed prophetic.

The next time I saw *Burning Days*, it was again shown at the Jerusalem Cinematheque. This time, it was introduced to the public as a cinematic fable of populist extremism and corruption in the post-truth and media manipulation era. The film's mesmerising portrayal of the attacks on the rule of law was presented as relevant to the understanding of contemporary political developments in both Turkey and Israel.

The 21st century has been challenging to liberal democracies, to the rule of law, and to egalitarian legal systems. Populism and the culture of "post truth" are the harbingers of what seems to be fundamental change. Countries that seemed to be moving toward liberal democracy have been pulling back, electing self-serving leaders who set out to limit the autonomy of legal systems and restrict human rights. Women's rights, LGBT rights, and ethnic minorities' rights have all been significantly curtailed in several countries as Hungary's Viktor Orbán has become the beacon of "non-liberal democracy", and Vladimir Putin has declared the revival of ancient regimes. In the United States as well, a conservative yet activist Supreme Court, strengthened by Donald Trump, has denounced its long-standing commitment to personal freedom, equality, and progress.

The law can hardly speak to its own demise. It cannot analyse its weakness in the face of growing nationalism, populism, and regressive conservative currents. But, law films can, and some do. By presenting the law in its social context, associating it with powerful imagery, and calling attention to its less obvious features, such films can evoke readings and interpretations that shed light on the contemporary regression of legal regimes.

In this chapter, I read the film *Burning Days* as attesting to the failure and deterioration of the rule of law. I suggest that by reading the film in cinematic context – more specifically, against a unique 1962 "town tamer" Western – it can be seen as depicting how, against its better judgment, the law might find itself wrapped up in an honour-driven showdown with political leadership. Trapped in such a head-on confrontation, the legal system compromises its moral standing as it becomes driven by self-interest. Locked in a political struggle, the law loses its integrity and good standing with the public and is likely to be defeated by its political opponent, who is always better positioned for such a duel. Read as a contemporary remake of John Ford's *The Man Who Shot Liberty Valance*, Alper's *Burning Days* can be interpreted as exposing its legal protagonist's dark, honour-bound aspects that bring about his failure. This cinematic commentary is highly applicable to real-life conflicts between populist regimes and legal institutions.

To lay the ground for this argument, I begin with short plot summaries of both *Burning Days* and the Western I read it against, *The Man Who Shot Liberty Valance*, followed by a brief presentation of honour and honour culture. This sets the stage for the close reading of *Burning Days*. Read against the backdrop of *Liberty Valance*, the film is shown to demonstrate how its legal protagonist's engagement with a strong honour system leads to the collapse of the rule of law. *Burning Days*'s young legal official steps into every honour trap laid for him by the strong, corrupt ruling class. The ground he stands on becomes increasingly shaky, until he finds himself trapped in a sinkhole, actual and figurative. *Liberty Valance* portrays an alternative route that, taken by Emre, might have led to the survival and perhaps even triumph of the rule of law.

Burning Days – Movie Plot and Imagery

Law Faces Wobbly Ground

Framing the film's subject matter, its opening scene confronts the audience with the image of a huge sinkhole in a bare, arid landscape. Young-looking Emre, the newly arrived prosecutor, stands at the edge of a cliff, accompanied by the local judge who acquaints him with the whereabouts of his new post. Looking down the sinkhole, the young legal official comments that it is scary.

Gun in the First Act

Returning to Yaniklar, Emre is sickened by a barbaric scene of hunters, townsmen and children joyfully chasing a large wild boar helplessly running for its life. The boar is later dragged by the hunters through the town's streets, leaving a distinct trail of blood.

Stepping in Honour Trap 1

In his spacious office, Emre is visited by Sahin (Erol Babaoğlu), the mayor's son and a local lawyer, accompanied by his sidekick, the local dentist. The two claim that boar hunting is an honourable tradition, insinuating that Emre might be too refined (sissy) for their tough (manly) customs. He responds harshly, reminding them that shooting is prohibited within the town limits and threatening that next time he will press charges.

Politics of Water and Power

Driving through the town, Emre notices people lining up with large plastic jerricans, as the mayor's campaign for reelection focuses on his role as their water supplier. These scenes reappear throughout the film, intensifying as the elections approach. When Emre drives to a nearby lake for a swim, Murat, the journalist, shows up, warning him that the lake is treacherous and can turn into a death trap. He informs Emre that his predecessor disappeared, perhaps in fear of accusing the mayor of overexploiting the groundwater and causing the sinkholes.

Stepping in Honour Trap 2

That evening, Emre accepts an invitation to the mayor's house. He is repelled by the countless photos of boar hunts that cover the walls. Emre finds himself with the mayor's lawyer son, Sahin, and his friend the dentist in the mayor's garden. When the locals taunt him, he succumbs and, against his better judgment, drinks their strong homemade *raki* (a Turkish alcoholic beverage). When a young Roma woman named Pekmez joins, the two men dance closely and sensually with her, daring Emre to show his manhood. Emre drinks until he feels sick, throws up, is laid down by the men, and loses consciousness.

The Law Entrapped

The following morning, Emre wakes up with a headache, noticing a mark on his neck. He has no recollection of the previous night's events. After visiting a new sinkhole, he is informed of a rape allegation: Pekmez was brutally raped and beaten and is now hospitalised. Her devastated father demands justice. Feeling he has been tricked, provoked and enraged, Emre orders the arrest of Sahin and the dentist, requiring that their semen be sent to a laboratory. As he examines the garden, he finds his pen on the ground and conceals it.

From this moment on, Emre desperately tries to recall the events of the night he spent in the garden. In a series of short flashbacks, he slowly recovers bits of memory of stumbling away from the garden, helped by Murat. Piece by piece, he remembers himself in Murat's house, in his shower, in his arms.

As Emre is trapped in his nightmarish attempt to restore his memory, the mayor's newspaper claims he is out to get the mayor and stop the water supply to Yaniklar and that he is implicated in an immoral relationship with Murat. Further, it insinuates that Emre was at the scene of the crime when Pekmez was brutalised and was either a witness to the crime or a participant. The growing public hostility towards Emre is evident as people block his way home and blockade the entrance to his house, piling empty jerricans on his doorstep.

The Law Loses Ground

On election day, the town is covered with the mayor's posters, his followers shooting their rifles in the streets in a show of support. The judge informs Emre that she released Sahin and the dentist after the lab report exonerated them both. On the streets of Yaniklar, they are received as heroes. Alone in his office, Emre looks defeated and humiliated. Meanwhile, the crowd shoots at Murat's house; the Roma camp is set on fire; the independent newspaper run by Murat is set on fire; and the judge informs Emre that Pekmez, the young Roma woman, is now accusing him of the rape. The judge urges him to surrender to the chief of police, saying that prison is the safest place for him as the riots in town are out of control, and the police cannot protect him.

Gun Goes Off and the Sinkhole Swallows Emre

Murat shows up at Emre's place, and they are both surrounded by growing crowds of young men, silently eyeing them with hostility and throwing rocks at the house. As the crowd closes in on them, the two men make their way to Emre's car, driving out of town. The townsmen celebrate the mayor's reelection. Spotted by Sahin and a group of hunters, Emre's car is chased by a line of cars as it makes its way out of town. Forced to stop at a police block, Emre and Murat abandon the car and run for their lives as the hunters gleefully follow. The camera cuts back and forth between the hunters' frenzied faces and the desperate expressions on Emre's and Murat's, as it did when portraying the boar chase at the film's opening. Finally, the hunters arrive at the edge of a sinkhole, only to see their prey standing, miraculously, on the other side of the abyss.

The Man Who Shot Liberty Valance

As Emre struggles to overcome his blackout and regain control of his life, as the streets of Yaniklar close in on him, forming an increasingly claustrophobic, suffocating sensation, *Burning Days* takes on the dark features of *film noir*. Adrian Martin rightly points out:

> Traditional *noir* elements – such as the paranoia of a stranger who is faced with the disquieting, sometimes violent rituals of a tightly-knit community – are evoked not only for the sake of an atmosphere of dread, but also to address the political reality of the "mob mentality" in today's world.[1]

1 Adrian Martin, 'Burning Days' blog <https://iffr.com/en/iffr/2023/films/burning-days>.

Burning Days is also an effective thriller, keeping its viewers on the edge of their seats. The possibility of a sexual attraction between the film's two leading men adds a gay erotic dimension; the *Thelma & Louise* ending, in which the two friends reach the precipice yet their image remains unscathed, echoes a dead-end road trip film. For my purposes here, I focus on the film's Western-like plotline. More specifically, I read *Burning Days* as a "town tamer" Western: a film in which an outsider brings law and order to a remote town, saving it from brutality, violence, and chaos and civilising it.[2] As in most Westerns, including town tamers, *Burning Days* depicts a man's world and features no women characters to speak of. Pekmez, the young Roma woman, is no more than a trap Sahin sets for Emre. Typical of Westerns, the only gender issue investigated by the film is the meaning of masculinity.

In classic town tamer Westerns, the town-taming hero is a gunfighter, such as Wyatt Earp in John Ford's *My Darling Clementine* (1946), Shane in George Stevens's *Shane* (1953),[3] and Will Kane in Stanely Kramer's *High Noon* (1952).[4] Accepting a sheriff nomination (as in *Clementine*), backing up the good people of the community (as in *Shane*), or forcing his will on a reluctant community (as in *High Noon*), the gunfighter uses his extraordinary professional skill to rid the town of the villains who terrorise it. Yet an exceptional and highly celebrated town tamer Western deviates from this pattern by replacing the gunfighter with a man of law, a lawyer. *The Man Who Shot Liberty Valance*[5] presents a plotline that resembles *Burning Days*'s so closely that the latter can be seen as a take on it.

John Ford's 1962 classic features a young, idealistic lawyer who arrives in a frontier town, aspiring to bring its residents law and progress. Finding

2 The term was coined by Richard Slotkin in his *Gunfighter Nation: The Myth of the Frontier in Twentieth-Century America* (U of Oklahoma P 1998) 379–404. It has since become a term of art in Western scholarship.

3 For a reading of *Shane* as a town tamer Western, see Slotkin (n 2) 396–400.

4 For a reading of *High Noon* as a town tamer Western, see Slotkin (n 2) 391–96.

5 For a detailed reading of *The Man Who Shot Liberty Valance* against *My Darling Clementine* as two outstanding, strikingly different town tamer westerns, see Timothy P O'Neill, 'Two Concepts of Liberty Valance: John Ford, Isaiah Berlin, and Tragic Choice on the Frontier' (2004) 37 Creighton Law Review 471, 479, 482–91. O'Neill claims that "While *Clementine* exhibits a sweet simplicity, *Liberty Valance* possesses a complexity that is far more challenging, even revisionist, in its view of the American frontier". 479. Cheyney Ryan Reads *Liberty Valance* against *High Noon*, pointing out similarities and differences between them as two remarkable town tamer Westerns. See Cheyney Ryan, 'Print the Legend' in John Denvir (ed), *Legal Reelism: Movies as Legal Texts* (U of Illinois P 1996), 23–43. "More so than *High Noon*, MSLV connects the problem of the legal order and its democratic context to the problem of *representation*. But it does so in a manner that deeply problematises the notion of 'representation', and with it the related notion of 'legitimacy'" (30). In like manner, most analyses of *Liberty Valance* treat it as a highly sophisticated and critical Western. I offer a twist on the film's sophistication and criticism in the chapter's last paragraphs. Here I refer merely to the basic, overt plotline.

himself at odds with the self-serving villain who enforces his rule of violence and fear on a weak community, the young lawyer forms a union with the town's independent journalist, attempting to expose the villain and enforce the law on him. The dramatic conflict escalates into a showdown, after which the young lawyer frees the town from the grip of the villain, ensuring the rule of law and its accompanying promise of progress. Read against this plotline, I suggest that *Burning Days* can be understood to reveal what went wrong in Emre's 2022 quest for law and justice and why it was he – the man of law – and not the villain who was forced out of town. To pursue this interpretation, I must add some detail to the presentation of *The Man Who Shot Liberty Valance*.

Law Faces the Rule of Violence

Ransom "Ranse" Stoddard (James Stewart), a young lawyer fresh out of law school, follows the ethos of the day: "Go West, young man!" A man of law, he refuses to carry a gun, holding tight to his law books instead. As the stagecoach that he rides in is held up by Liberty Valance (Lee Marvin) and his gang, Ranse is robbed as well as flogged cruelly for intervening on behalf of a lady fellow rider. Left to die, he is found by Tom Doniphon (John Wayne), a local rancher who brings him to the Ericsons' restaurant in Shinbone, a frontier town in the desert.

Avoiding Honour Trap 1

As Ranse slowly recovers, he begins to wash dishes and bus tables at the restaurant. Despite Valance's mockery and ridicule of him for wearing an apron, Ranse refuses to be dragged into an honour conflict. He repeatedly demands that the sheriff arrest Valance and bring him to trial. But the sheriff knows all too well that the only law in Shinbone is the one enforced by Liberty Valance with his threats, whip, and gun.

Integrating Into the Community

Meanwhile, discovering that Hallie (Vera Miles), with whom he works at the restaurant, is illiterate, he starts a school, teaching children as well as adults English, basic history, and civics. He teaches them democracy and that all men are created equal. Classes are held in the backroom of the local newspaper, *The Star*, where Ranse befriends and assists the paper's eccentric editor and lone reporter, Dutton Peabody (Edmond O'Brien).

The townsmen assemble to elect two delegates to the convention that will determine whether the territory that Shinbone is situated in will become a state. Valance, working for the statehood-opposing cattle barons, tries to bully the men into electing him. But thanks to Tom Doniphon's dominant presence and the community's solidarity, the men elect Ranse and Peabody.

Responding to Honour Trap 2

Vengeful Valance challenges Ranse to a duel and goes on to ransack *The Star* and injure Peabody severely. Finding his friend badly wounded, Ranse decides to accept Valance's challenge. As they stand in the dark street, Valance wounds Ranse, but just as he aims at him again, saying, "This time, dud, right between the eyes", Ranse shoots, and Valance is dead.

Rule of Law Triumphs Over Rule of Violence

Ranse later learns that Tom, hiding in the shadows, was the man who shot Liberty Valance, following Hallie's request that he aid Ranse. Remaining in the shadows of the dramatic event, Tom allowed Ranse to take credit and become a local hero and legend. Ranse marries Hallie, who was Tom's sweetheart, and is chosen to represent the territory in Washington, DC. He goes on to develop a distinguished political career and become governor. Shinbone, now ruled by law, joins civilisation and enjoys peace and prosperity. Tom Doniphon lives and dies impoverished and forgotten. Twenty-five years after Tom's shooting of Valance, Ranse and Hallie attend his funeral and attempt to tell his story. But it is of no interest to the town.

Honour, Shame, Honour Code, and the Law

The protagonists of both *Burning Days* and *The Man Who Shot Liberty Valance* are aspiring young lawyers determined to serve the rule of law and enforce it. They both find themselves attempting to do so, against all odds, in remote desert towns. Each of them is supported by the local independent press as he confronts the town's corrupt, powerful, ruthless villain. In Ford's 1962 Western, the young lawyer succeeds spectacularly, turning wilderness into garden, as Hallie phrases it in the film's concluding moment. In Alper's 2022 *noir* Western, he fails miserably as the local villains gain power.

One obvious difference between Ranse and Emre is that the former is a hero of an epic: "*The Man Who Shot Liberty Valance* is a tale about mythical actions, the building of a new society, the cosmicization of chaos".[6] Emre is the protagonist in a *noir* tale of corruption, stagnation, and doom. However, I suggest that a more intriguing point of reference is the protagonists' relationships with honour. Both young lawyers arrive at places beyond the reach of their countries' rule of law. The sheriff in Shinbone and the chief of police in Yaniklar know better than to try and enforce state law. In each of these

6 Victor Bruno, 'Mythology and Anti-Mythology in John Ford's *The Man Who Shot Liberty Valance*' (2021–2022) 15–16(59–60) Studii şi Cercetări de Istoria Artei. Teatru, Muzică, Cinematografie, Serie nouă 102.

towns, residents adhere to a set of norms that is distinct from and outside the law: a local honour code.

Ranse and Emre are both men of law confronting strong honour cultures. Their responses to the respective honour cultures are worlds apart: one securing the rule of law, the other dooming it. I suggest that law's engagement with the system of honour is an overlooked aspect of the inherent conflict between liberal democracy's rule of law on the one hand and non-liberal, authoritarian, populist forces on the other. Non-liberal cultures are often steeped in honour mentality, which they use to rally their supporters. Ranse's and Emre's distinct responses to the honour cultures they encounter represent choices facing legal systems as they confront non-liberal forces. A close reading of the movies from this perspective offers an insight into the consequences of coping strategies that legal systems may choose in response to populism.

Honour and its terminology were common and widely familiar in previous generations but have been deemed politically incorrect in most parts of the Western world for several decades. It is no wonder that discussion of honour is facilitated by a contemporary Turkish movie and a Hollywood Western from 1962. Most people in the Western world no longer recognise honour's logic and mentality. They are unaware of its strategies, tactics, and power. To refer to it and present an argument addressing it, I must acquaint readers with its basic terms.

An honour code is the unwritten set of social norms that governs an honour-and-shame society.[7] It contains the rules of conduct that derive their logic from the fundamental value of honour. Most traditional societies in most parts of the world adhered to honour – and often still do – together with its foundational attitudes, logic, psychology, economy, and code of conduct.

In honour-and-shame societies, honour is the fundamental value, the organising principle, and the value each member of society attributes to himself and to others. (I use the masculine because honour is a manly thing, strongly associated with patriarchy.) Honour is the relative value attributed to and felt by a member of society vis-à-vis his peers; it implies comparative social status, prestige, rank, and standing in the hierarchical structure of a specific group. It is neither innate nor egalitarian. On the contrary: it is something one works hard to achieve and maintain, and the more of it you have, the more valuable you are. Its accumulation promises superiority over others: hence, better living and improved prospects of survival and prosperity. Shame is dishonour: the absence of honour due to inherent lack or circumstantial loss.

7 The following description of honour is based on my study and research of the topic. See Orit Kamir, *Betraying Dignity: The Toxic Seduction of Shaming, Social Media and Radicalization* (Fairleigh Dickinson UP 2020) 17–48.

In an honour-and-shame society, every player's main goal is to gain honour, which is done through a careful and disciplined adherence to the norms defined by that society's honour code. Failure to do so inflicts shame. Honour is ceaselessly achieved, enhanced, accrued, and inevitably lost while shame is constantly dreaded and avoided at all costs.

The logic of the honour competition is, as Bill Miller aptly put it, that of a zero-sum game.[8] Since social hierarchy is a pyramid and honour corresponds to a position in the pyramid, one member's promotion must entail another's demotion. Each player's every move affects the honour and relative standing of others. Shaming and humiliation of a peer robs him of honour, an honour that goes to the player brave enough to do the shaming. The victim of shaming will do everything in his power to avenge himself and clean the stain of shame from his honour. He must bring his opponent down and humiliate him even more than he himself was humiliated. Honour conflicts are the means of social mobility. They are escalating in nature and highly dangerous.

Different honour societies adhere to different honour codes: that is, to different sets of social norms. In many traditional honour societies, bravery, proud self-assertion and self-reliance, and loyalty to the group and its leaders were prevailing honour norms. Since most honour societies are patriarchal, manhood is constructed as honour bound, dictating militant competition and aggression. In these societies, the terms "honourable" and "manly" are interchangeable: the manlier one is considered to be – the more honourable he is, and vice versa. The cinematic Wild West, the Japanese Bushidō culture, and Europe's duelling aristocrats are familiar examples of such societies.

Societies organised around state law and its rule established themselves by combatting local honour codes and subduing them. In contemporary liberal democracies, state norms are not derived from honour, but from human dignity.[9] A dignity-oriented culture ascribes every human being absolute, universal, immeasurable worth. Human value is not viewed as relative to others' and does not depend on manliness, loyalty to a code, or shaming of competing peers. The law treats all humans as imbued with identical, innate value. It therefore treats them equally, acknowledging their identical basic human rights. In order for state law to rule, it must overcome some peoples' adherence to honour and its code. For liberal democracies to flourish, human dignity must prevail over honour.

Law Versus Honour in *Burning Days* and *The Man Who Shot Liberty Valance*

Both *Burning Days* and *The Man Who Shot Liberty Valance* portray a clash between the rule of law – embodied by a young lawyer protagonist – and a

8 William Miller, *Humiliation* (Cornell UP 1993) 116.

9 See Kamir (n 7) 73–106.

local honour code. The law arrives in a remote town that is and has always been ruled by a crude, machoistic honour code based on overt militant violence and aggression. The law of the land requires abandonment of old norms and unconditional acceptance of its authority. It demands superiority and absolute obedience. Unsurprisingly, in both films, these uncompromising requirements are met with fierce resistance. Yaniklar's mayor and Shinbone's Liberty Valance, both claiming superiority within their respective honour hierarchies, have a lot to lose if the law and egalitarian human dignity replace honour. They fight back to protect their interests, relying on the majority's fear of their threats, as well as its investment in the familiar existing order.

Arriving in Shinbone, Ranse is at the very bottom of the local honour hierarchy. Penniless, no horse to his name, a stranger to guns and to shooting, he sleeps in a restaurant kitchen and wears an apron as he serves customers. No wonder Liberty Valance mocks his unmanly, honourless appearance and conduct. But Ranse does not attempt to climb up the social ladder by adhering to the honour code. On the contrary, he sets out to overthrow it.

One of the Western's most dramatic scenes occurs when Valance trips Ranse as he is carrying Tom Doniphon's order. Ranse falls to the ground, as does Tom's steak. Defending his honour, Doniphon demands that Valance pick his steak up. Valance refuses, calculating whether Doniphon can shoot before he does. The tension between the two men is building up, and the honour conflict is about to burst into a showdown. Ranse could wait for Doniphon to shoot Valance and rid the town of his presence, but he refuses to legitimise the honour code at the root of the conflict and the violence it entails. Picking up the steak from the ground and placing it on Doniphon's table he shouts, "What's the matter? Everybody in this country is kill-crazy?"

By wearing an apron, bussing tables, refusing to carry a gun, and devoting himself to words and books, Ranse blatantly places himself outside the honour hierarchy. Doniphon and Valance disagree on the exact norms derived from the honour code that rules Shinbone. Doniphon reads the code as requiring integrity, honesty, generosity, fairness, and other chivalrous qualities while Valance's conduct makes it clear that self-assertion, self-reliance, raw power, and professionalism are the only honour norms he acknowledges. As Doniphon and Valance compete for honour-based supremacy, each promoting a different honour code, Ranse rejects the premise of their competition as well as the type of masculinity associated with it. Even as he is denigrated and mocked, he refuses to adhere to the standards of any honour code, demanding that it give way to the rule of law.

Resisting the world of honour, Ranse suggests an alternative. His is a firm, unyielding, yet soft-spoken and completely nonviolent masculinity. He protects a woman passenger in the stagecoach but does not attempt to fight back when Valance flogs him. Rather than plan a violent revenge, he assembles the town's least honourable residents, empowering them through education and insisting on their equal human dignity and rights. His manner is gentle, and he radiates modesty, moderation, and comradery. He forms a union with the town's other man of words and progressive ideas, the journalist and newspaper editor, Peabody, encouraging him and offering positive feedback on his journalism. Even when he returns to Shinbone 25 years later, now a distinguished senator, he treats the retired local sheriff, as well as Doniphon's black farmhand, with respect.

Embodying the law, Ranse offers Shinbone a new perspective. In the world he stands for, all men are treated equally as fellow citizens, all possessing human dignity. They are each considered valuable, addressed, and taken into consideration. They are not trampled by powerful men who use them to promote their own interests and status. Instead of hierarchy, Ranse suggests solidarity; instead of ruthless competition, community life built on empowerment of every member, on mutual empathy, comradery, and common fairness.

Emre is a world away. Arriving from the big city, he is clearly anxious in his first position, yet his demeanor communicates superiority. When, over dinner, the judge suggests that he date local women, Emre instinctively sneers, causing her to raise a brow. In his scarce interactions with the locals, mostly his landlady's son, he is polite yet condescending. In his professional dealings with the chief of police, Emre systematically ignores his professional experience, advice, and requests, commanding the chief time and again to act against his better judgment. Emre creates no social ties and does not seek to befriend the locals. He is aloof. His tense relationship with Murat is initiated and nearly forced on him by the journalist. Influenced by the pejorative gossip surrounding Murat, Emre never fully trusts him, and rather than forming an alliance with him, he remains ambivalent and suspicious towards him. The sexual tension between them, which Emre seems unable to come to terms with, further complicates the relationship.

With Sahin, the mayor's sleazy lawyer son, Emre immediately enters into a power struggle framed as an honour conflict. When Sahin first appears in Emre's office to welcome him to town with a box of sweets, he asks whether the locals' hunting practices scare him. Emre understands this as an insult, a mockery of his delicate, big-city disposition, and as skepticism of his masculinity. He could brush off the innuendos, indicating that he is above the politics of honour. But he chooses to enter the honour arena head on. Determined to set the record straight and put Sahin in his proper place, Emre responds that the hunting is not merely barbaric and repulsive but also prohibited by law within the town limits. He adds harshly that this time, he will not arrest the participants, indicating that next time he might; the big stick of law is his to use at his discretion. Emre sends Sahin and his friend a clear message: the man of law is no sissy; he holds his ground and will not be trampled on. He is in charge of the powerful force of the law and will use it to override his rivals.

Unlike Ranse, Emre does not position the law outside the honour game, marking it as an alternative. Rather, he arms himself with it within the boundary of the honour norms. Sahin wears his father's status, political power and wealth, as well as his hunting reputation; Emre wears his right to use the almighty law to restrain Sahin and disarm him. Emre uses the law as a trump card within the honour code and in his honour conflict with Sahin.

Emre once again feels slighted at the dinner party in Sahin's garden. Sahin and his friend note that their homemade *raki* is stronger than the commercial *raki* Emre is used to. Emre hears this as an honour challenge and rises to meet it by continuing to drink the *raki*, even as he feels he is incapable of absorbing it. Eager to prove his manly competence and ensure his honourable standing, he puts himself in harm's way. When regaining recollection of the night's events, Emre realises that Sahin once again goaded him, when Emre was already incapacitated, posing yet another honour challenge. Insinuating that Emre is not "a real man", Sahin invited him to refute the rumors of his homosexuality by having sex with Pekmez. The suspicious mark Emre notices on his neck the following morning suggests to him – and to the film's viewers – that he might have accepted this challenge as he did the previous one.

As he learns of the brutalising of Pekmez, Emre treats it as yet another challenge posed by Sahin. He realises that Sahin has trapped him, daring him to use his legal prowess as he boasted he would, with his own reputation and freedom at stake. Emre responds immediately: he accepts the challenge and orders Sahin's arrest and semen test.

Having gone this far, Emre must now protect his reputation at all costs. This brings him to conceal evidence (his pen, which he finds while examining the garden) and corrupt the investigation. He is now personally implicated and motivated by self-interest. His pure, superior legal standing is compromised and tarnished. Having entered the honour arena, he is a player in the honour game, not an alternative to it. As a player, he is doomed to lose: Sahin has his father's power and reputation, his standing within the community, his newspaper echoing his narrative, and the loyalty of his supporters. A lone outsider, a newcomer to the community, cannot beat the local man of honour at his own game. He might have stood a chance had he bonded with the locals and formed ties of solidarity and mutual care. But Emre has not formed a school for the community's downtrodden, nor has he befriended a local woman and her family, as Ranse did. Emre stands alone, counting on the superior power of the law. He has failed to understand the limits of that power and, hence, has lost.

Read against *The Man Who Shot Liberty Valance*, *Burning Days* depicts the inevitable failure of the law when it enters the arena of honour and becomes party to an honour contest, rather than offering an alternative to the honour system. When the law remains condescendingly aloof and alienated from its public, it stands no chance of overcoming strong local traditions.

Tom Doniphon, Law's Secret Weapon

The reading of *The Man Who Shot Liberty Valance* I suggested would have been compelling if, after Ranse's victory at the Shinbone assembly, Valance had accepted the democratic procedure. But rather than transform into a law-abiding citizen, Valance challenges Ranse to a shootout, clarifying that his only other option is to leave town. Tom Doniphon advises Ranse to leave and offers him his carriage. But finding Peabody nearly dead and his newspaper ransacked, Ranse decides to accept Valance's challenge and meet him for a duel. Appearing to relinquish his commitment to law and his disdain for violence, he enters the honour arena, much as Emre does in *Burning Days*.

Indeed, it is in an honour-bound, violent confrontation that Valance loses, and Ranse wins. Ranse does not rid Shinbone of Valance and of his rule of terror through a deliberate judicial proceeding pronouncing humanistic ideals; it is a gun that liberates the town from Valance. Interestingly, the man pulling the trigger is not Ranse but the town's man of honour, Tom Doniphon. It is by skillful use of violence that Tom enables Ranse to represent the town in the territorial convention and bring about statehood and its legal order.

The rule of law, the movie appears to suggest, cannot establish itself by its own power. Left to his own devices, Ranse would have either been forced out of town or shot dead. Valance would have prevailed. Law can only be established if a powerful man within the honour society is convinced of its necessity, and – against his own self-interest – turns on the honour system, using its own violence against it and helping replace it with a new, nonviolent system.[10] This is what Tom Doniphon does when, in a spectacular act of self-sacrifice, he chooses to give up his future as Shinbone's most esteemed citizen. Helping Ranse destroy the honour system in which he excels, Tom paves the way for its replacement with an order in which Ranse thrives and Tom fades away.[11]

The big enigma at the core of the film is Tom's choice. Why does Tom shoot Valance? Why does the rule of law prevail through an honour confrontation, when its champion, the man of law, is incapable of winning such a confrontation? The simple answer, given by Tom himself, is that it was for Hallie, who had sent word to Tom asking him to look after Ranse. Indeed, it is thanks to Hallie's request that Tom is present on the street, holding a gun. However, I suggest that there is more to his altruistic choice.

10 In a previous article, I suggested that this is the case made by another, more contemporary western: Clint Eastwood's *Unforgiven*. Orit Kamir, 'Law, Society and Film: *Unforgiven*'s Call to Substitute Honour with Dignity' (2006) 40 Law and Society Review 193–235.

11 "When, out of 'love' for Hallie, Doniphon decides to shoot Liberty Valance, allowing Stoddard to receive the credit, his whole *kosmos* is destroyed, and Doniphon sets fire to his own house, bringing about a process akin to *ekpyrosis* that razes his existence to the ground. To the day of his death, Doniphon becomes an ossified man – literally a fossil of a being that lived in a previous era". Bruno (n 6) 100.

By stepping into the street for a shootout with Valance, it might seem that Ranse is giving in to honour and violence, betraying the rule of law. But as Tom hides in the shadows, watching the aproned Ranse, his wounded arm folded, aiming a gun Tom knows full well Ranse could never shoot straight, Tom – and the viewers sharing his point of view – know that it isn't honour driving Ranse.

What Tom sees is a man whose substantial commitment to human dignity, to comradery, to solidarity is stronger than his procedural commitment to nonviolence and the rule of law. In a tragic moment, in which he cannot hold on to these two commitments simultaneously, he chooses human dignity, loyalty to a friend, and the duty to stand up to a bully. His choice clarifies that the nonviolent rule of law is, for Ranse, merely a means to the greater end of ensuring human dignity and solidarity. His commitment to these values is dearer to him than life itself. There could have been no doubt in Ranse's mind that Valance would shoot faster and aim better. What Tom sees is a man sacrificing his life for humanistic, communal values that are the core of his being.

Witnessing this honourable self-sacrifice, Tom is now faced with his own dilemma: side with Valance and their honourable self-reliance, allowing it to kill Ranse and all he stands for? Or side with Ranse and his humanistic, community-oriented values, committing the shameful crime of shooting a man from the shadows as he is engaged in a duel with another man? Tom's dilemma is every bit as tragic as Ranse's, and his choice is just as heroic and self-destructive. With a single shot, Tom forfeits the world of honour in which he has excelled and flourished, and chooses Ranse's human dignity, comradery, standing up to bullies, and eventually nonviolence and the rule of law. Realising that Ranse's world is the better choice for the citizens of Shinbone, he destroys the honour system and himself with it, paving the way for a new beginning. Just as Ranse's integrity drives him to face Valance with a gun he cannot shoot, Tom's drives him to choose Ranse and everything he stands for over himself. Indeed, soon after the shooting, Tom sets fire to his house, and his life is saved only thanks to his farmhand, who pulls him out of the flames.

In *Liberty Valance*, the rule of law prevails not merely because a trigger is pulled and Valance is killed. It prevails because Ranse is willing to sacrifice the rule of law and even his very life for the communal values he cherishes, and because Tom realises that this man and the values for which he stands would serve his community better than he can. They both truly love Hallie, the film's emblem of Shinbone and its citizens. Their bonding over this love brings about the rule of law.

Read against *Liberty Valance*, it is clear that *Burning Days* features neither a Ranse nor a Tom Doniphon. Emre never tries to teach the local residents of Yaniklar and convince them that the rule of law would bring them emancipation and progress. The film gives no indication that his commitment to the rule of law is a means to the promotion of higher values. In fact, a plausible reading of the film suggests that Emre cherishes the rule of law because it is the basis of his honour. His status, standing, prestige, and power all rely on his authority to enforce the rule of law. It is clearly important for him to tackle corrupt, powerful forces, but when his life is threatened, Emre attempts to run, never considering sacrificing it for moral principles.

Equally important, Yaniklar features no true man of honour, no insider who could have joined Emre and brought about an end to the rule of honour and corruption. In the absence of a Tom Doniphon, the man of law is unlikely to conquer the forces of honour. Furthermore, *Burning Days* features no love. Emre and Murat may be erotically attracted to each other, but neither of them – nor any other character – manifests empathy, care, or compassion, let alone love. The complete lack of these feelings signals Yanikar's doom. It characterises *Burning Days* as a *film noir* and a cautionary tale. Triumph and redemption, like those achieved in *The Man Who Shot Liberty Valance*, require an epic, legendary morality tale.

Burning Days can be read as departing from and commenting on *Liberty Valance* and its heroic, fairy-tale portrayal of both the frontier and its men of honour, as well as the founding of the rule of law. Emin Alper's film seems to claim that both Ranse and Tom, the knights in shining armour, are no more than figments of our mythological imagination. Yaniklar, together with Emre, Murat and Sahin, is the real world. Emre's fall is inevitable. There is no moral substance behind his zealous enforcement of the rule of law, no sincere dedication to human dignity, comradery, and solidarity. It is merely honour that motivates Emre, not empathy and love of the community. He stands empty handed in the struggle against brutality and corruption and is thus doomed to lose.

Yaniklar and Our Contemporary World

The analysis of Emin Alper's 2022 film from an honour-sensitive perspective, coupled with its reading against John Ford's 1962 *The Man Who Shot Liberty Valance*, renders some insights regarding the challenges legal systems face when confronting honour cultures. I suggested that through the said lens, the movie cautions legal systems and legal officials not to step into honour traps laid out for them by political players. Once the law of a liberal democracy responds to an honour challenge, becoming a player in an honour game, it is doomed to compromise its neutrality, distance, integrity, and claim to stand for an alternative value system. It is bound to lose its standing and the hope of securing public faith in the rule of law. It enters an arena in which it cannot win. A legal system and its representatives, even when threatened, mocked, or provoked by political powers, must refrain from engaging in an honour conflict with them. Taking on an honour challenge is stepping into sinkhole territory.

Furthermore, for a liberal legal system to survive a strong, honour-based opposition, it must be fully and deeply committed to its substantial values:

human dignity, liberty, equality, community solidarity, and plurality. Legislators, justices, judges, law professors, prosecutors, and lawyers must feel and display sincere, acute dedication to humanity and the social structures designed to protect and promote it. They must present the legal system to the public as promoting the well-being of all individuals and the community at large. Condescending, aloof legal officials who come across as using their legal authority to secure their own honour, privilege, status, and power stand no chance of winning public trust and support.

The comparison to *Liberty Valance* highlights another ingredient missing in *Burning Days*: steadfast support of the legal system, the rule of law, and humanist values professed by upstanding, respectable community members. Legal officials must express sincerity in their devotion to the principles of humanism and liberalism, but so must additional community leaders as well. For a community to rally around the rule of law and human dignity and overcome strong forces promoting honour, it must have admirable advocates beyond the legal community. Writers, artists, performers, athletes and religious, spiritual, and other community leaders must stand with the law and the liberal values it manifests. They must show that the liberal world of humanism is fiercely backed by strong sponsors.

A film, even when viewed as a law film, is not a commentary on contemporary issues. I will not attempt to read *Burning Days* as an immediate reference to the political situation in Turkey nor as a guideline for legal systems worldwide confronting non-liberal political powers immersed in honour cultures. Each reader may apply the film's insights as I presented them here to legal and political situations they are familiar with. To facilitate such discussion, I will conclude with some general comments regarding honour-based tactics of contemporary non-liberal, populist forces.

Non-liberal, populist politicians everywhere evoke honour-based arguments and sentiments. The propaganda for Brexit in 2016 relied on rhetoric of national honour: proud Brits were to regain their independence from Brussels, break the humiliating shackles that bonded them to Europe, and once again be masters of their borders and their fate. The flood of foreigners, outsiders, Others, taking over the British economy and threatening Britain's culture and identity would be stopped as Britain regained the control it had lost.

Extreme right-wing parties all over Europe use similar rhetoric to rally their supporters around national honour. Demanding the right to exclude outsiders who, they claim, infiltrate their countries, denigrate their cherished traditions, and threaten their cultural heritage, these parties incite honour-based sentiments. Women's and LGBT rights are portrayed as undermining honourable national concepts of masculinity and family. The liberal state and its egalitarian humanism, defined, defended, and enforced by the rule of law, are universally blamed for weakening proud nations. They are portrayed as traitors, undermining national honour by allowing outsiders entry, by securing their social benefits and rights, by allowing them to denigrate national costumes. They are the ones encouraging women and the LGBT community to humiliate manhood, disparage it. Hungary under Orban's rule, Poland under the rule of the Law and Justice party, Israel under Netanyahu's 2022 government all targeted, first and foremost, their countries' legal systems, attempting to curtail their independence and their ability to enforce human rights and defend the rule of law. As in the 1930s, honour cultures seem to be strengthening at the expense of the rule of law.

Have legal systems in these countries refrained from accumulating honour and flaunting it? Have they reassured the public of their integrity? Have legal officials in these countries, together with community leaders, taken a strong stand, sincerely and passionately, in support of the liberal legal systems and their values? Have they formed Tom Doniphon-Ranse Stoddard partnerships? Or do they echo Emre's condescending, self-centred stance?

As I write, the American legal system is reviewing many cases brought against former president Donald Trump, some of them openly attempting to prevent him from running for the presidency in 2024. Trump, a macho populist, deeply invested in crude honour mentality and rough masculinity, has, for a long time, been accusing the legal system of abusing its power to curtail his political success. He claims that the legal system is a player in a feud against him. Many of his supporters accept his portrayal of the legal system's conduct.

Scrutinised closely, have the legal system, its prosecutors, and its judges fully resisted the honour traps set by Trump? Is the legal treatment of the cases brought against him free of honour considerations? Have prosecutors and courts shown full self-restraint, and committed strictly to the rule of law and its humanistic, liberal values? Are there enough distinguished leaders who lend their fierce, unrelenting support to the legal system and the values it stands for? These are the questions *Burning Days* invites us to consider.

Based on such close scrutiny, is Alper's film right in claiming that, in the third decade of the 21st century, the rule of law is represented by the Emres of the world and will be crushed by populism and corruption? Is there hope, as *Liberty Valance* insisted 60 years earlier, that genuine dedication to human dignity and sincere love of community do exist and may yet work miracles and save the day?

Reference List

Bruno V, 'Mythology and Anti-Mythology in John Ford's the Man Who Shot Liberty Valance' (2021–2022) 15–16(59–60) Studii şi Cercetări de Istoria Artei. Teatru, Muzică, Cinematografie, Serie nouă

Kamir O, 'Law, Society and Film: Unforgiven's Call to Substitute Honour with Dignity' (2006) 40 Law and Society Review

Kamir O, *Betraying Dignity: The Toxic Seduction of Shaming, Social Media and Radicalization* (Fairleigh Dickinson UP 2020)

MartinA, 'Burning Days' <https://iffr.com/en/iffr/2023/films/burning-days>

Miller W, *Humiliation* (Cornell UP 1993)
O'Neill TP, 'Two Concepts of Liberty Valance: John Ford, Isaiah Berlin, and Tragic Choice on the Frontier' (2004) 37 Creighton Law Review
Ryan C, 'Print the Legend' in John Denvir (ed), *Legal Reelism: Movies as Legal Texts* (U of Illinois P 1996)
Slotkin R, *Gunfighter Nation: The Myth of the Frontier in Twentieth-Century America* (U of Oklahoma P 1998)

Chapter 4

Violence as Law

Reading *Dirty Harry*, *Unforgiven*, and *Gran Torino* as Comments on Vigilantism

Günter Frankenberg

The Liberal Script: Relating Law and Violence

The liberal narrative of rights and law has achieved the prominence of *A Thousand and One Nights* in terms of its magical elements and global proliferation. It causes the subjective factor – or, more precisely, the personal bearers and agents of *rule* in the rule of law – to disappear elegantly in the fog of the ideological formula of "government of laws and not of men", which appears for the first time – as anything, after Aristotle, of course – in the Constitution of Massachusetts in 1780.[1] *Rule of law* camouflages semantically the physical violence and the definitional force on which any legal order and its rule are based.[2] In a consistent continuation of the narrative, in the US context, the police operate as "the law". Both in *the* law and in *law*, violence is allowed to appear only in the abstract as the idea of rule-directed and rule-controlled proportional coercion. Also in prisons, even on death row, justice is officially administered, not force applied.[3]

Rule of law, État de droit, Rechtsstaat, etado derecho, stato di diritto, or *constitutional state* – these terms of trade swap reality for a product of ideological world-making. They invariably suggest that violence was magically withdrawn from society, that the morass of feud, fist law, blood revenge, and vigilantism has been drained so we can concentrate on conventional forms of moderately violent self-help and civilised self-justice framed and monitored

1 Art XXX: "In the government of this commonwealth, the legislative department shall never exercise the executive and judicial powers, or either of them: the executive shall never exercise the legislative and judicial powers, or either of them: the judicial shall never exercise the legislative and executive powers, or either of them: to the end it may be a government of laws and not of men".

2 Jacques Derrida, 'Force of Law: "The Mystical Foundation of Authority"' in D Cornell and others (eds), *Deconstruction and the Possibility of Justice* (Routledge 1992) 3 ff.

3 German constitutional/public law breaks through this coding; in continuation of its statist tradition, it uses concepts such as *Staatsgewalt* ("state force") and *besondere Gewaltverhältnisse* ("special relationships of force", like incarceration, schools, the military service), by modern doctrine replaced as *Sonderrechtsverhältnisse* ("special legal relationships").

DOI: 10.4324/9781003461180-4

by Max Weber's "monopoly of legitimate violence of the state",[4] executed by legislators, judges, administrative agencies, and, notably, the police. The idea of a monopoly of force dates back to Jean Bodin, *Les Six livres de la République* (1576) and Thomas Hobbes, *Leviathan* (1651). Weber elevated it to the level of a defining criterion and legitimising conception of the state.[5]

In consequence, quasi-judicial vigilante justice is frowned on, while quasi-executive self-help is permitted, if only by way of exception and under special circumstances: in emergency situations, in cases of legitimate self-defense, in the war on terror (rescue torture!),[6] or if needed to protect private property. In liberal theory, the citizenry is disarmed and, in return, obtains rights as weapons. This is the first part of the liberal narrative.

The official agents and agencies of the state are also entitled to execute their measures – laws, ordinances, decrees, administrative acts – by force as long as they follow the script of the law within the authorising frame of legally assigned tasks, powers, and duties, all the while preserving the civil rights of people and perpetrators and always heeding the key principle of proportionality. This is the second and complementary part of the liberal narrative.

The realism of this constitutional script for law rule and its exercise have come under attack from three different corners: first, the violence embedded in the structure of rule, which Max Weber almost casually labels a monopoly of legitimate violence, is revealed systematically in situations of crisis or distress (war and civil war, state of siege or of kinds of exception) and displayed selectively in comparable conflict situations that are limited in space and time. In contrast to the rule of law preserving the legitimacy of legality, raw violence emerges here from the situational and individualising limitation – the singular case. It is betrayed routinely in executive action *extra legem*, east of law's Eden, so to say. Then violent executive action becomes conspicuous and raises the threshold of justification or, if a justification is not at hand, delegitimises coercion and repression as violence and manifests an authoritarian feature of government.[7]

The second threat has to be coped with when the routines of law rule are challenged by the disorderly exercise of judicial state power. Arbitrary judgments or the denial of justice by a court or judge miscarrying/abusing the rule of law, and thus the "man" (as acting persona) emerges all too visibly

4 Max Weber, 'Politics as a Vocation' in Tony Waters and Dagmar Waters (trs and eds), *Weber's Rationalism and Modern Society* (Palgrave Books 2015) 129–98.

5 Jean Bodin, *Les Six Livres de la République* (Forgotten Books [1576] 2018); Thomas Hobbes, *Leviathan* (CUP [1651] 1996).

6 Günter Frankenberg, *Political Technology and the Erosion of the Rule of Law – Normalizing the State of Exception* (Edwar Elgar Publishing 2014) Ch VI with further references.

7 For a more detailed analysis of the structural components of authoritarian regimes, see Günter Frankenberg, *Authoritarianism – Constitutional Perspectives* (Edward Elgar Publishing 2021).

from behind the government of laws and not of men. More importantly, the corruption of judicial justice encourages those who have been denied fair procedures or a just decision to act as judges on their own behalf.

Finally, the constitutional script of law rule may be threatened by the public denial of the state monopoly of justice on the part of either the citizenry at large or significantly powerful groups. The latter are usually referred to as "organised crime", the Mafia, or vigilantes.[8] The act of breaking a norm, and even more the act of social violence, undermines the magic of the liberal narrative. Whoever cannot read civil disobedience as an affirmation of a democratic legal order or an attempt at legal interpretation[9] but as deliberate resistance or vigilante justice is likely to react nervously to any deliberate, if considerate, norm violation. Even more dangerous, of course, are regimes of the "law of the street" or spectacular cases of blood revenge and honour killings, because their protagonists dismiss law rule's law and take the law script they have written into their own hands. They execute a "law of men" (which is to be taken literally) that is claimed to have been dictated by the honour code of a Mafioso organisation, an obscure tradition, a misogynous religion, or the ethical codex of the military. Invariably, these varieties of "dark ethics" establish an extra-legal order. It is quite illuminating that in the movie trilogy here under review – in *Unforgiven* and *Dirty Harry* and *Gran Torino* – directed and/or re-presented as main character by Clint Eastwood, well known also for his rather conservative politics, the actions of the hero (always Eastwood as detective, gunslinger, or retired soldier) imply that extra-legal "honest revenge" or "adequate atonement" is justified.[10] In each of these movies, uncivil disobedience – that is, breaking the law or, rather, criminal action – opens the door to vigilantism. In every case, law rule is replaced by man rule and, in the final analysis, street rule. In *Gran Torino*, the aged and wiser Eastwood, having realised the dynamics of vigilantism, appears to distance himself from the ethics of honour and revenge. More on this later in the chapter.

Law's Power and Powerlessness

Power and powerlessness are equally captured in the paradoxical metaphor of law "taken into your own hands" – by victims, their (self-appointed) protectors, or third parties. Through this change of personnel in the

8 Instructive: the US movie drama *Vigilante* by Olivia Wilde (2018), in which the main character is dedicated to revenge against perpetrators of domestic violence.

9 See the brilliant study by Samira Akbarian, *Ziviler Ungehorsam als Verfassungsinterpretation* (Mohr Siebeck 2023).

10 *Dirty Harry* (Directed by Don Siegel, Warner Bros (Universal Pictures) 1971); *Unforgiven* (Directed by Clint Eastwood, Malpaso Productions 1992); and *Gran Torino* (Directed by Clint Eastwood, Warner Productions 2008).

moment of execution, the law (admittedly it differs from the one that has been originally intended) acquires the power to stand up to and, if it succeeds, correct injustice. However, once taken into your own hands, not only the law's law but also this non-legal law changes its nature and modality.

Whenever the official, positive law fails, the door opens for the entry of the law of the fist or self-justice, and citizens who are supposed to be disarmed become judges in their own causes. In this way, the legal project of modernity – in essence, its principle of legality – is suspended for the time being so that certain ends may be pursued. Where the power of crime is about to triumph over the powerless because civilised, legal fights against crime and fantasies of just violence are set free, and so are archaic longings for the saving angel with the sword. Intoxicated by the odor of a just cause, the avenger replaces the sober script of police or criminal law and rewrites it in a more or less persuasive way to provide the stuff for printing press and screen. Max Weber is replaced by Hollywood.

Into the dark tradition of self-empowerment *contra legem*, for the purpose of rescue or some other justified end, director Don Siegel inscribed his film *Dirty Harry* in 1971. After its surprising success, four significantly weaker sequels followed, always with Clint Eastwood in the leading role of police inspector Harry Callahan. In accordance with the rule of Hollywood, he finally replaced Don Siegel as director in *Dirty Harry IV*. Of these, only two scenes from *Sudden Impact* (*Dirty Harry IV*, 1983) are actually worth remembering, which, in turn, pick up the vigilante motif. To quote Harry Callahan: "We are not gonna let you walk out of here". Robber: "Who's we?" Harry: "Smith, Wesson, and me". And also the legendary, albeit borrowed, provocation: "Go ahead, make my day!"

The star of *Dirty Harry*, Clint Eastwood, has made great contributions to the Hollywood project of preventing crimes from going unpunished and the criminal from remaining uncaught. (Maybe that is why he believed his embarrassing support for Donald Trump, if only lame, would remain unsanctioned.)[11] Clint Eastwood's politics and his theory of law become more ambivalent in *Unforgiven* (1992) and *Gran Torino* (2008), his very successful later films. Where *Dirty Harry* plays with prejudice (the evil villain; the good, albeit not strictly law-abiding detective), William Munny's melancholy in *Unforgiven* and Harry's revenant, Walt Kowalski, in *Gran Torino* rise to the highest – the Oscar – level of Hollywood rule. They celebrate the morally superior (white) individual (man/hero/Eastwood), still not trusting the rule of law, like Detective Callahan in *Dirty Harry*. However, gunslinger emeritus

11 Always a staunch Republican, Eastwood later withdrew his support for Trump and shifted it to Mike Bloomberg. <www.nbcnews.com/politics/2020-election/just-get-mike-bloomberg-there-clint-eastwood-distances-himself-trump-n1141066/> accessed 14 October 2021.

William Munny in *Unforgiven* returns to his single parenting and moves to California, not trusting that the law will protect him from organised crime. And finally Korean War veteran Walt Kowalski in *Gran Torino*, still not trusting the administration of justice, supports its workings by producing the evidence needed to arrest and imprison the gang members. Law-rule only works if helped by a strong individual – Eastwood's epiphany.

First Take: *Dirty Harry* and *Unforgiven* From Drive to Persuasion

Dirty Harry *I*

The plot of *Dirty Harry* (in legalese: the facts of the case) is based on "true events", which promises authenticity and adds an additional thrill effect: wow, it did happen in real life! The serial murders of the never-captured Zodiac Killer in San Francisco in the late 60s serve as a matrix. As "in real life", two driven people meet in *Dirty Harry*: the detective and the serial killer. The random victims of Scorpio are, among others, a young woman in a pool, a priest, and finally a schoolgirl. The killer is not propelled by any logic one might recognise from the outside. In cases of this kind, a dark instinct or generalised evil is rather helplessly held liable for the bad deeds. Police detective Harry Callahan lets himself be driven by what might be called unconventional methods of investigation that border on the fanaticism of revenge. As one person crosses the line into the area of crime, the other is urged to break legal forms, procedures, and guarantees. Scorpio keeps a city, San Francisco, in suspense with murders and death threats. By his unruly actions, Dirty Harry constantly makes his superiors fear violations of the script for law enforcement. Their warnings remain unheard, or at least not heeded. And the experienced *film noir* viewer soon enough recognises the impending shift from law rule to the triumph of man rule, stripped of the cloak of legal legitimacy.

Director Don Siegel translates and breaks down the dynamic of being driven into three chases. In the first, Callahan takes up the hunt after the murder of the young woman in the pool on the roof and chases the murderer across the rooftops and dark back stairs of the city. Whether carelessness during the shoot of the movie or a symbol for the failure of this first chase, in a much later take after the murder, the blood still floats unchanged, as if clotted on or glued to the surface of the water. In the second sequence, Scorpio turns the tables. He has kidnapped (and already murdered) a fourteen-year-old girl but is blackmailing the mayor for ransom for her release. His pursuer, Callahan, is charged with delivering the ransom but soon finds himself being chased all over the city from one possible ransom delivery point to another.

In the third sequence of scenes, towards the end of the film, Callahan takes up the pursuit of the school bus with children captured by Scorpio.

Although the mayor is willing to pay the ransom demanded and forbids him to obstruct the handover, Harry operates according to his own script, contrary to instructions. He succeeds in ending the kidnapping. Having freed the children, the detective as hunter, beyond all legal powers of investigation, chases the murderer-extortionist-kidnapper like a piece of game in a self-created garden of emergency. The final showdown takes place at a gravel pit. Here, *Dirty Harry* dramatically deviates from the template of real life. Whereas the Zodiac Killer had never been caught, Scorpio ends after a final hostage taking: a group of innocent children – a standard trope – increases the justification for the detective to take the law into his own hands and act on his own. According to Hollywood grammar, a manipulative provocation of self-defense provides the makeup for a flimsy legitimisation of the final salvation shot and paves the way for the liberal legal script's healing – to the audience's and the producers' relief.

Unforgiven

While *Dirty Harry*'s dynamic is fueled by protagonists who are out of control and driven by justice, revenge, and evil urges in a kind of raw state of nature, *Unforgiven* comes across as a more pensive plot with hesitant and out-of-shape protagonists: retired gunslingers who need to be persuaded to act rather than being driven to take up arms again. William Munny lives on a farm, singly parenting his two children after the death of his wife. While Dirty Harry comes across as a macho daredevil, Munny long ago withdrew from the stage as a celebrated gun hero. Now he needs to be convinced by the extremely shortsighted Schofield Kid and his African American buddy of the old times, Ned Logan (played by Morgan Freeman) to take up arms again. The living legend can be persuaded, we are to believe, for economic reasons. After a swine flu has almost ruined his farm, he is in dire straits. And he needs the bounty of 1,000 US dollars, advertised by two prostitutes for whoever would revenge their colleague, whose face had been disfigured with a knife after she poked fun at one of her customers (because of his small penis). The local sheriff, "Little Bill" Daggett (Gene Hackman), who ran Big Whiskey with a strict law-and-order regime, ordered the cowboys to bring several horses as compensation for the brothel owner. The prostitutes, outraged by the sheriff's decision, offered the reward to anyone who would kill the cowboys.

Initially, Munny is disoriented and demotivated. He needs to get drawn into the revenge mood after having been beaten up by Sheriff Little Bill (for carrying a gun in the saloon and thus violating the social contract, i.e. the gun regulations for Big Whiskey) and, more importantly, seeing, upon his return from having killed the cowboys and letting the Schofield Kid have the bounty, his former co-outlaw and friend Ned Logan's corpse displayed in a coffin outside the saloon with a sheriff's sign warning that this is what happens to assassins in the town of Big Whiskey. Violence as law, executed by Big Whiskey's Leviathan.

Munny's former ego and alcoholism return and paradoxically steady his hand so he can go ahead and avenge the prostitute's mutilation and, with enhanced legitimation, Ned's brutal murder by shooting the sheriff and his helpers. Violence as law? In the end credits, the audience is informed that Munny returned to his children, and they moved to San Francisco. In default of a legal order, Munny cannot feel safe.

Second Take: *Dirty Harry* and *Unforgiven* as Diagnoses of the Hero and Anti-hero

From the perspective of a story that happened around 1881, Harry Callahan's late–Wild West cynicism reflects the Republican reaction to the zeitgeist of the era of the Vietnam protest and the Watergate scandal – a blowback from decades of deceit.[12] The widespread distrust of established institutions and conservative critiques of the cultural liberal hegemony, especially as political correctness, civil rights, the civil rights rulings of the (Warren) Supreme Court and of "Washington" in general are depicted in reverse, in contrast to numerous Hollywood productions of the time and before.

In the role of the larger-than-life gunslinger à la John Wayne, Harry Callahan represents right-wing conservative ideals and their supposedly innocent political screenplay. Unlike the role model for Zodiac, *Dirty Harry* presents the Hollywood version of a serial killer, interestingly enough a psychopathic, long-haired, rather colourful hippie. The stronghold of hippie high culture, San Francisco, was carefully chosen as the location for the plot and not Seattle as originally planned because Zodiac had ravaged there. The film articulates the protest of the silent, pro-law-and-order majority against this (all-too-liberal or libertine) culture, a majority who had to wait until the Reagan presidency for their political turn.

The (petty) bourgeois imagination of evil and its punishment is brought into play, in not a time-diagnostic but a timeless way. It allies itself with a (perhaps again time-bound) anti-liberal affect against Freudian theory, in which the police chief suspects at the end of his short lecture about "sick guys" and their behavioral patterns, "It must appeal to their superego". However, it is precisely the superego that is the psychic instance which prevents or should prevent people from giving in to the desire to do evil and commit crimes.

The hero fascinates and functions only in the backlight of the anti-hero. Harry Callahan's brilliance lives from Scorpio's dark aura, from the vividness of the evil in perpetrators and their crimes. In the film, Don Siegel invites

12 See Karl Malantes, 'Vietnam: The War That Killed Trust' *The New York Times* (7 January 2017); more generally Jeffrey C Goldfarb, *The Cynical Society* (U of Chicago P 1991).

us to look over the shoulder of the evil when it is committed: how Scorpio prepares and executes the murder of the young woman in the pool. How Dirty Harry hunts, tortures, and finally liquidates Scorpio in the brightly lit nocturnal stadium. The invitation is toxic, so to say; it turns the viewer into an accomplice, as it were, who, in the end, willingly lets themself be purified by this moment of voyeuristic murderous lust.

By the same token, director-actor Clint Eastwood presents the metamorphoses of hero and anti-hero in *Unforgiven*. The three avengers, Munny, the Schofield Kid, and Ned Logan, each in his way, demystify the image of the hero, often reiterated and much celebrated in most Wild West movies, who fights the battles at the frontier and inaugurates the American tradition of regeneration through violence.[13] They are by no means impressive gunslingers but reformed alcoholics with serious health defects and economic problems. Where *Dirty Harry* thrives on prejudicial concepts of good and evil and comfortably serves the majoritarian zeitgeist, *Unforgiven* frontally (or is it tongue in cheek?) challenges the Hollywood genre in Hollywood and deconstructs the mythology of the "Wild West", Billy the Kid and the like, and US-Western frontier justice. *Unforgiven* lets the once-wild West end in a torrential, seemingly endless rainy night, when violence, bereft of its regenerating force, ends in total destruction.

The script and the film dare to lay bare the ambivalent and unequal distributive logic of law rule, in particular the law-and-order concept represented by the sheriff, Little Bill, who accommodates his understanding of the rule of law to the strong (the cowboy gang) and crushes the weak, notably Ned Logan. While it is clear from a legal point of view that the cowboys should have been brought to justice and not killed by the Schofield Kid and Munny, it seems morally comprehensible and even acceptable that the avengers did not trust the sheriff's law rule as personal rule. Even if Munny is likely to have most viewers' sympathies, few will come away from this movie with the conviction that justice has been served. The end credits tell the audience, to repeat, that Munny has to take his children and leave for San Francisco, which implies that no problem has been solved by the crescendo of violence, and he cannot be certain to be protected from revenge.

Third Take: On Constitutional Criticism and the Turn to Institutions

The scriptwriter and the director of *Dirty Harry* do not take (legal) plausibility seriously. Scorpio, despite the problems discussed later in this chapter, could not only have been charged for murder and kidnapping but would also

13 See the brilliant analysis by Richard Slotkin, *Regeneration Through Violence: The Mythology of the American Frontier* (U of Oklahoma P 1973) especially 268 ff. and 313 ff.

most probably have been convicted, based on the facts shown in the film, for assault on an on-duty officer (he knocked Harry unconscious when delivering the ransom), assault with intent to kill (shooting Chico, Harry's assistant), and illegal possession of an automatic firearm. The film bypasses this with aplomb for the sake of its "populist" or rather right-wing critique of how justice was/is administered in the US, notably by the civil rights–oriented, liberal Supreme Court.[14] Scorpio had to be released before because Callahan had violated a number of procedural rights during his arrest: house search without a court order, right to a lawyer, no Miranda instruction on the right to refuse to testify:

> The person in custody must, prior to interrogation, be clearly informed that he has the right to remain silent, and that anything he says will be used against him in court; he must be clearly informed that he has the right to consult with a lawyer. If the individual indicates in any manner, at any time prior to or during questioning, that he wishes to remain silent, the interrogation must cease.[15]

According to the "fruit of the poisonous tree" doctrine,[16] the evidence obtained by Callahan was not likely to be admitted at trial and therefore unusable for the case against Scorpio. Which is to say that standard procedure in a reasonably functioning constitutional state is denounced as a scandal in *Dirty Harry*. Don Siegel's diagnosis of the times, which just a moment before had taken sides with the silent majority, here allies itself consistently with the criticism circulating in the conservative camp and also in the police camp at the end of the 1960s and the beginning of the 1970s of the (much bemoaned) civil rights "excesses" of the liberal Warren Court.[17] Effective criminal prosecution and victim protection, as the thesis states, must fail because the rule of law favours the perpetrators. At his first arrest, Scorpio, the epitome of brutality and unscrupulousness, formulates the paradox of perpetrators' rights and the powerlessness of the law: "I have rights. I want a lawyer". Two sentences that make any police officer cringe and almost any conservative or US Republican shiver in disgust.

14 See e.g. James Elston, 'The Warren Court and Civil Rights: Positive Constitutionalism' (January 1973) 8 Journal of Thought 19–39; Robert Longley, 'The Warren Court: Its Impact and Importance' *Thought & Co* (2 February 2021) <www.thoughtco.com/the-warren-court-4706521/>; Isidore Silver, 'The Warren Court Critics: Where Are They Now That We Need Them' (1976) 3 Hastings Constitutional Law Quarterly 373.

15 US Supreme Court, *Miranda v Arizona*, 384 US 436 (1963); the Miranda rules were in later decisions "relaxed", see *Harris v New York*, 401 US 222 (1971); *Rhode Island v Innis*, 446 US 291 (1980); *New York v Quarles*, 467 US 649 (1984). Also Escobedo.

16 First elaborated in *Silverthorne Lumber Co v United States*, 251 US 385 (1920). Also used by other courts: see e.g. European Court of Human Rights in *Gäfgen v Germany [GC]*, no 22978/05, § 25, ECHR (2010).

17 See Morton J. Horwitz, *The Warren Court and the Pursuit of Justice* (Hill & Wang 1998).

Contemporary criticism of the Warren Court and its civil rights adjudication claimed that the law falls on the arms of the police and obstructs their work. This criticism has a tendency to "overshoot": by stylising Harry Callahan, the specialist for dirty jobs he carries out beyond the confines of legality, as a glamorous hero and the sole positive identification figure, the film makes its contribution to the legitimisation of police action through the effective act rather than simply the lawful application of law. A red line leads from Dirty Harry to police officers killing George Floyd, Michael Brown, Eric Garner, Freddie Gray, and others today. Moreover, criticism of a judgment (*Miranda*) is boosted to a fundamental critique of the institution and its judicial practice. In the end, it takes on almost Schmittian traits of contempt for the liberal legal paradigm, when Siegel/Eastwood want the viewers to believe that the law prevents effective police work and justice to be realised. As a result, the abstract general legal rule is replaced by the concrete individual "law" of the act/measure that leads to a certain, more or less arbitrarily defined end.

Gran Torino – *The Avenger as Epiphany*

Unforgiven and *Dirty Harry* were followed by *Gran Torino*.[18] The sequel illustrates that Eastwood's politics and possibly also his theory of the Constitution and law may have changed or at least softened a bit. *Unforgiven* is as far removed from everyday police work and legal practice as *Dirty Harry* is close to a police operation in the Bronx. With *Gran Torino*, the mature or rather aged Eastwood introduces a new perspective: the potential avenger sacrificing himself so that the law may rule. *Unforgiven* unfolds in the realm of the everyday philosophy of a handicapped retired gunslinger, whereas *Dirty Harry* celebrates a fairly straightforward, right-wing critique of liberalism and the importance of extraordinary police action and powers, covered with a Schmittian frosting. Whereas *Dirty Harry* invokes the state of exception dominating the streets of San Francisco and condones a policeman's right to literally execute justice single-handedly, the *Unforgiven* Eastwood does not clearly reveal his concept of law and the rules of police work. *Unforgiven* does not affirm or critique the liberal paradigm of law rule but echoes the call for executive action, albeit with the charm of demythologising frontier justice. It is true that the sheriff posts half a dozen rules at the gate to Big Whiskey, in particular the prohibition against carrying guns; however, Little Bill is not only the lawmaker but also the executive agency that decides which violations of the law to tolerate (or not) and how to sanction violations of his rules. So he is the Leviathan, bent on containing the state of nature (with his gun regulations) and forcing the people of Big Whiskey under the yoke of his despotic autocracy.

18 It is certainly no coincidence that Dirty Harry's Ford Torino returns as Walt Kowalski's fancy and cherished Gran Torino Sport.

William Munny takes the law in his own hands, once he has realised that this Leviathan is deeply corrupt and his administration of justice anything but just and not constraining the "mortal God's" arbitrary executive power. By torturing, killing, and openly displaying the corpse of Ned Logan, the sheriff deconstructed his law's claim to legitimately order life in Big Whiskey. In such state of lawlessness, Munny's moral conviction could easily take the lead. In a way, *Unforgiven* renders a comment on Derrida's statement that justice cannot wait (in the movie: for a just Leviathan observing the imaginary social contract). In default of a speedy and reliable administration of justice and in the presence of a lawless law that honors property but not the mutilated prostitute, Munny acts on his own accord – his sense of justice being his moral compass. Just as Dirty Harry executed the criminal because he was convinced that, in court, the serial killer would go free on the grounds of some liberal doctrine far from reality and be a danger to society again, William Munny evens up the score for his dead companion, all the while aware that he is releasing the dragon of violence.

Eastwood's final turn comes in *Gran Torino*. After the critique of (liberal) institutions and trusting instead in his own sense of justice, the director-actor finally turns to the institutions he condemned in *Dirty Harry* and didn't even mention in *Unforgiven*. In a grand gesture, the notoriously xenophobic, racist, and grumpy war veteran Walt Kowalski sacrifices his life to provide the police with clear evidence that the gang members who terrorised his Asian neighbors would shoot him in plain sight and, hence, could be arrested and tried for murder. Thus, he protected his neighbors from being further harassed, threatened, and attacked. Riddled with bullets, Walt dies a martyr for the rule of law and the law.

Fourth Take: Violence as Law, Eastwood as Benjamin

The perpetrator's paradox becomes obvious in one of the dramatic highlights of *Dirty Harry*. After Callahan arrests Scorpio in the stadium of the San Francisco 49ers, the law of necessity supersedes ordinary secular law in order to rescue the still-kidnapped girl. Harry Callahan repeatedly kicks the whimpering Scorpio's severely injured leg and asks, "Where is the girl?" Scorpio's answer, "I have a right for a lawyer". Callahan repeats, "Where's the girl?" The irony of this scene: the serial killer invokes the liberal paradigm of law rule, whereas the detective violates one of its fundamental taboos. Whereas conservatives would not bat an eyelid, (liberal) lawyers and the ACLU raised their voices in protest against the torture scene in the stadium and the execution of Scorpio in the end, branding it as "fascist medievalism" and "a right-wing fantasy".[19]

19 Joe Street, *Dirty Harry's America: Clint Eastwood, Harry Callahan, and the Conservative Backlash* (UP of Florida 2018); Matt Lohr, 'Dirty Harry' <www.loc.gov/static/programs/national-film-preservation-board/documents/dirty_harry.pdf/> accessed 14 October 2021.

Since the mid-1990s, torture has experienced a remarkable renaissance as a practice, a metaphor, and a soon-to-be doctrine of justification in the juridical discourse on "rescue torture" and "modern torture", "rescue shooting" (of renegade planes in the power of suspected terrorists), and the "final rescue shot" (targeted fatal shot by the police).[20] In particular after 9/11, liberal constitutional scholars agonised over the justification of (modern/political) torture and torture methods, and quite a few seemed to be content with restricting them to "extreme situations" covered by "strict conditions" as defined by the principle of proportionality and special procedural precautions. While they were arguing (and trying to protect the liberal paradigm), these scholars did not realise that torture had already been normalised: that is, semantically camouflaged (by being called "modern" and "for rescue") and, step by step, integrated into the ordinary legal regime since the "war on terror" had begun in the mid-1990s and continued, especially in the aftermath of 9/11.[21] Interestingly enough, scholars bent on justifying torture time and again referred to the fact that in difficult situations of danger (top of the list: terrorism followed by "organised crime"), someone had to be the Dirty Harry to save human lives.

Unforgiven did not generate legal doctrines, nor could Munny's revenging the prostitute and his friend Ned Logan be adopted as a normative matrix for police action. Here is where the paths of Dirty Harry, William Munny, and Walt Kowalski as Eastwood's various egos part company. The angry critic of liberal legal reform and civil rights celebrates Harry Callahan's official vigilantism, whereas Munny is desperate and melancholy rather than a desperado. However, he cannot tolerate a sheriff's crime *in officio* at the expense of his friend Logan, who, in the hands of the Wild West Leviathan, suffered the fate shared by generations of slaves and African Americans. Munny's altruistic violence shatters the pillars of a rotten legal regime and thus tried to restore – or, better, could have restored – the dignity of law in the service of justice. *Unforgiven* may be read as a narrative of doubt: the director-actor-hero doubting the conventional truths about law dispensing the monopoly of legitimate violence, liberal law rule, and its conservative critique. In good – or, rather, bad – American tradition, he seeks refuge with the mythical individual, this time a non-hero turning out to be a hero after all without feeling heroic. Still, he might be understood as having fulfilled the honorable task of Walter Benjamin's critique of violence "as that of expounding its relationship to law and justice".[22]

20 For references, see Frankenberg (n 6) Ch 7.

21 See Philippe Sands, *Torture Team, Rumsfeld's Memo and the Betrayal of American Values* (St. Martin's Press 2008) – an incisive, albeit selective value analysis of the Cheney/Bush administration and the torture practice in Guantanamo. For a more complete value vision, see Slotkin (n 13). Regarding the concept of normalisation, see Frankenberg (n 6) Ch 1.

22 Walter Benjamin, 'Critique of Violence' in Marcus Bullock and Michael W Jenning (eds), *Selected Writings, vol. 1, 1913–1926* (The Belknap Press 1966) 236.

Clint Eastwood uses (or, rather, plays with) two concepts of violence as if he had read at least the first part of Benjamin's essay. The violence of *Dirty Harry* is historical and social. The dominant (liberal) opinion would criticise its means from the vantage point of positive (liberal) law. Callahan challenges the law by disobeying what legality requires. For good reasons, liberal constitutionalism and legal theory argue, modern law divests the individual executive of the state of the power to make law. Therefore, Dirty Harry is dangerous because he, the policeman, threatens that divestment by deciding that executing the helpless Scorpio is a just means because the administration of justice would not produce "justice" but would let him go to enjoy ever after the fruits of the poisonous tree. Yet, *Dirty Harry* I and the next sequels do everything possible in Hollywood to confirm the belief that Callahan's illegal violence is, in fact, from his perspective, a "law-preserving violence".[23]

By contrast, William Munny's violence seems to originate in a realm that is generally referred to as natural law. One could criticise its ends, but the critique runs into the void because, from his perspective, which is likely to be shared by many viewers, his (personal) violence serves just ends. However, this is not the narrative Eastwood tries to tell us. Clearly, Munny sees that there is "something rotten in the law" revealed by *Unforgiven*. So Munny's violence cannot preserve law but has to establish a kind of new law beyond the realm of positive and natural law. It might be called the LAW in capital letters. According to Benjamin, it transcends the antinomy of natural and positive law, and it is – or, rather, can be – created through mythical violence. It resides in the third dimension of transcendental law or mythical law created by the lawmaking power of violence or transcendental earthly justice generated by a voluntary victim like Walt Kowalski.

Conclusion

Dirty Harry is a spectacular *film noir*, full of suspense, with unforgettable scenes that reveal the paradox of law rule and its means-ends-rationality – and a logic than could be exploited by the law-and-order campaigns of politicians like Ronald Reagan (in his bid for governor of California and later president of the US). *Unforgiven* is a masterpiece: first, it deconstructs both the mythology of the Western frontier and its law by displaying the human defects and deficiencies of anti-heroes and by allowing a no-hero hero and prostitutes (no innocent children)[24] to take center stage. Second, *Unforgiven* visualises the antinomy between natural and positive law. Third, it reconstructs a situation

23 Walter Benjamin, *Toward a Critique of Violence: A Critical Edition* (Stanford UP 2021).

24 Their role and need to be rescued by men, as well as Mundy's persona, call for a critique from a feminist perspective. See Tania Modleski, 'Clint Eastwood and Male Weepies' (2010) 22 American Literary History 136 ff.

of mythical lawmaking against a "mortal God" (Gene Hackman as the sheriff of Big Whiskey). Munny knows he cannot remain in his world because the evil forces will haunt him and the law cannot protect him where guns rule. He is doomed because he killed the Leviathan, incidentally also the cowboys.

Both Dirty Harry and William Munny return in the guise of Walt Kowalski to fulfill their fate and stop their urge to take the law into their own hands. Walt Kowalski sacrifices himself and the memory of Harry Callahan for "the law" to do their job and "the LAW" to be respected, very likely in court. Walt Kowalski, the veteran, delegitimises Dirty Harry and William Munny because, in the final showdown, he does not resort to mythical or raw violence. Neither does he run away. Accepting death, he stays in his world and helps "the law" bring down a gang with the force of LAW.

Reference List

Benjamin W, 'Critique of Violence' in M Bullock and MW Jenning (eds), *Selected Writings, vol. 1, 1913–1926* (The Belknap Press 1966) 236

Bodin J, *Les Six Livres de la République* (Forgotten Books [1576] 2018)

Derrida J, 'Force of Law: "The Mystical Foundation of Authority"' in D Cornell and others (eds), *Deconstruction and the Possibility of Justice* (Routledge 1992) 3

Elston J, 'The Warren Court and Civil Rights: Positive Constitutionalism' (January 1973) 8 Journal of Thought 19–39

Frankenberg F, *Political Technology and the Erosion of the Rule of Law – Normalizing the State of Exception* (Edward Elgar Publishing 2014)

Goldfarb JC, *The Cynical Society* (U of Chicago P 1991)

Hobbes T, *Leviathan* (CUP [1651] 1996)

Horwitz MJ, *The Warren Court and the Pursuit of Justice* (Hill & Wang 1998)

Longley R, 'The Warren Court: Its Impact and Importance' *Thought & Co* (2 February 2021) <www.thoughtco.com/the-warren-court-4706521/>

Modleski T, 'Clint Eastwood and Male Weepies' (2010) 22 American Literary History 136

Sands P, *Torture Team, Rumsfeld's Memo and the Betrayal of American Values* (St. Martin's Press 2008)

Silver I, 'The Warren Court Critics: Where Are They Now That We Need Them' (1976) 3 Hastings Constitutional Law Quarterly 373

Slotkin R, *Regeneration Through Violence: The Mythology of the American Frontier* (U of Oklahoma P 1973)

Street J, *Dirty Harry's America: Clint Eastwood, Harry Callahan, and the Conservative Backlash* (UP of Florida 2018)

Weber M, 'Politics as a Vocation' in T Waters and D Waters (trs and eds), *Weber's Rationalism and Modern Society* (Palgrave Books 2015) 129

Chapter 5

The Impossible Truth in Law and Films

The Female Gaze of *Saint Omer* and *Anatomy of a Fall*

Séverine Dusollier

Introduction[1]

A significant part of law and film scholarship focuses on how movies represent courtroom or legal proceedings or engage with issues generally addressed by law ("law in film"), thereby guiding viewers in forming a judgment. The cinematographic language also operates to impose some construction or interpretation of the facts, as law does. The combination of framing, angle and the situation of subject/object, camera movement, lightning, length of shots, sequences, and editing, all choices made by filmmakers, organises the narrative in order to position viewers to identify with some interpretations. Films tell stories with a normative effect by weaving implicit meanings and judgments in their very fabrics. To that extent, movies are normative tales and could be studied as such ("film as law").

Law is immediately understandable as a normative regime while film appears to be primarily an entertainment product, yet "as socio-cultural formations, both law and film create meaning through storytelling, performance and ritualistic patterning, envisioning and constructing human subjects and social groups, individuals and worlds".[2] One can say that "what is seen on the screen is so manifestly shown",[3] in a similar manner as what is said by law is so manifestly told. Yet the way the norms are built and imposed by legal and filmic languages operates in a largely more invisible way.

It is particularly interesting to analyse this normative construction with courtroom movies in which the key question of the film is to determine the culpability of an accused person and to unfold how the judge or jury and the viewer alike are making their opinion. The visual rhetoric here intersects with

1 My thanks to Mikhail Xifaras for helpful comments on an earlier version of this chapter.
2 Orit Kamir, 'Why "Law-and-Film" and What Does It Actually Mean? A Perspective' (2005) 19 Journal of Media & Cultural Studies 255, 257.
3 Laura Mulvey, 'Visual Pleasure and Narrative Cinema' (1975) 16 Screen 6, 9.

DOI: 10.4324/9781003461180-5

the deployment of the judicial truth to create the celluloid "truth" that the director and the scriptwriter want to narrate. The particular cinematographic vision then adds a supplementary dimension to the often-discussed distinction between the facts-based truth and the judicial or legal truth by deploying specific tools for the interpretation of facts.[4]

The present chapter aims to reveal such operation of judgment making in film and in law, based on my perception as a legal scholar with a limited knowledge but an insatiable enjoyment of cinema. I will add another twist to that plot by analysing two recent movies on criminal proceedings, *Saint Omer* by Alice Diop and *Anatomy of a Fall* by Justine Triet. Both films tell a story of a woman accused of having killed someone. *Saint Omer*, winner of the 2022 Grand Jury Prize in Venice and of a César for best first feature, is based on a real case of a woman who killed her 15-month-old child. *Anatomy of a Fall*, which won the Golden Palm at the 2023 Cannes Film Festival and a few Oscars and Cesars, is a fiction about a woman accused of having killed her husband after a dispute. Both films are made by female French directors and have been praised by the critics. They also rejoice in how they construct the accused woman as a subject, going well beyond the usual question of guilt or the performance of lawyers that we regularly see in courtroom dramas. In that sense, Alice Diop's and Justine Triet's movies adopt a "female gaze" that rejects the objectification of the woman character and focuses instead on her story.

This chapter will first examine how truth and judgment are achieved in law and in films, including by building an objectifying and judgmental gaze on female characters. Then the indeterminacy of truth and the regained subjectivity of accused women, which are observations one can equally make about law, will be illustrated by the films *Saint Omer* and *Anatomy of a Fall*. More interestingly, these films stand out from legal and court processes, as well as from the majority of courtroom movies, in their refusal to pass judgments and impose their truth.

Truth Between Facts and Storytelling in Law and Film

Legal rhetoric engages legal subjects into judgment and adherence (or not) to legal constraints, order, and norms. Before courts, the legal argumentation uses facts and evidence, glued with legal formal rules, to form a judgment that is reputed to declare the truth. Likewise, the visual rhetoric of cinema engages viewers in some interpretation, narration, and judgments, and each film creates a normative system of its own, unfolding a story while

4 Duncan Kennedy, 'A Left Phenomenological Alternative to the Hart/Kelsen Theory of Legal Interpretation' in Duncan Kennedy (ed), *Legal Reasoning, Collected Essays* (The Davies Book Publishers 2008) 158.

guiding the viewer through the narration and, as demonstrated by feminist film studies, assuming a male gaze that objectifies women. Unsurprisingly, courtroom movies offer a fascinating scene for the combination (and the construction) of legal and cinematographic narratives.

The Construction of Truth in Courts

Law is a regime of production of truth in a Foucauldian sense, meaning that truth is not "an essential and original attribute of [reality] that we simply have to discover . . . [but] is always produced in relation to a specific reality".[5] The regime of truth produced by law relies on mechanisms, techniques, and procedures, particularly in the instances of a trial, that aim to obtain the truth and distinguish it from what is considered false.[6] How the judiciary process seeks to "say the truth" – i.e. to produce some judgment that will consist in a discourse of truth and its particular relationship to reality and facts – has been studied in legal theory. The judiciary truth is distinct from the factual truth (assuming that such truth inherently exists) as it is necessarily a process of reconstruction from facts, testimonies, recollections, investigations, expertise, and perceptions that leads to a sort of "fictive truth".[7] The use of fiction also plays a significant role in the pragmatics of the law.[8]

Looking for truth in the many facts, uncertainties, and unknown or unrevealed elements requires a storytelling that privileges some interpretations over others to overcome the facts and result in a solution to the trial in the form of a judgment that will be authoritative (*faire autorité* in French). Even if such truth is fictive,[9] such fiction is based on consensus and plausibility,[10] two accommodations with reality that are indispensable to delivering justice. The elaboration of a judiciary truth follows strict procedures, particularly in criminal trials,

5 Daniele Lorenzini, 'Foucault, Regimes of Truth and the Making of the Subject' in Laura Cremonesi and others (eds), *Foucault and the Making of Subjects* (Rowman & Littlefield 2016) 66.

6 Michel Foucault, 'The Political Function of the Intellectual' (1977) 17 Radical Philosophy 13.

7 Alexandre Frambéry-Iacobone, 'Vérité judiciaire, vérité factuelle et élément moral: Perspectives d'histoire pénale contemporaine' (2020) 19 CLIO@Themis, Dossier Vérité judiciaire 62, 77.

8 Yan Thomas, 'Fictio Legis – L'empire de la fiction romaine et ses limites médiévales' in *Les opérations du droit* (Seuil/Gallimard 2011) 134. See also Mikhail Xifaras, 'Fictions juridiques – Remarques sur quelques procédés fictionnels en usage chez les juristes' (2011) 3 Annuaire de l'Institut Michel Villey 451.

9 Thomas (n 8) 153.

10 Frambéry-Iacobone (n 7) 77: 'Loin d'offrir le règne du *justement vrai*, c'est bien celui du *consensuellement vrai* parce que *vraisemblablement vrai* qui l'emporte ici. Par ces mécanismes, nous quittons le monde du véridique pour pénétrer dans le crédible, ne nous fondant plus sur le savoir, mais sur les croyances les plus étayées, les plus vraisemblables, donc les plus consensuelles'.

supported by the acquisition of evidence and the verification of hypotheses by the contradictory debate.[11] Such information-gathering and decision-making processes might appear elusive but are predicated on rules of evidence that define what can be considered as a fact to be taken into account in the forming of a judgment, as well as procedural rules that organise the collection of testimonies, expertise, and the questioning of the accused persons and the witnesses.

As Yan Thomas wrote, after the exposition of facts (*narratio*) and evidence (*argumentatio, probatio*), the judge (or the jury) needs to "decide, not the truth but the dispute"[12] and reduce the many explored ways and interpretations to a unique and constrained question in order to say what will be the truth.[13] The *chose jugée* or *res judicata* then accedes to the status of (judiciary) truth, fabricated only partially from reality.[14] The law needs to evacuate the doubt "to create or to undo determinacy",[15] and "the requirement to reach a decision suspends the requirement of truth, after having been subjected to it".[16] The dialogic and contradictory process of the trial is essential to the construction of the truth as it helps in choosing among the diverse interpretations, versions, and convictions, all equally defendable.[17] The judgment (but it could be said of the law too) merely makes as if it relies on reality by fabricating a pseudo-truth on the mode of fiction and storytelling.[18] A comparison with cinema that expressly refers to fictional worlds is then particularly enlightening.

Normative Storytelling in Films

Films tell stories with a complex visual rhetoric that assembles framing, lightning, choices of shots, camera movements, montages, and other tricks like voice-over or offscreen action that give a distinct meaning to each sequence and to the course of the story. Even spectators not particularly educated in

11 Christiane Besnier, 'Le travail de la vérité en cours d'assises' (2020) 19 CLIO@Themis, Dossier Vérité judiciaire 97.

12 Yan Thomas, 'La vérité, le temps, le juge et l'historien' (1998) 5 Le Débat 17, 19.

13 See also Kennedy (n 4) 158 ('[Legal work] aims to transform an initial apprehension of what the system of norms requires, given the facts, so that a new apprehension of the system, as it applies to the case, will correspond to the extra-juristic preferences of the interpretative worker. . . . Often, once the facts are found, no one will even advert to the possibility of legal work directed at the interpretation of the norm that defines and punishes murder. The facts will be understood to establish guilt or innocence "of their own accord", as the norm "applies itself" seemingly without any agency of the interpreter').

14 Michel van de Kerchove, 'Vérité judiciaire et para-judiciaire en matière pénale: Quelle vérité?' (2013) 84 Droit et société 411, 421.

15 Kennedy (n 4) 159.

16 Thomas (n 8) 134.

17 van de Kerchove (n 14) 424.

18 Xifaras (n 8) 453; Stefan Goltzberg, 'De quoi la fiction indique-t-elle l'absence?' in Anne-Blandine Caire (ed), *Les fictions en droit* (PU de Clermont 2015) 107.

film studies will get the emotion or sense of a sequence shot in the way the filmmaker intended so as to convey a particular interpretation of the scene, such as the position (as subjects or objects of action) of some actors in the narrative, their honesty, their feelings, and the double entendre or hidden meaning of some dialogue. Through a vast array of filmic techniques, good films express tension, fear, joy, desire, domination, and trouble better than words.

Combined with the storytelling, script, and dialogue, the employed visual rhetoric participates in the consented "suspension of disbelief" that is required from viewers to accept the narrative as it is told to them, without doubting its reality, plausibility, or logic. Truth in movies is thus a fabricated process that mixes several narrative, visual, sound, and performance schemes. Even in documentary films, the visual and editing choices of the filmmaker separate the filmed reality from its filmed rendering. Whether fiction or documentary, movies are normative framings: similar to what happens in law, they impose a narrative with limited room for interpretation, at least within the room the filmmaker has created and allowed, in the same way as the interpreter of legal materials aims at convincing "an audience of some kind (and himself as well) that an initial apprehension (his or that of another) of determinacy or indeterminacy was wrong".[19]

Cinematographic storytelling resembles legal processes, as beautifully argued by Jessica Silbey:

> Cinema's play on the hermeneutics of seeing/knowledge and critique/judgment, parallel those of the courtroom jury trial. As with film, the trial process is based on the believability and privileged status of observable phenomena – on seeing, bearing witness, and judging. Also like film, legal processes are self-reflexive. The essence of the trial is the existence of debatable stories, facts that fit into conflicting versions of events, all being retold and represented for an audience asked to compare and judge their relative faithfulness to a past reality. Trials and their verdicts are then themselves appealable and exposed to retellings that may have equal or greater persuasive force. This process exposes law's own fictions of determinacy and finality, ideological commitments that political order requires. Despite the contingencies of both legal and filmic accounts, both law and film are nonetheless authoritative representational forms. Both are perceived to tell a particularly persuasive account of "what happened" because they fortify the "knowledge" produced (a verdict or a filmic rendition of an event) with the practice of first-person witnessing, reflexivity and self-critique, and the accumulation and sorting of multiple perspectives.[20]

19 Kennedy (n 4) 160.

20 Jessica M Silbey, 'American Trial Films and the Popular Culture of Law' in *Oxford Research Encyclopedia of Criminology* (OUP 2017) 5–6 <https://papers.ssrn.com/sol3/papers.cfm?abstract_id=3151795>.

Moreover, feminist film scholars have particularly explained how movie language has moulded the spectator's gaze around unconscious ways of seeing and looking. Laura Mulvey has influentially developed the concept of male gaze,[21] which she borrowed from John Berger in his BBC series and later book *Ways of Seeing*, which analysed how the female nude in painting represents women as desire objects for the pleasure of the heterosexual male viewer.[22] Likewise, says Mulvey, cinema as a representation system commodifies women as objects to be seen for the gaze of the filmmaker and of the spectator, who is assumed to be male. Female spectators, on the other hand, look at female characters on the screen to be looked at. In narrative cinema, the male gaze organises the visual choices and sightline of the filming and presents the male character as active and the female character as passive and displayed as the object of desire, reproducing longtime representations and aesthetics of the dominant patriarchal order.[23] As said by John Berger on female representations in painting,

> *[M]en act* and *women appear*. Men look at women. Women watch themselves being looked at. This determines not only most relations between men and women but also the relations of women to themselves. The surveyor of woman in herself is male: the surveyed female. Thus she turns herself into an object – and most particularly an object of vision: a sight.[24]

Based on the Freudian psychoanalytic concept of scopophilia, or the aesthetic pleasure drawn from looking at an object or a person, Mulvey explains:

> [I]n a world ordered by sexual imbalance, pleasure in looking has been split between active/male and passive/female. The determining male gaze projects its phantasy on to the female figure which is styled accordingly. In their traditional exhibitionist role women are simultaneously looked at and displayed, with their appearance coded for strong visual and erotic impact so that they can be said to connote *to-be-looked-at-ness*.[25]

The combination of the male gaze and the objectification of women relies on several filmic mechanisms that have been identified by feminist movies studies, such as the establishment of characters as subjects and objects by the script, the camera angle and movement, the framing choices, and the lightning, which might differ for male and female characters.[26] In particu-

21 Mulvey (n 3) 11.
22 John Berger, *Ways of Seeing* (Penguin Books 1972) particularly Ch 3.
23 Mulvey (n 3) 9.
24 Berger (n 22) 41.
25 Mulvey (n 3) 11.
26 See the conference *Sex and Power, the Visual Language of Oppression* by Nina Menkes, turned into a film, *Brainwashed – Sex-Camera-Power* 2022.

lar, close-ups of body parts or faces, a fragmented body, travelling along the naked body, and silencing female characters are typical cinematographic choices that transform women into passive objects subjected to the gaze and desire of viewers.

The concept of the male gaze became popularised in the last decades, beyond academic feminist and cinema studies writing, though it was also criticised for its too-simple and heteronormative reading of films and viewers' position. Mulvey herself eventually attenuated the relevance of the concept and insisted on the contemporary ambiguity of the spectator's gaze, particularly as it is now informed by race and queer theories.[27]

Yet this objectivation and sexualisation of women through and for a male gaze can be seen in many mainstream movies throughout the history of cinema. There is a long tradition of the representation of "woman as spectacle" in Hollywood that we can find as well in courtroom movies.[28] As written by Laura Mulvey again,

> [T]he popular cinema, itself a commodity, can form a bridge between the commodity as spectacle and the figure of woman as spectacle on the screen. This, in turn, leads on the bridging function of woman as consumer, rather than producer, of "commodities".[29]

Objectivation of women as objects of desire also forbids them to be agents and subjects in the film: they are either passive objects or have to identify with the male protagonist. Courtroom movies, a specific genre in cinema, similarly proceed through filmic and narrative devices to induce the viewer's judgment on the case and the accused on trial. Here also, women assume a predefined and constrained role.

Storytelling and Male Gaze in Courtroom Films

It comes as no surprise that courtroom movies have always been a favourite topic for study in law and film. Trials on the screen open an interesting space for playing with facts, narratives, and interpretations by using cinematographic vocabulary and language to empower the viewer to form a judgment in the pursuit of justice.[30] Neither law nor film reveals the truth, but both declare it, based on a combination of facts and rhetoric that guides some

27 Laura Mulvey, 'Introduction: 1970s Feminist Film Theory and the Obsolescent Object' in L Mulvey and A Backman Rogers (eds), *Feminisms – Diversity, Difference and Multiplicity in Contemporary Film Cultures* (Amsterdam UP 2015) 17–27.

28 Heidi Slettedahl Macpherson, 'Spectacular Expectations: Women, Law and Film' (2007) 41 Journal of American Studies 641–58

29 Laura Mulvey, *Fetishism and Curiosity* (BFI Publishing 1996) 8.

30 Kamir (n 2) 268.

interpretation and judgment. Courtroom movies seek even more to perform the process that would lead viewers to engage in the act of judging through seeing and believing.[31] As Orit Kamir writes, "[A] law film can be read as passing cinematic judgment when, in addition to portraying a fictional legal system, it offers distinct normative constructions of subjects and societies, of justice and judgment, inviting a judgmental viewing process".[32] While the law builds justice by relying on evidence, rules, and interpretations of multiple conflicting stories, a trial film, in addition to the display of facts and testimonies that could count as evidence, actively creates meaning through narrative, editing, framing, and shooting choices.

Similar to what happens in a courtroom, the film is presenting facts, plots, and stories told through witnesses or people involved, raising in the viewer a first intuition and opinion about what has happened. This *a priori* conception can then be modified and destabilised by new twists in the scenario and story, new evidence, or interventions. Contrary to actual legal proceedings, a movie has the liberty to move outside the tribunal and make spectators aware of events that have not reached the court, making them more knowledgeable than the judge, lawyers, or detectives of the film. The actual scene of the crime can be seen by spectators, even if it occured without any witnesses; preliminary or posterior events can be shown and told and give light to the intentions or feelings of the protagonists. The spectators can hence form their apprehension of the case, the suspect, the guilt, and the motive based on elements that only need to meet the procedural and aesthetic conditions of the cinematographic language and the fictive truth decided by the director. The verdict of the spectator will be influenced or even manipulated by elements of filmic vocabulary they have been accustomed to perceiving as producing some meanings over others.[33] For instance, a close-up of the accused person might reveal his anxiety, hence his likely guilt; a shot/reverse shot can elevate tension between two characters; contrasted lightning can put some roles in the spotlight and induce their dark personalities.

Legal proceedings and cinematographic choices reveal to the viewer their essential fictive and storytelling nature and that their

> truth tale has as its aim not to tell (what in documentary jargon would be) a true story based on the culmination of multiple perspectives, but instead to cultivate and accommodate multiple notions of truth based on irreconcilable points of view.[34]

31 Jessica Silbey, 'Truth Tales and Trial Films' (2007) 40 Loyola of Los Angeles Law Review 551, 560.

32 Orit Kamir, *Framed: Women in Law and Film* (Duke UP 2006) Introduction.

33 Orit Kamir, 'Judgment by Film: Socio-Legal Functions of *Rashomon*' (2000) 12 Yale Journal of Law & the Humanities 39–40.

34 Silbey (n 31) 567.

A quintessential film about the indeterminacy or relativity of truth is *Rashomon*, by Akira Kurosawa.[35] This 1950 Japanese movie is famous for its multivocal narration of a crime, in which four persons tell different stories about a murder: the presumed murderer, the victim's wife, and the victim himself, all of them claiming their guilt, and finally, the person who discovered the body. Each testimony is filmed in close-up in a similar setting with very contrasted light and is mixed with the representation of the story as it is told. Neither the judge nor the recipient of the four narrations is ever visible, and there is no visual trick that induces the viewers to believe one story over another. The close-ups emphasise the emotion and nervousness of each character, which scatters their presumed innocence even more. The verdict of the court is not revealed either. The film has generally been interpreted as showing that no reality ever exists beyond the subjective and contradictory representations persons make of it.

The scenery of the film, which oscillates from the bare settings of the court to the ruins where the story is told once again to a priest and a vagabond, who express their disenchanted views of each version, arguably representing morality and ordinary sense, does not deploy any visual rhetoric to guide the interpretation. *Rashomon* is a perfect allegory of the truth unattainable by a legal process, including unreliable and self-centered narrators, witnesses, victims, and accused persons, whose diverging stories can only be subjected to evaluation and comparison.

The male gaze I explained earlier also operates in courtroom movies as they rarely display a woman as an active agent of the narrative, except when they are lawyers defending their clients.[36] In *film noirs* and trial movies alike, women are mostly "guilty objects responsible for the destruction of men, though themselves denied full subjecthood and agency".[37] In *Rashomon* particularly, the woman is the sexualised victim whose rape is depicted as seduction or something induced by the woman herself. She is the object of desire and the reason for the crime, but she is ultimately excluded from the story as a victim and as a subject, silenced, and offered to the judgment of men.[38] The spectator here assumes a male gaze and a specific socio-legal narrative that displays the woman as an object of desire and of repression or blame. Likewise, in *Anatomy of a Murder* by Otto Preminger, from which Justine Triet borrows the title for her film, which I will discuss in the following section, the woman's rape is used as the possible motive and excuse for the murder

35 For a comprehensive analysis of the film from a legal point of view, see Kamir (n 32).

36 See Orit Kamir, 'Anatomy of Hollywood's Hero-Lawyer: A Law-and-Film Study of the Western Motifs, Honor-Based Values and Gender Politics Underlying Anatomy of a Murder's Construction of the Lawyer Image' (2005) 35 Studies in Law, Politics and Society 67 (analysing the association of the figure of the lawyer in movies with gender politics).

37 Kamir (n 32) Preface.

38 Kamir (n 32) Preface 82–83.

in a patriarchal honour-based paradigm, not as an act to be compensated in itself for the victim.[39] The existence of a rape is unsurprisingly minored and doubted in the light of the enticing clothing and amorality of the woman (and of all women?), one concern of the judge even being that using the word "panties" to evoke the underwear that the raped wife lost in the assault would be too lightly connoted for the jury.[40] Even in what is considered a feminist trial film, *Adam's Rib*, in which Katherine Hepburn acts as a lawyer defending a woman accused of shooting her adulterous husband, against her own spouse (played by Spencer Tracy), who is the prosecutor in the case, the indicted woman is portrayed as a simple-minded housewife taken by her emotions and reduced to the object of a legal defence of gender equality, deprived of any subjectivity of her own.

This is where the two recent films I will discuss next diverge and restore the subjectivities of women and their stories while refusing to impose "truth" about their guilt.

The Female Court Gaze in *Saint Omer* and *Anatomy of a Fall*

Now that I have laid down the many tropes of this chapter (i.e. the striking parallel between law and film in engaging judgment; the key features of courtroom dramas and the way they construct, as law, a fictive truth around facts and testimonies without ever getting rid of ambiguities and contradictory interpretations; and a feminist reading of cinematic gaze in most films, including trial movies, that objectifies women and denies them subjectivity), let me turn to the analysis of two recent films that completely renew and subvert such lines.

Saint Omer by Alice Diop and *Anatomy of a Fall* by Justine Triet jointly rejuvenate the genre of courtroom movies by embracing the indeterminacy of truth and interpretations and constructing instead the complex subjectivity and agency of the accused woman. Contrary to *Rashomon*, the perplexity of the viewer as to the impossibility of forming an opinion about what has really happened (rather, as to what the film narrative seeks to tell) is not at the expense of the female character, who would assume the moral guilt whether she was the victim or the criminal. Instead, both films are examples of what

39 Kamir (n 32).

40 This gives a particularly funny all-men dialogue between the judge and the three attorneys, one married, one bachelor, and another one telling about his experience in France during the war, about how to name such panties. When the judge finally says to the court that the undergarment is a pair of panties, the whole attendance burst into laughter, which the judge corrects by saying that there is "nothing comic in a pair of panties which figure in the violent death of one man and in the possible incarceration of another". The rape of a woman seems to be only a minor detail one could laugh at.

Iris Brey has conceptualised as a "female gaze" in films.[41] Starting from the notion of male gaze developed by Laura Mulvey in the 70s, as explained earlier, Brey does not reverse it to mean that a female gaze in cinema would merely be the possibility for a film to grant female spectators some viewing pleasure of male (or, incidentally, female) objects of desire. Instead, the notion of female gaze Brey invokes insists on the representation of women as subjects and agents of the narrative: in a movie that could be said to adopt a female gaze, female characters are given a voice and agency and not just a body to be looked at or actions to be judged.[42]

In both *Saint Omer* and *Anatomy of a Fall*, the subjectivity given back to the accused women is paired with the recognition of the complexity and relative opacity of their actions and intentions and underlines how neither law nor film can fill the inherent gaps between juridical truth and psychological and material reality. Diop and Triet do not assume a position of omniscient and dominant narrators whose filmic tricks would impose a story. Instead, their films aim at developing the truth of the accused woman, however elusive it might be, over the reality of the facts and the determinacy of the judiciary truth. Neither film lands on a definitive truth.

Saint Omer

Alice Diop's movie, released in 2022, retraces the trial of Laurence Coly, a Senegalese woman accused of the infanticide of her 15-month-old daughter, played by a fantastic Guslagie Malanda. Based on a real-life *fait divers* whose trial in the city of Saint-Omer was attended by the filmmaker,[43] the film does not raise the question of the guilt of the accused, which is without doubt, but lets the viewers follow her defence to try to understand her motives and trajectory. The real case and trial startled the French press and public as they discovered, in the courtroom, a woman whose complexity, language, and mind did not meet the racist and misogynistic prejudice they had assumed against the story of an African infanticide.[44]

41 Iris Brey, *Le regard féminin – Une révolution à l'écran* (Points 2020).

42 Iris Brey, *Le regard féminin – Une révolution à l'écran* (Points 2020) 36.

43 Note that the title of the film is borrowed from the name of the city where the real trial took place but with the omission of the hyphen, which introduces some reminiscence of the "sea" which took the baby and of "mother", both words in French ("mer" and "mère") being homophones of the "mer" in Saint Omer.

44 The filmmaker, Alice Diop, also confessed that she went to the trial with her own prejudices, even though they were different from those entertained by the media. See her interview in *Trois Couleurs* (24 November 2022) <www.troiscouleurs.fr/article/entretien-alice-diop-saint-omer>.

This is not the first film by Diop, who was already a recognised documentary filmmaker, and this first fiction feature shows an evident continuity with her previous films that constantly challenges our ways of looking at the black body, particularly black women, and the lack of some narratives.[45] In *Saint Omer*, she again unfolds the rarely told and seen story of an African woman, made invisible by French society (and, in the film and reality, by her older companion), by offering the testimony of a form of life that is only fantasised and racialised by our European assumptions.[46] This storytelling is intersected in the film with other counternarratives: the reality of motherhood compared to its idealised vision and the indeterminacy of guilt compared to the judiciary force of evidence.

These multiple narratives are seen through the eyes of Rama (played by Kayije Kagame), a scholar and writer who attends the trial for a book she is writing. This "narrator", another Senegalese woman, who has a successful professional career as a university professor and novelist, reflects on thoughts the trial brings about her own uneasy relationship with her mother and her motherhood about to come.[47] Diop thus literally installs a female gaze: the accused woman is seen through the eyes of the writer, and the subjectivity of the former mirrors the subjectivity of the latter. The only interaction between the two women happens at mid-film, when Laurence directly gazes at Rama with a smile, which makes the writer cry and exit the courtroom. This is also the only time where the indicted woman, mostly a sphinxlike figure throughout the trial and the film, looks at the attendees or the jury, for she generally directs her gaze to the president of the court and, when not being interrogated, stares fixedly in front of her.

The first two sequences of the film are, on the one hand, a dream made by Rama that represents a woman leaving something on the beach as a sort of vision of the crime[48] and, on the other hand, a lecture she gives to her students during which she screens a scene from *Hiroshima Mon Amour* by Marguerite Duras, which shows head-shaved French women at the Liberation. That reference to Duras, her voice-over, and the literary language sublimate the humiliated and condemned women.

45 As in her documentaries *La Permanence* (a Wiseman-like film of a medical consultation receiving migrants), *Vers la Tendresse* (an exploration of masculinity in Paris's northern outskirts), and *Nous* (portraits of people along the RER-B line, which is a busy train line that crosses the poorest neighbourhoods north of Paris).

46 In an interview, Alice Diop refers to the well-known text by Gayatri Spivak, *Can the Subaltern Speak?* (1998), that "questions whether a subaltern woman of the past can be given voice by historians of the present without becoming a collage of their own projections" <www.filmcomment.com/blog/interview-alice-diop-on-saint-omer/>.

47 The mothers of Laurence and Rama also appear in the film in a very interesting way.

48 Alice Diop refrained from representing the abandonment of the baby in the film.

Likewise, Diop does not want to dictate our judgment or opinion as viewers. She said in an interview:

> The film does not seek to pass moral or judicial judgement. I'm not interested in the verdict, which is not presented in the film. We know she is guilty. But what we don't know is who she is. What the film does is to enable us to listen to the life story of a black woman in all its complexity. The film also leaves a lot of room for the viewers, allowing them to change their minds, to doubt, to move from one feeling to another. I do not want, through my editing choices for example, to lock viewers into my own vision.[49]

Indeed, the storytelling is left to Laurence, who pleads not guilty: though admitting what she did and the horror thereof, she doubts her responsibility. What is striking is that, far from the stereotypes assumed by the press and the audience of the trial, she is an articulate, lucid, intellectual woman who uses sophisticated language and references. In her answers to the judges, she quotes Descartes and Wittgenstein (the latter being the invented topic of a PhD, as she lies about that as well as about her director recommending instead a PhD topic closer to her culture). Amongst her many lies, she pretends that she is possessed by witchcraft and demons, as if she wants to confirm the post-colonial fantasy of Black female subjectivities.[50]

The filmmaker does not take sides; she unfolds the different stories based on the testimony of the protagonists – namely, the absent father of the child, alternating with the questioning of the accused – and, without showing the verdict, stops the film after the pleadings by the defence attorney, who reproduces the text of the actual trial. The lawyer, a new narrator and a new gaze, has no explanation or excuse for what her client did and no way to plead her innocence. Instead, she evokes the figure of chimaera to describe the maternal body as cells pass between mothers and children, creating a hybrid organism. The chimaera also relates to Medea, the mythological infanticidal mother, who is the topic of the book Rama wants to write when attending the trial. "We women, we are all chimaeras; we bear in us the cells of our daughters and of our mothers; we are all monsters, but terribly human monsters", ends the attorney, before taking the crying accused in her arms, the only moment in the film when she loses her impassibility, as if the image of a monster, needed by criminal law to condemn, is finally liberated in all its humanity, a hybrid of a victim and a perpetrator. The camera then moves on to the many women in the room – the judge, the members of the jury, and the attendees – all with tears in their eyes, all filmed in close-ups shots. No men are shown.

49 Interview of Alice Diop, *Trois Couleurs* (author's translation).

50 The witchcraft took more importance in the actual criminal case than in the film, where it is only mentioned at the end, as if it was another way to make her motivation undecipherable.

Anatomy of a Fall

In the awards-winning *Anatomy of a Fall*, the verdict is shown and acquits Sandra Voyter, a writer played by Sandra Hüller, of the homicide of her husband. Contrary to *Saint Omer*, her guilt or innocence is never known throughout the film, nor is it demonstrated by it, and at the end of the film, the viewer does not have a firm opinion of what truth to believe. The film rather analyses the many perspectives and views of what could have happened, notably in their couple relationship, that could explain the fall of the victim from the second floor. The anatomy operated by the film is of the fatal fall and of the couple alike.

A substantive part of the movie revolves around the process during which the prosecutor relentlessly tries to convince the judge, the audience, and the spectators of Sandra's guilt. He does so by pointing out how she is not the "perfect wife" who would sacrifice her career to give time to her husband and son and how she is resolutely and successfully focusing on her writing and having sex with others, including women, not out of love but mostly out of need. Similar to the accused in Alice Diop's movie, she is not particularly likeable but appears somewhat selfish and egocentric as she remains unapologetic for the independence she has gained as a woman.

The inquiry and the trial, as well as the preparatory discussions of Sandra with her lawyer, all seek to reveal the facts that led to the death of her husband. Discrete forms of languages are mobilised in pursuit of the truth: the testimony of the accused, in imperfect French and English, and that of other witnesses; the demonstrations by experts; one recorded conversation between the spouses; the conviction of the advocate general; and also the literary writing of the novelist, used by the latter as it was not a complete fiction. The voice of Sandra herself and her own (counter)narrative are also heard, though she continuously struggles to express herself and to rectify how others portray her. She tells her story and the story of her couple and the difficulties they encountered, first to her lawyer, then to the court. But her tale is fiercely opposed by the many discourses that pretend to tell the truth: the legal discourse, the media discourse, the psychiatric discourse, the literary discourse.

As in *Saint Omer*, Justine Triet does not want to impose some cinematographic truth by using the regular tricks and devices of courtroom dramas, interlaced with the operation of the law. In an interview, she declared:

> It was very important to me that truth cannot emerge in the courtroom. It won't and it doesn't. I was interested in this couple exactly for the fact that they are the face of something that goes beyond a kind of Manichean good and evil: there's a bad guy and a good guy, and a victim and not. I think the most interesting thing that I have been told about this film is that she can be responsible without being guilty, or she could be guilty

> without being responsible. She could be responsible for having driven him to suicide without being guilty of having killed him, or she could have killed him without having wanted to – whether in an impulsive way or in however we can try to imagine that. So truth exists, but it's too complex to be grasped here.[51]

Anatomy of a Fall is a film about how difficult it is to attain truth and to decide about guilt or liability. The law does not help much here, despite its process of accumulating and scrutinising elements of facts and evidence. A crucial moment of the film is when the judiciary assistant taking care of the son of the couple, Daniel, while his mother is on trial, tells him: "The law is not your friend". Daniel, who could not really see what happened, both because he is blind and because he was walking his dog at the time of the fall, has started to doubt his mother and her implication in his father's death and makes some dangerous experiments to try and corroborate some elements of her testimony. So, if law and facts do not help, sometimes one has to decide by oneself about the truth one wants to believe.

This is what he does, by giving one final testimony to make the jury decide what is undecidable. We will never know if what he tells is the truth and really happened or whether he invents what he pretends his father told him, which could explain a possible suicide. Justine Triet literally films the boy putting words in his father's mouth with a fabulous filming trick.[52] This last and decisive testimony decides on a possible truth but also moves the attention away from the accused woman, whose own story was mostly not heard or heard with some misogynist disdain for her independence, success, and lack of care, to focus on the victim, the father, and his fragility, which is a much more convenient truth.

The pleadings by the lawyers and the prosecutor are not part of the film, which leaves all freedom to the viewer to decide which interpretation to adopt without being encumbered by this traditional dialectic phase of the trial, generally shown in courtroom films with a lot of emphasis. We have seen that Alice Diop equally declines to use such emphatic pleadings, showing only a moment of the defence pleadings, marked by calm and emotion.

Another rejection of an emotional filmic device, the close-up, is found in both films. Close-ups of female stars have been analysed as a cinematographic convention commodifying and eroticising the female body.[53] While

51 Interview of Justine Triet <www.cbc.ca/news/entertainment/justine-triet-anatomy-of-a-fall-interview-1.7000741>.

52 The victim in the film is never directly heard or seen. He is offscreen with his loud music in the first scene, then he appears in two trial moments: the first through a sound recording found in his computer that is rendered by a scene of dispute, and the second being the testimony of his son in a scene in which the son's voice replaces that of the father. This lack of flashbacks showing the victim and giving him his own voice before the fall is ingenious.

53 Mulvey (n 27), particularly its Ch 3, 'Close-ups and commodities'; see also Brainwashed, a film by Nina Menkes (n 26).

in courtroom movies, close-ups of the accused person often seek to decipher the emotions of the convicted and their sincerity, both Alice Diop and Justine Triet largely avoid close-ups of their female protagonists. Preferring medium or long shots, they refuse to objectify the women indicted for murder or to explore in their faces their possible guilt. The only close-up in *Saint Omer* takes place when Laurence tells about the night she left her child on the beach, which, interestingly, gives her back some subjectivity: she is now the narrator of her tale. In *Anatomy of a Fall*, Sandra is mostly filmed in medium shots from the waist up when she tells her story, with a few close-ups, whereas she is filmed with longer shots when she has to listen to the other forms of discourse about her and her actions. Close-ups are rather on the attendees, particularly the son in *Anatomy of a Fall* and Rama, the writer, in *Saint Omer*, as if to focus on the viewer of the case, who needs to make their own decision, however indecisive it will necessarily be.

Such absence of close-ups on the accused women conveys a refusal to dissect their stories and emotions without their consent. Both directors opt instead for the complexity and inscrutability of their lives and their right to opacity, as developed by Edouard Glissant,[54] which doubles the opacity of the truth that the films support.

Conclusion

Two of the best films of the last years are radically troubling the genre of courtroom movies, hence raising fascinating issues for the law and film discipline. *Saint Omer*, released in 2022, and *Anatomy of a Fall*, released in 2023, could be said to develop a female gaze about law and truth, not because they are directed by women, but because they decline to objectify the truth and the women accused of a crime, opting instead to let the female character tell her own narrative, however undecipherable it may be.

In neither film do we know what to think of the guilt of the accused women, and the filmmakers refuse to decide for us whether we should sympathise with them or condemn them. Many questions as to their guilt, their motives, and their sanity remain unanswered. The very concept of truth is put on trial.

Most courtroom movies pass judgments through narratives and cinematographic choices, leading the viewer to form an opinion on the spectacle of justice and the character accused of a crime. When the latter is a woman, such films reinforce the (mostly Hollywood) "tradition of positioning woman as a spectacle"[55] and multiply filmic devices to such an end. Feminist film scholars have demonstrated that women in film are the object of the viewer's gaze, mediated and manipulated by the director to be looked at. This is only

54 See Edouard Glissant, *Poétique de la relation* (Gallimard 2009). Such opacity is particularly relevant in *Saint Omer*, which adopts a stimulating post-colonial perspective.

55 Slettedahl Macpherson (n 28) 641.

reinforced with women in trial films, fiction and documentary alike, through excessive use of close-ups and other cinematographic strategies and tricks, combined with the lack of their voices and narratives.

By refraining from objectifying the accused woman and embracing their unreadable subjectivity, *Saint Omer* and *Anatomy of a Fall* intentionally refuse to tell a definitive story and decisive counternarrative. Indeterminacy and the destabilisation of the truth are privileged over an interpretative fiction. By departing from the fictive reconstruction generally achieved by law and judiciary processes, both movies reveal the very truth of the law: that is, its incapacity to tell the truth and its likely indifference towards it.

Reference List

Berger J, *Ways of Seeing* (Penguin Books 1972)

Besnier C, 'Le travail de la vérité en cours d'assises' (2020) 19 CLIO@Themis, Dossier Vérité Judiciaire 97

Brey I, *Le regard féminin – Une révolution à l'écran* (Points 2020)

Foucault M, 'The Political Function of the Intellectual' (1977) 17 Radical Philosophy 13

Frambéry-Iacobone A, 'Vérité judiciaire, vérité factuelle et élément moral: Perspectives d'histoire pénale contemporaine' (2020) 19 CLIO@Themis, Dossier Vérité Judiciaire 62

Goltzberg S, 'De quoi la fiction indique-t-elle l'absence?' in A-B Caire (ed), *Les fictions en droit* (PU de Clermont 2015)

Kamir O, 'Judgment by Film: Socio-Legal Functions of *Rashomon*' (2000) 12 Yale Journal of Law & the Humanities 39

Kamir O, 'Anatomy of Hollywood's Hero-Lawyer: A Law-and-Film Study of the Western Motifs, Honor-Based Values and Gender Politics Underlying Anatomy of a Murder's Construction of the Lawyer Image' (2005) 35 Studies in Law, Politics and Society 67

Kamir O, 'Why "Law-and-Film" and What Does It Actually Mean? A Perspective' (2005) 19 Journal of Media & Cultural Studies 255

Kamir O, *Framed: Women in Law and Film* (Duke UP 2006)

Kennedy D, 'A Left Phenomenological Alternative to the Hart/Kelsen Theory of Legal Interpretation' in D Kennedy (ed), *Legal Reasoning, Collected Essays* (The Davies Book Publishers 2008)

Lorenzini D, 'Foucault, Regimes of Truth and the Making of the Subject' in L Cremonesi and others (eds), *Foucault and the Making of Subjects* (Rowman & Littlefield 2016)

Macpherson HS, 'Spectacular Expectations: Women, Law and Film' (2007) 41 Journal of American Studies 641

Mulvey L, 'Visual Pleasure and Narrative Cinema' (1975) 16 Screen 6

Mulvey L, *Fetishism and Curiosity* (BFI Publishing 1996)

Mulvey L, 'Introduction: 1970s Feminist Film Theory and the Obsolescent Object' in L Mulvey and A Backman Rogers (eds), *Feminisms – Diversity, Difference and Multiplicity in Contemporary Film Cultures* (Amsterdam UP 2015) 17–27

Silbey JM, 'Truth Tales and Trial Films' (2007) 40 Loyola of Los Angeles Law Review 551

Silbey JM, 'American Trial Films and the Popular Culture of Law' in *Oxford Research Encyclopedia of Criminology* (OUP 2017) <https://papers.ssrn.com/sol3/papers.cfm?abstract_id=3151795>

Thomas Y, 'La vérité, le temps, le juge et l'historien' (1998) 5 Le Débat 17

Thomas Y, 'Fictio Legis – L'empire de la fiction romaine et ses limites médiévales' in *Les opérations du droit* (Seuil/Gallimard 2011) 134

van de Kerchove M, 'Vérité judiciaire et para-judiciaire en matière pénale: Quelle vérité?' (2013) 84 Droit et société 411

Xifaras M, 'Fictions juridiques – Remarques sur quelques procédés fictionnels en usage chez les juristes' (2011) 3 Annuaire de l'Institut Michel Villey 451

Chapter 6

Teaching Law and Feminism Through Cinema

A Proposal

Helena Alviar García

Introduction

Imagine you enter any classroom in Latin America or Europe where a course on law is being taught. More likely than not, the space will be a setting where students are sitting in rows, looking straight at the professor to impart knowledge (when they are not staring at their screens). They listen to a lecture in which the content of a very particular branch of law is discussed, ending with a period in which they are graciously allowed to ask questions. Their engagement with the materials is marginal and very seldom critical. Normally, there is only a final exam, in which they are expected to repeat whatever wisdom the professor imparted.

This model asks little from either teacher or student. The teacher owns the knowledge, has the power to impel or prevent individuals from pondering the limits or possibilities of law, and frequently uses the same notes for years on end (unless the content of legislation changes). The student can passively sit; observe the professor or stare at their screen; memorise knowledge at the end of the term (sometimes without truly grasping it, as if it were mathematical formulas); and disengage intellectually, politically, and emotionally. Thinking about law as a student and teaching it are all about imparting and reproducing a rational, logical, benevolent, neutral system.

As professors and students with a critical stance would argue, law is political, indeterminate, and at times irrational. It shouldn't be taught in the way it is taught. The classroom should be a politicised space where participants (including the professor) are thinking about an idea; feel passionate about the limits and possibilities of its content; are aiming to link the ideological framework of a legal regime to economic and social particularities provided by its context; and are engaged in relevant discussions about what law is, what it does, and how it manifests itself while, at the same time, embracing uncertainty and accepting that there is cruelty, irrationality, and pain in the content of the law.

DOI: 10.4324/9781003461180-6

Teaching and thinking about law in this way demand much more from everyone. They ask the professor to relinquish authoritarian power; to democratically engage; to accept that pupils have many perspectives, readings, or interpretations that are valuable and enriching; and to be willing to be challenged and unsettled. They ask students to get involved, autonomously learn, critically explore, and decide where they stand from an ideological perspective on any given topic.

This chapter proposes a specific counterpoint to mainstream law teaching by discussing the use of cinema in a course on feminist legal theory. It understands movies as the perfect frame to start a debate about relevant legal topics, their limitations, the context in which they operate, and the way they distribute resources. In order to do this, the text outlines the elements of critical legal thinking and radical, socialist, and post-colonial feminism, along with movie suggestions that promote a fruitful discussion regarding these schools of thought.

How to Think About Law in a Critical Way and What This Means for Teaching

There are many ideas about law that, as professors aiming to advance critical thinking, we should aim to debunk. What follows is a synthesis of critical insights that are fundamental to the purposes of this chapter.

Let us first take the idea of the neutrality of law. From a liberal legal theory perspective, legal arrangements are a set of instruments democratically debated and formally passed by Congress. They are tools to arbitrate human interaction – as in the case of contracts and property – or mechanisms to promote social transformation, as in the case of decriminalising abortion or allowing same sex marriage. Consequently, they reflect a plurality of interests at a specific period in history. From this theoretical outlook, if law is complicit in the creation of inequality, it has to do with bad legislation, a congress coopted by certain economic actors or corrupted in some form, a gap between the law in the books and the law in action, or a lack of political will on the part of the ruling elites. From a Marxist perspective, law is a tool with which capitalist elites dominate and exploit the working class. In this interpretation, law is not only complicit in stacking the deck against the downtrodden and the disenfranchised but also irrelevant, since it is determined and shaped by the forces of production. From a critical perspective, both liberal legal theory and Marxism are insufficient to explain the law and its role in society. Liberal law underestimates the force of economic and social forces, and Marxism overestimates their power.

Another critical insight is related to the divisions and subdivisions within law: not only the separation between the public and the private but also the differentiation between labour law and property or criminal law, family law and labour or property. Compartments also distort how the past (even legislation that has been revoked) influences the present. In fact, legal architecture is composed of layer after layer of reforms and regulations. It can be described better with words borrowed from geology than from positivism. Partly for this reason, but also because of historical context, economic background, and the geopolitical space a country occupies, it is impossible to separate, for example, the public from the private, contracts from criminal law, family law from labour law, and the local from the global.

Along the same lines, law is not a static set of rules that are clearly written and applied in a consistent and predictable way. Rather, it is a battlefield where, at any given moment, there are competing interpretations: actors who are trying to promote their particular vision of what it should be, institutions filled with bureaucrats who have discretionary power to decide its content, and judges who will disentangle its meaning differently according to their theoretical backgrounds.

Unpacking the actors, institutions, and possibilities unveils the idea that the application or exercise of power granted by law is not natural or invisible; it is determined by specific decisions: political choices at every turn that end up benefiting some and affecting others. Therefore, an adequate metaphor for law is not a photograph but a movie.

In sum, law is neither an instrument to promote change; an impartial, neutral frame; nor a rigid cage. Rather, what this chapter is proposing is that law is indeterminate; it entails more bargaining than adjudication, it is shaped by many forces as well as diverse rules, and as a consequence, it is foundational to the distribution of resources.

Bringing in Cinema

Not all movies about law trigger a discussion about its political bias, the uncertainty and indeterminacy of its content, or how actors struggle to give it meaning or narrate the harms they suffer through its language.

In fact, traditional trial movies depict law as a force for good, with a clear and correct interpretation that empowers heroes and serves society. The common narrative arc is represented by a struggling lawyer who takes a case unwillingly, throughout the movie is slowly convinced that the cause is worthwhile, faces a series of setbacks, and wins the case in a moving finale, and the whole of society ends up in a better position.

The perfect example is the movie *Philadelphia*,[1] a 1993 film that deals with discrimination based on sexual orientation and the diverse dimensions of exclusions produced by the HIV/AIDS pandemic. It is centered on the character of Andrew Beckett (played by Tom Hanks), a prestigious lawyer who is fired from a recognised law firm after his employers discover he has

1 *Philadelphia* (Directed by Jonathan Demme 1993).

AIDS. Beckett is certain he has been removed from his job solely because of his sickness and sues the law firm on the grounds of wrongful termination. He hires an initially homophobic lawyer, Joe Miller (played by Denzel Washington). As the film progresses, we witness the transformations and difficulties that both the protagonists encounter as they face the ingrained biases and limitations of the legal system. They end up developing a strong friendship, and Miller leaves his homophobia behind. The progressive power of law triumphs.

If only life in general, or the life of law, was that easy. When the goal is to teach how law is determined by structural exclusions and the limitations of discrimination as a tool to face exclusion, this is not the movie to trigger those insights or conversations. Rather, I would suggest the film *Saint Omer* (also discussed in this volume) as a perfect example that encourages students to debate and think about the indeterminacy of law, its structural biases in terms of race and gender, and its limitations as an instrument of emancipation.

Saint Omer is inspired by true events that happened in 2013, when Fabienne Kabou, a French-Senegalese woman, was indicted for murdering her infant daughter.[2] The movie personifies the perspective of two women: Rama (played by Kayije Kagame), a novelist and professor who is following the trial, and Laurence (played by Guslagie Malanda), the accused.[3] Even though it is set in a courtroom and could evolve as a traditional trial movie, it is distant in the way it presents the power of the law, the way the different participants engage with the law, and the racial biases ingrained within the system. *Saint Omer* doesn't picture the law as a neutral, emancipatory force that solves disputes. Instead, it only poses questions. Under what circumstances does a mother kill her child; what led her to do it? The circumstances and causes are inexplicable. What is the fair resolution of the trial? It is hard to tell, and when Laurence (a character inspired by Kabou) is asked, "Madame Coly, do you know why you killed your daughter?" She answers: "I don't know; I hope this trial will give me the answer". The fact that going through the process of law provides no answers but opens universal questions about motherhood and femininity beautifully was explained by director Alice Diop:

> Throughout the trial I sat riveted, shocked, overwhelmed, disturbed, and dumbfounded by this real woman's story, connecting her life to my own

2 For more on the case and its effect on the director, see Esther Zuckerman, 'For the Documentarian Alice Diop, Only Fiction Could do Justice to a Tragedy' *The New York Times* (16 January 2023) <www.nytimes.com/2023/01/16/movies/alice-diop-saint-omer.html> accessed 2 February 2024.

3 *Saint Omer* (Directed by Alice Diop 2022).

> experience, to that of my mother, to the lives of so many Senegalese women I know. When, on the last day, I saw every other woman in the courtroom in tears as well, I understood that we'd shared something profound and unspeakable, which made the story universal.[4]

In sum, a dialogue between the two movies surfaces both traditional and critical ideas about law.

An Example of Legal Transformation: Exploring the Roots of Gender Inequality Through Movies

As a scholar coming from the Global South, debates about law have always been grounded in ideas about social transformation. In Latin America, policy makers on the right and on the left have deployed law as a tool to achieve economic and social change. This instrumentalisation has, at times, required transforming the understanding and interpretation of law by changing the way it is taught. Thus, critical legal scholars have been engaged in discussion about how to transmit knowledge about existing social and cultural conditions, along with aiming to grasp the contemporary needs of a particular nation and the different ways in which law impacts society (or fails to do so).[5]

One of the most pressing issues is the unequal access to power and resources across gender lines. Different strands of feminist legal theory explore what causes inequality and what legal tools should be used to combat it. It is a diverse and vibrant field of knowledge, and for the purpose of this chapter, four perspectives will be discussed: liberal, radical, socialist, and post-colonial.

Liberal Feminism

For liberal feminists, there are two legal roots to the problem. The first one is existing laws and regulations that purposefully exclude women from certain rights. The solution is to change them or shift their interpretation. The second cause is the historical and cultural legacy of exclusion. From this perspective, even if they have the right to vote or there is a nondiscrimination clause in the Constitution, women have difficulty accessing certain jobs or professions. This can be solved by changing cultural patterns (through popular culture, including movies) or establishing quotas. As with the traditional

4 Ben Croll, 'Venice Prizewinner Alice Diop on the Haunting Nature of "Saint Omer"' *Variety* (10 September 2022) <https://variety.com/2022/film/festivals/venice-alice-diop-saint-omer-1235367521/> accessed 1 February 2024.

5 For a discussion on legal education, see 'The Classroom and the Clinic: The Relationship Between Clinical Legal Education, Economic Development and Social Transformation' UCLA Journal of International Law and Foreign Affairs, Los Angeles, 2008.

views about law described in the first part of the chapter, liberal feminists see both the problem and the solution as issues that can be solved by changing the content or adjudication of law.

Among the many movies that illustrate this approach, two will be discussed here: *On the Basis of Sex*[6] and *North Country*.[7] Both of them celebrate the power of law. *On the Basis of Sex* is about the early life of Ruth Bader Ginsburg. The film very directly and without much subtlety shows how Ginsburg (played by Felicity Jones) experiences constant discrimination. She is surrounded by a wave of men at Harvard Law School; her job interviews are humiliating; it is difficult for her to get employed. Everything about her life is depicted in the public sphere, and the glimpse of her private life is perfect: she lives with an adoring husband in a beautiful home with two lovely children. Eventually, she decides to take a case to court regarding gender discrimination; her husband is the one that nudges her attention to it. The case revolves around a single man living in Denver (Charles Moritz), who often traveled for work and had filed a lawsuit regarding his taxes. He had filed for a tax deduction for the amount of money he had paid a caretaker for his elderly mother. The deduction was denied, and Mr Moritz argued in court that a single woman in the same situation would have been given a tax break. The law included the benefit for women but did not include it for men as men are not traditionally considered caregivers. The court decided in favour of Moritz, arguing that the tax code discriminated on the basis of sex.[8]

North Country tells a messier story. The movie is framed within progress narrative tradition. It takes place during the 1970s, when mining companies in Minnesota signed a document with the US Department of Justice agreeing to assign 20% of their new jobs to women and minorities. Working in the mine paid three times more than any other job in the region, and the women needed these jobs because they were single mothers or needed to support other members of their family. The men who were employed by the mine violently opposed these hirings and manifested their disagreement as it is depicted in the film through threats of rape, harassment, assault, and stalking. When the women complained, either they were ignored or ostracised or their job degraded. As in the movie, they decide to craft a class action and take the company to court. What the movie can't show in detail is the physical and emotional toll that the case took upon the plaintiffs. They had to face violent opposition in the workplace, and the expensive lawyers hired by the company were ruthless in the defense of their interests. The case took more

6 *On the Basis of Sex* (Directed by Mimi Leder 2018).

7 *North Country* (Directed by Niki Caro 2005).

8 Lila Thulin, 'The True Story of the Case Ruth Bader Ginsburg Argues in on the Basis of Sex' *Smithsonian Magazine* (24 December 2018) <www.smithsonianmag.com/history/true-story-case-center-basis-sex-180971110/> accessed 25 January 2024.

than ten years to be decided in their favour, and which point they were sick, exhausted, and bitter. Each of them received a small amount of money.[9]

In a course on feminist legal theory, the films adequately illustrate the experience of discrimination and the arguments that are deployed to change it. It is a useful way to start a conversation about the structural conditions that allowed Ruth Bader Ginsburg to advance her quest (having graduated from a prestigious university and being married to a successful lawyer, among others) or how the interaction between the public and the private determine women's capacity to access and maintain a job in the case of *North Country*. From a more critical perspective, it could also trigger a debate about the limitations of liberal feminism, how it interprets equality in relation to men, how it is centered on the public/political and leaves the private/economic in the background, and the blind spots created when emancipation is only understood in the limited terms encapsulated in rights discourse (right to anti-discrimination, in these particular cases).

In response to liberal feminism, there are other perspectives that both critique it and propose different tools to overcome inequality. The following section starts with quotes from Catherine MacKinnon, Nancy Fraser, and Chandra Talpade Mohanty to explore the different perspectives. The quotes are meant to trigger fundamental questions about feminist theory: Is it possible to grasp the root of gender oppression? Marxist-inspired feminists such as Catharine MacKinnon and Nancy Fraser seem to argue that it is, whereas Chandra Mohanty critiques the premises of the inquiry and shed light on the futility of the feat.

Radical Feminism

Catherine MacKinnon, a central figure in radical feminism, interprets the submission of women as the result of male domination over the production of knowledge, the exercise of state power, and the enactment of desire. Her intellectual objective is to rebuild the foundations of society from the female perspective. In order to do this, she needs to illuminate the gendered dimensions of the exercise of power. Radical feminists describe liberal and socialist feminisms as the direct application of liberal or Marxist political theory to women. Liberal feminism is too centred on formal equality, and socialist feminism is too hooked up to class struggle and care. Therefore, according to radical feminists, the only feminist approach that contains an autonomous theory is radical feminism. MacKinnon interprets women's difficulty accessing power and resources as a structural issue, impossible to solve through amendments in law (as liberal feminists would argue). The root of

9 National Women's History Museum, 'Real Women of North Country' (6 May 2006) <www.womenshistory.org/articles/real-women-north-country> accessed 26 January 2024.

women's oppression is the appropriation of women's sexuality by men (by what and how they desire, but also the way they represent women and how they try to dominate the outliers who don't abide by the rules through violence). MacKinnon herself synthesises radical feminism and its relationship to liberal feminism in the following way:

> Where liberal feminism sees sexism primarily as an illusion or myth to be dispelled, an inaccuracy to be corrected, true feminism sees the male point of view as fundamental to the male power to create the world in its own image, the image of its desires, not just as its delusory end product.[10]

A masterpiece that allows students to engage with the male gaze (essential to sexual appropriation) is Agnes Varda's 1962 film *Cléo de 5 à 7*. The movie follows a young singer, Cléo Victoire (played by Corinne Marchand), who is waiting for the results of a medical exam which will establish if she has cancer. It develops over the course of two hours as she wanders through the streets of Paris, reflecting on her life, her fears, and her relationships while coming to terms with her own mortality, the possibility of death, and the uncertainty of her future. The film (where the beauty of Paris navigates between the foreground and the background) delineates the oppressiveness of men's way of observing women and women's acceptance of it, of the search for meaning that comes after becoming aware of life's finite quality, of the complexity that characterises identity. Instead of being a film about female courage or strength (as *On the Basis of Sex* and *North Country* are) it explores the contradictions, paradoxes, and ambiguities that Cléo faces in the social (patriarchy), spatial (the city of Paris), and political contexts (the specific historical context) that frame her life. In fact, Cléo is depicted as an object of desire through her interactions with others and what she buys. The use of mirrors also foregrounds the centrality that beauty plays for her own sense of worthiness. As the movie progresses, we experience her transformation from passive and shallow to an exploration regarding the value of beauty while facing the possibility of death. Varda herself explained her feminist approach in an interview in 2018:

> Yes, when the film starts, she's just there to be looked at. When she takes off her wig and puts on her black dress and goes out, she's the one who starts to look. Looking at others is the first step of feminism – not being selfish, not being mirror-oriented. Looking at other people. Discovering what they do to make a living. Or how they behave. Cléo, in the shock of being afraid of death, starts to see things differently. The shock is very

10 Catharine MacKinnon, 'Feminism, Marxism and the State: Toward Feminist Jurisprudence' (1983) 8 Signs: Journal of Women, Culture and Society 640.

good for her. She starts to listen to other people. She sees her friend differently. The soldier she meets, she wouldn't have gone with him another day. Bad situations do something for people. Maybe she'll die of cancer. But that day, especially that time, those 90 minutes – it was hard to believe that in 90 minutes someone can change so much but it is true. But some moments in life are like this. That's why Cléo could go with this solider who was in the [Algerian] war, that stupid war. . . . I try to make films that are related to society but not totally in it. It's not a film about the Algerian War. It's not a film about cancer. It's a film about finding threads in the world. The theme of death and beauty is a terrible one. We want to protect beauty. Lots of painters paint beauty; me, I made a film about it. There was an ancient German painter, Hans Baldung Grien, who for a time was painting beautiful naked women with tits and a skeleton. That mental image was with me all the time [while making *Cléo*], because that's the flesh, the sweet flesh and the dryness of the bone. That beautiful woman is fragile because she's afraid, but in the film we make it something that happens to her to make her stronger.[11]

In this sense, it provides the ideal starting point for an exploration of radical feminism as it illustrates the many dimensions of the patriarchal male gaze (depicted through the obsession over beauty and its representation, observing and being observed, and women's adequate place in society), the process through which women can break free from it, and what it takes from them (including the certainty of death).

Socialist Feminism

For socialist feminists, gender oppression can be explained by embracing what MacKinnon calls a "three-dimensional account of injustice", which includes lack of redistribution, recognition, and representation. While she sheds light on the co-optation of second-wave feminism by neoliberalism, she also proposes an agenda to move towards the social recognition of reproductive work, the strengthening of participatory democracy, and the building of transnational alliances.

For feminists influenced by Marxism, the issue that is at the root of women's oppression is not formal access to rights as in liberal feminist theory or the appropriation of sexuality for radical feminists. What really determines women's fate is the sexual division of labour which has marginalised them and forced them to limit their work to caretaking and subsistence production with little or no access to wages, resources, or property. Their research is inspired by the work of Fredrich Engels, *The Origins of the Family: Private*

11 Kiva Reardon, 'Curiosity Is a Good Thing: Interview with Agnes Varda' (2019) 6(1) Cléo a Journal of Film and Feminism <https://cleojournal.com/2018/04/11/curiosity-is-a-good-thing-an-interview-with-agnes-varda/> accessed 2 February 2024.

Property and the State,[12] in which he argues that initial capitalist accumulation was male dominated. The text describes how the surplus of wealth created in agriculture and exchange was dominated by men. The accumulation of this surplus, in turn, was the foundation of private property. Women were conspicuously absent from these two processes as they were mostly in charge of the survival of the household through cooking, cleaning, and generally taking care of others: in other words, producing goods not for exchange but for subsistence. As a result, women had little access to resources outside the household, and this increased their dependency on men.

According to this interpretation, it is this unpaid family work, which guarantees the reproduction of the labour force, that makes it possible to pay workers very low salaries, which paves the way for capital accumulation. The fact that women and children at times enter the labour market creates a surplus of labour, which, in turn, undermines the solidarity of the working class. Marxists are keen to highlight that capitalist accumulation occurs partly as a result of the separation of the worker from what he produces, which makes survival dependent on the erratic conditions of wage work.

A necessary outcome of Marxist emphasis not only on capitalist accumulation but also on reproductive work has been the study of domestic labour and household production and the patriarchal structure that promotes and strengthens it. Domestic work is the combination of goods bought in the market transformed through labour. It also includes duties such as child rearing and the taking care of older adults. Reproductive labour interacts with the market as commodities are necessary to advance a part of it. It also is characterised by being unpaid, invisible, and mostly advanced by women. In modern urban societies where labour work is at the center of resources for family subsistence, domestic work is essential. Marxist feminists argue that women will only be truly equal when housework as well as the education and care of children and older adults is understood as a national, public affair. It doesn't matter how many anti-discrimination policies you pass or how many equality clauses exist for the productive sphere, if you don't eliminate women's burden in the reproductive sphere and the patriarchal system that allows it, no law or policy will make a difference.

Understanding the oppressiveness of domestic work is the starting point when discussing socialist feminism. The structural limitations it imposes and the stress, ambivalence, and pain it produces in women is aptly showcased in the movies *À Plein Temps*[13] and *Elena Sabe*.[14]

À Plein Temps is a 2021 French film which follows single mother, Julie, who works a difficult, strenuous job as room cleaner at what appears to be a five-star

12 Fredrich Engels, *The Origins of the Family, Private Property and the State* (Penguin Classics 2010).

13 *À Plein Temps* (Directed by Éric Gravel 2021).

14 *Elena Sabe* (Directed by Anahí Berneri 2023).

hotel in Paris. Her intense day includes waking up early to arrange everything for her children, commuting from a remote suburb into Paris, and trying to change her job into one that is better paid and considers her university diploma. Her hectic schedule is significantly disrupted by a transportation strike which forces her to arrive late to work and later to pick up her children from their caretaker. The husband's alimony payments don't arrive. The pressures coming from the interaction between the demands of her job and her care responsibilities give the movie the pace of a thriller. This double pressure is at the heart of what socialist feminists describe as the root cause of gender oppression.

Elena Sabe (based on the novel by Claudia Piñeiro) is an incisive, severe, bitter account of a mother/daughter relationship, of the costs that age bears upon our bodies, of what it takes from us to take care of others. It follows Elena (played by Mercedés Moran) as she sets out to investigate and prove that her daughter Rita (played by Ërica Rivas) was assassinated and did not commit suicide. On this journey, we see flashbacks of her cruelty toward Rita, the pain and contained rage it produced, and the sacrifices and incredible patience it demanded from her. We also see the indignities of traversing the city of Buenos Aires as an older woman with Parkinson's (the shoving in the metro, her invisibility and frailty, the lack of empathy and solidarity typical of urban settings), as well as the uncertainty that comes from knowing your body will only work slightly a few hours after taking medication. Both of them are overwhelmed by the challenges of their economic conditions (not poor, but not rich either) and the extreme heartlessness of the health-care bureaucracy.

Post-colonial Feminism

For post-colonial feminists, the issue of gender inequality is impossible to answer in traditional feminist perspectives because it is encapsulated in rigid terms, it is reductionist, and it suffocates difference and the fluidity of how we understand and experience gender, desire, and agency. Chandra Talpade Mohanty, one of its central thinkers, synthesises this debate with other feminisms in the following terms:

> While radical and liberal feminist assumptions of women as a sex class might elucidate (however inadequately) the autonomy of particular women's struggles in the west, the application of the notion of women as a homogenous category to women in the third world colonizes and appropriates the pluralities of the simultaneous location of different groups of women in social class and ethnic frameworks; in doing so it ultimately robs them of their historical and political agency.[15]

15 Chandra Talpade Mohanty, 'Under Western Eyes: Feminist Scholarship and Colonial Discourses' (Spring–Autumn 1984) 12 Boundary; reprinted in *Critical Theory: A Reader for Literary and Cultural Studies* (Robert Dale Parker ed 2012) 710.

Mohanty is foregrounding the artificial differentiation between first-world and third-world women in order to show how this characterisation flattens difference, distributes resources, and seems to suggest that third-world women are one-dimensional victims who cannot act, decide, strategise, or engage, in a way, posing challenges when thinking programmatically.

Post-colonial feminism is centred on a critique of colonialism and its effects on gender relations. It proposes interpreting the problems of women less as a division between Global South and Global North and more in terms of the connection between capital accumulation, class formation, environmental degradation, gender relations, and care work. As women lose control over land, water, fuel, and food because of changes in models of production (from subsistence to producing for the market or for export), they have also seen an increase in their workload as they have to look farther for water, fuel, and in some cases food, or they have to migrate within or outside their countries to work in care work (another way of subsidising capitalism). In sum, the global dimensions of capital accumulation and how they affect work opportunities and gendered bodies are foregrounded.

The perfect movie to explore these dimensions is the film *Babel*.[16] In it, we follow four stories that simultaneously take place in Morocco, Japan, Mexico, and the United States. For the purposes of exploring the feminist angles, the stories developing in Mexico and the US are crucial. Richard and Susan Jones (played by Brad Pitt and Cate Blanchett) are an American couple on vacation in Morocco; the tension and distance in their marriage are evident. Susan is accidentally shot, and one of the consequences is that their nanny Amelia (played by Amelia Barraza) is forced by Richard to extend her stay taking care of the children. It is impossible for her to stay longer as her son is getting married in Mexico. After unsuccessfully trying to get someone to take care of them, she decides to cross the border and take them to the wedding with the illusion of bringing them back after the celebration. The film directly critiques the limitations imposed by family law by including Amelia (an irregular migrant in the United States) as a central figure close to the children, with whom she lives more intimately than with her own and takes care of as if she were their mother. The comparison between the two borders and countries couldn't be more striking in aesthetic and political terms, but the artificialness of the line separating the countries is also called into question. The wealthy couple depends on the cheap labour of the nanny, and the nanny depends on the precarious conditions offered by work in the US. Global capital accumulation is evident at every turn, from the tourist bus traversing Morocco to the wealth in Tokyo.

16 *Babel* (Directed by Alejandro Gonzáles Iñarritu 2006).

Conclusion

If, as professors, we oppose a view of law as a force to preserve existing conditions and, to the contrary, believe it is an instrument to make the world a fairer place, then we must start out by transforming the way we think and go about transmitting knowledge. This includes making university spaces more egalitarian and less authoritarian; opening spaces to explore the uncertainty and indeterminacy of law; bracketing ideas about law's rationality and neutrality and instead experiencing the rage, cruelty, and pain present in any legal system; critiquing the progress narrative; and following the setbacks that are produced after what appear to be triumphs.

This chapter has attempted to foreground relevant ideas about law in general and feminist legal thought in particular through a range diverse of films, from more mainstream Hollywood ones such as *Philadelphia*, *On the Basis of Sex*, and *North Country* to more artistic, marginal ones such as *Cléo de 5 à 7*, *À Plein Temps*, *Elena Sabe*, and *Babel*. The use of movies in a classroom has the goal of aiding students in embracing more questions than answers, more confusion than certainty. This ambitious agenda is never achieved, of course, but bringing art into the classroom (in the form of cinema) is an apt tool on this journey.

Reference List

Caro N, *North Country* (Film 2005)

CrollB, 'Venice Prizewinner Alice Diop on the Haunting Nature of "Saint Omer"' *Variety* (10 September 2022) <https://variety.com/2022/film/festivals/venice-alice-diop-saint-omer-1235367521/> accessed 1 February 2024

Demme J, *Philadelphia* (Film 1993)

Diop A, *Saint Omer* (Film 2022)

Diop A, 'Only Fiction Could Do Justice to a Tragedy' *The New York Times* (16 January 2023) <www.nytimes.com/2023/01/16/movies/alice-diop-saint-omer.html> accessed 2 February 2024

Engels F, *The Origins of the Family, Private Property and the State* (Penguin Classics 2010)

Fraser N, 'Feminism, Capitalism and the Cunning of History' [2013] Fortunes of Feminism 211

Gravel E, *À Plein Temps* (Film 2021)

Iñarritu AG, *Babel* (Film 2006)

Leder M, *On the Basis of Sex* (Film, Focus Features Production 2018)

MacKinnon C, 'Feminism, Marxism and the State: Toward Feminist Jurisprudence' (1983) 8 Signs: Journal of Women, Culture and Society 640

National Women's History Museum, 'Real Women of North Country' (6 May 2006) <www.womenshistory.org/articles/real-women-north-country> accessed 26 January 2024

ReardonK, 'Curiosity Is a Good Thing: Interview with Agnes Varda' (2019) 6(1) Cléo a Journal of Film and Feminism <https://cleojournal.com/2018/04/11/curiosity-is-a-good-thing-an-interview-with-agnes-varda/> accessed 2 February 2024

Sabe E (Directed by Anahí Berneri 2023)

Talpade Mohanty C, 'Under Western Eyes: Feminist Scholarship and Colonial Discourses' (Spring–Autumn 1984) 12 *Boundary*. Reprinted in *Critical Theory: A Reader for Literary and Cultural Studies* (RD Parker ed 2012) 710

ThulinL, 'The True Story of the Case Ruth Bader Ginsburg Argues in on the Basis of Sex' *Smithsonian Magazine* (24 December 2018) <www.smithsonianmag.com/history/true-story-case-center-basis-sex-180971110/> accessed 25 January 2024

Chapter 7

Holy Motors

Law and Technology

Nathan Moore

Introduction

The 2012 film *Holy Motors* is perplexing. As film theorist Dominic Lash relates, Carax's film can be understood as offering us a cinema of disorientation, in which what is in question are the operations of coherence, consistency, and cohesion.[1] If so, the viewer of *Holy Motors* is put in a position in which they must question or, at least, review how it is that a film presents us with something meaningful. This encompasses how it maintains a minimal level of self-relatedness in its images and narrative to form a whole or an entity that, hopefully, adds up to something more than the sum of its parts. In other words – and here Carax is, of course, not the first to do so – the film *Holy Motors* can be considered a film about film, inasmuch as it destablises the general norms of film narrative, making the viewer aware of conventional cinematic habits in the process.

If so, using film to comment on film offers us one way to address the apparent confusions of *Holy Motors*. My contention is that this can only take us so far in our understanding of the film. *Holy Motors* plays with the conventions of film narrative (I will return to this later), but it is also a narrative in its own right, with its own narrative and internal consistency. As Lash writes, "[The relationship between fate and chance] is certainly of great importance [in Carax's work], but part of its importance lies in the fact that the characters' responses to contingent events are crucial".[2]

The significance of this is to highlight that understanding Carax as using film to make films about films provides only a very restricted understanding of what they potentially offer. Rather, it is more useful to view *Holy Motors* as a more traditional film, with traditional characters (as it were). What is different are the situations these characters find themselves in and their responses to those situations. If so, we can think of *Holy Motors* as being an

1 Dominic Lash, *The Cinema of Disorientation: Inviting Confusions* (Edinburgh UP 2020) 73.
2 Dominic Lash, *The Cinema of Disorientation: Inviting Confusions* (Edinburgh UP 2020) 74.

DOI: 10.4324/9781003461180-7

example of something quite classical in cinema, albeit rather unconventional in execution: to use the characters' predicaments as a means to explore the nature of our world and, more broadly, human "nature".

If so, then the confusions and disorientations posed by *Holy Motors* reflect something of the contemporary world, and the film can be viewed as attempting to say something about that world. Of course, even here, it is not possible to give a satisfactory summation of what *Holy Motors* (and film generally) is about. To reduce it to a lesson about the world as it is entails its own limitations, not to mention an air of instruction or pedagogy that often sits uncomfortably with artistic practice in general. Nevertheless, what I wish to do in this chapter is to present *Holy Motors* as "saying something" about the world: in particular, that it is a film about a transitional phase, when the world finds itself moving out of the age of machines and energy and into one of communications and information.

This might all seem a long way from matters of law, but taking a legal theoretical view, I will argue that this transition – from machine to electron – has far-reaching consequences that impact directly on our politics, economics, and sociality. In short, this transition goes to the heart of what it means for humans to live *together*. Consequently, it must then also go to the heart of law, inasmuch as law is concerned with the regulation and stabilisation of human "being together". The theme of human living together is what I take *Holy Motors* to be about. More specifically, the film investigates this in light of the transition from machine to electron and, for this reason, resonates with the distinction Deleuze outlined in his brief but influential paper "Postscript on Control Societies".[3]

In that paper, Deleuze remarked that we were moving out of disciplinary societies and into control societies. This is not to say that the techniques and rationalities of discipline disappear, but that they are subsumed within a new ordering – one in which norms become more mobile and more productive, and the distinction between the "normal" and the "abnormal" is continuously breaking down. This breakdown is not an error or a malfunction; rather, control operates through such breakdowns, constantly re-structuring and innovating in the pursuit of entrepreneurship and aspiration. To clarify this, I begin by presenting four dualities as a way to describe the difference between the regimes of the machine and the electron, which I also take as being loosely equivalent to the regimes of discipline and control. This will give the broad theoretical framework for my account of the film. From there, I will go on to outline what I consider to be the significant themes of the film in connection with law. This will be framed with an emphasis on law and technology, superimposing the technological shift from machine to electron over the juridical one from discipline to control.

3 Gilles Deleuze, *Negotiations 1972–90* (Martin Joughin tr, Columbia UP 1997).

Part One

Four Dualities

Leos Carax's 2012 film *Holy Motors* does not deal explicitly with the theme of law. Yet the questions raised by the film do have an important connection to legal concepts and at quite a fundamental level. Therefore, it is an interesting film to consider from the perspective of legal theory.

Central to this interest is the overarching concern of the film to ask about the status of the subject. More specifically, the status of the subject in a transitional time, during which the world of the machine is being displaced by the world of the electron. *Holy Motors* takes a broad thematic approach to this displacement which, given the breadth and speculative nature of its subject matter, is entirely appropriate. However, it is useful to highlight certain dualities present in the film to provide some orientation for a legal theoretical consideration of the issues raised.

The first such duality is that of energy and information. On the side of energy, it is the machine that operates through differentiated parts that interact via energetic displacements of friction and pressure. The origin of the word "machine" is, inevitably, militaristic, but it also contains, etymologically, the sense of trickery or deception. This is explained by the transformative nature of the machine: it takes energy as an input of one kind and transforms it to output it as energy of a different kind. The overall quantity of energy remains equal, so the machine works to move it, as it were, from one site of application to another. At the same time, energy is also dissipative, tending towards an equal distribution across all sites. The steam engine is, of course, the exemplary figure of an energetic machine, but it would not be too much of a stretch to consider the metabolism of cells as operating in a similar way. If so, the machine is not necessarily "mechanical" only but can also be found in the realms of biology and chemistry.[4]

At such a point, the figure of the machine begins to take on the aspect of its partner, information. I mean by this that the transformation of energy, carried out by a machine, can be modelled as an informational process. This follows from Gregory Bateson's definition: information is the difference that makes a difference.[5] All the same, there is an important distinction between energy and information that also flows from this definition. Rather than differential components held in tension to distribute energy, informational difference is more a matter of perception: the differences Bateson was referring to are perceived differences, and this obviously requires an apparatus capable

4 Humberto R Maturana and Francisco J Varela, *Autopoiesis and Cognition: The Realization of the Living* (D Reidel Publishing Company 1980) 77–84.

5 See Gregory Bateson, 'Form, Substance, and Difference' in *Steps to an Ecology of Mind* (U of Chicago P 2000).

of such perception.[6] However, at the level of information, such perception does not need to be conscious or, indeed, human. Rather, information implies a self-organising system[7] in which – as a matter of contingency – certain elements enter into a dynamic equilibrium of attraction and repulsion to produce an effect. We might then say that, if the machine produces energy, then information produces effects. Information makes a difference to the system in question, causing it to react and develop (hence, its dynamism) so as to, simultaneously, maintain its particularity (hence, its equilibrium).

As Weiner noted, "[I]nformation is information, not matter or energy".[8] Yet the truth of this statement might be dependent on the type and level of analysis being undertaken. There is certainly a conceptual difference between information and energy – and this difference is, as we will see later, important for *Holy Motors* – but the implications of Bateson's definition (particularly when read in light of Maturana's work) suggests that at a more fundamental level, the difference between information and energy might ultimately collapse into a singular operation.

The second duality by which we can orientate ourselves relative to the themes of *Holy Motors* is the difference between the mechanical and the electronic. This duality is obviously connected to the first but pertains more directly to the question of technology. Mechanical technologies are those – such as the steam engine or motor car – that operate according to the laws of energy transfer. Electronic technologies are also constrained by those laws, but the difference in speed and scale is indicative of a difference in kind: electronic technologies tend to be much smaller than motors and also much faster in terms of the range and amount of information they can respond to and process. This has led to the innovations that many of us now take for granted, in terms of easy access to data and communications, most of which have either superseded earlier, mechanical technologies, or have integrated the latter into new, "informatised" systems of operation, such as in an internet of things.[9]

6 Perhaps more neutrally, the English translation of Maturana and Varela (n 4) 75 refers to "relations" so as to preserve a materialistic account. However, this raises the question: What is the materiality of a relation? At some point, we must encounter the difficulty implicit in Bateson's definition: a relation is, after all, an interaction between differences, therefore requiring some base element of "perception" in order that a relation might occur. See Bateson (n 5) 5.

7 Following Maturana and Varela (n 4), such a system can also be referred to as a "machine".

8 Quoted and discussed in Peter Janich, *What Is Information?* (Eric Hayot and Lea Pao trs, U of Minnesota P 2018) 39–47.

9 See, for example, Michael Hardt and Toni Negri, *Multitude: War and Democracy in the Age of Empire* (The Paragon Press 2004) 112–13. The seemingly materialistic/mechanistic process of seeds becoming crops has been subsumed within an immaterial regime of patents and intellectual property. With the internet of things, more mundane day-to-day tasks also become informatised. For example, empty fridges can communicate with a grocery website to purchase goods and arrange for their delivery, callers at buildings can be monitored and interacted with remotely through pre-formatted communications systems, and so on.

Connected to this is a third duality: the visible and the invisible. The energetic machine tends to be easily discernible (if not so easily understood) by the majority of humans, suggesting a relative scale of operation in which the physical human dimension can be taken as the basic measure of relativity and size: machines are "big" or "small" relative to human size. This often also allows the purpose of the machine to be grasped, inasmuch as its human scale implies a human purposefulness: What does this machine *do*? The significance of this is that, whilst a visible machine can be treated as a "black box" (when I switch it on, it does this), its "internal" workings are potentially accessible to anyone with the relevant mechanical knowledge. The machine is precise, but it can also be tinkered with by the hobbyist.

More broadly, it could be said that the machine is the thing which connects humans to their environment. Such technologies reveal the potentials of the environment to us, allowing us to further imagine and explore other possible potentials: we know the environment through our machines and technologies. As a result, an entire cosmology is implied by the energetic machine, one in which secrets can be discovered and understood, suggesting an apparent progress in line with human purpose. On the other hand, electronic technology is not only miniaturised but also, in its very operations, imperceptible to the normative scales of human interaction evident in the mechanical world. If we open up a digital watch, we cannot see its workings in the same way we could if we opened up an old wind-up clock (even if, lacking the appropriate expertise, we did not understand what we were seeing). In terms of relative scale, electronic technology is invisible in its operation.

A final duality: given what has been said in relation to the visible, the energetic mechanical world is a world conducive to surveillance. Bodies, machines, and operations can be overseen in their workings and, assuming the requisite knowledge, understood by the observer. The informational electronic world is, instead, one of communication. Surveillance more or less remains what Foucault described it as being in *Discipline & Punish*: a power, applied externally, that causes a change in the interiority of the subject. The point of this change is to bring the subject to an acceptance of and integration with the particular normative standards relative to the field in question. This normalisation then produces appropriate actions and efficient performances which are observable and thus measurable from an overseer's point of view. In other words, surveillance is a technique for improving human activity. It presupposes a visible (or directly measurable) energy transfer that understands the human as itself being akin to a machine, to the extent that the human body is integrated into a possibly dispersed (but nevertheless visible) apparatus of energy transfer (such as the prison, the school, the hospital, etc.).

With communications, visibility becomes less significant. If Foucauldian discipline is an observation of a body's conformity to (and thus, also divergence from) an established norm, communication is only indirectly visible (and even then, only through quite sophisticated systems of registration).

This is because, rather than marking a point or activity relative to a standardised norm, communication is concerned with an information exchange that is statistical in essence[10] and so always distributed and variable. In line with what was said previously, we might say that what happens with informatic communications is that disciplinary normativity is miniaturised, made less universal and more specific, and put into a continuous feedback loop, through which outputs keep the relevant standards in a constant state of flux. If it is the difference that makes a difference which is informative, then communicated information is that which is not statistically likely but which, despite its improbability, nevertheless happens.[11]

Information cannot be understood as overseeing a mechanical energy transfer reducible to a chain of cause and effect; rather, the statistical unlikelihood of information means that it is not anticipated precisely because it is not easily predicted from a given set of causes. Indeed, one could go so far as to say that, with information, causes are not essential; what matters is the effect that a differentiating difference makes. To be informed is to then immediately feed back such effects into the system itself so as to re-distribute probabilities and transform the anticipation of what is and is not likely to occur. Through communication, normative conformity is superseded by the (hopefully) controlled reaction to a surprise. So diversity and divergence become much more important than straightforward conformity.

The Subject: Energy and Information

As mentioned earlier, the concern of the film *Holy Motors* is with the status of the subject as it transitions from a world of energy to a world of information. The subject of the mechanical age is probably best described as being an individual – an indivisible unit that then serves as a point of attraction for rights, obligations, capacities, dreams, creativity, and so on. It is the figure we can see emerging during the 17th century in the work of thinkers such as Hobbes and Locke, who mark it, in legalistic terms, as an entity capable of contracting and owning property. Indeed, these two legal techniques are at the centre of the idea of the individual as an entity capable of knowing its interests and how to achieve them; and is also able to use its energies to acquire objects and land as the fruits of its own labour. The individual is an entity that takes action, and this will be its defining feature up to our own time.[12] As Foucault will subsequently point out, it is discipline that makes the

10 Tiziana Terranova, *Network Culture: Politics for the Information Age* (Pluto Press 2004) Ch 1.

11 Vilém Flusser, *Into the Universe of Technical Images* (Nancy Ann Roth tr, U of Minnesota P 2011).

12 For an account of the *vita activa*, see Hannah Arendt, *The Human Condition* (U of Chicago P 2018).

individual: it does not drop from the sky but has to be fashioned. Specifically, the subject must become capable of exchanging, meaning both that it has something to exchange (property) and that its promises to do so are rendered reliable (contract).

Symbolically, it is arguably Hobbes who provides the fundamental account of the subject-become-individual, which results from a social contract that sees the subject exchange freedom for protection. Of course, it is irrelevant that no such contract was ever made; what is important is the image of it, as a *grundnorm* by which the parameters and capacities of the individual can be worked out and defined. Under the protection of the sovereign, the individual reduces risk sufficiently that they are able to interact with others of their kind: contractual alliances are guaranteed and property and patrimony vouchsafed. Needless to say, it is not all plain sailing – the very fact that the individual is an historical construction points to both its artificiality and the tremendous work that must go into maintaining it. The toll of this effort will find its best expression in psychoanalysis, which might be considered the apex of the concept of the individual. Psychoanalysis will discover a split in the individual, but crucially, this split will not entail a necessary dispensation with the form of the individual but, rather, show how individuality is the task of holding the conscious and the unconscious together by making the latter the responsibility of the former. Consequently, it becomes clear that the individual is akin to a collection of symptoms that have to be managed therapeutically for the good of (socially contracted) society.

From the perspective of information, the individual is a cumbersome and perhaps outdated notion. Deleuze pointed out in the 1990s that it is the "dividual" that is emerging in place of the individual, being an entity that can not only be divided but also finds its very mode of being through such constant division. It is as if the individual explodes into a collection of uncoordinated tendencies and passions by which the subject becomes a site of divergence no longer to be disciplined (because, after all, the idea of a stable, normative centre has given way to a flux of provisional operations) but, rather, managed and controlled. Your perversity, dishonesty, inability, and other "shortcomings" are now all fine, so long as they can be properly managed and expressed. Or, more to the point, they take on propriety if they can be effectively communicated. As Erickson and Heggerty aptly described it, following Deleuze, the subject becomes a "data-double"[13] of itself (except, of course, that there is no "itself" behind the double; there is only ever the data or the copy without an original).

The subject as dividual is an ever-evolving site of probable preferences and dispositions. It is much freer than the disciplinary individual but at the cost of greater uncertainty and precarity. The successful dividual is one who makes

13 Kevin D Haggerty and Richard V Ericson, 'The Surveillant Assemblage' (2000) 51 The British Journal of Sociology 605–22.

of life a sort of portfolio,[14] in which abilities are acquired and dispensed with as needed, without ever becoming "core characteristics" of the subject itself. Here, exchange gives way to exposure and property to access. By exposure, I mean an incommensurability between what is provided and what is received. Of course, such disparity is evident in theories of exchange, most importantly in Marx, but here I mean something more, inasmuch as, with exposure, there is not even the pretence of any equivalence between what is exchanged; rather, exposure is the temporary linkage between two discrete and operationally un-combinable systems (for example, that of the worker and their employer through the so-called "uber-isation" of work). The dividual subject is simply exposed to uncertainties that they must navigate the best they can, without the support of a broader social and civic context of which they could consider themselves a "part". The social contract has given way to an ever-evolving matrix of discrete instances of contracting which, rather than enforcing a promise, can only seek to minimise risk in the particular circumstances of their making.

By access, I simply mean that, increasingly, property will be both out of the reach of many people and, consequently, will become less significant to them. Rather, it will be a matter of being able to access resources as and when they are needed, irrespective of whether this is cloud-held data or medical interventions. Access entails a sort of enforced nomadism through which the dividual surfs through life, whether from luxury hotel to luxury hotel, from sofa to sofa, or some level in between. This does not mean to say that property will disappear but that it will become increasingly inaccessible as the primary means by which subjects relate to objects. Either the object (such as data) will become temporary or access to it will (whether a room to stay in or a place in which to work). Consequently, the conceptual distinction between property and contract will become less significant as both are subsumed within a much more complex array of administrative and managerial measures that will be, at best, tailored to specific situations but, in most cases, will see pre-formatted "solutions" crudely applied to situations on a "best-fit" basis. At worst, of course, certain sectors of dividuality will likely find themselves simply not provided for and abandoned.

Part Two

Technologies

In many ways, the transition set out here is organised in *Holy Motors* around visibility: mechanical power (such as the motor) involves a Newtonian understanding of how energy is transferred and preserved. As noted, this type of energy is something visible: some act or event serves as the input for

14 Ivan Ascher, *Portfolio Society: On the Capitalist Mode of Production* (Zone Books 2016).

a machine which, through its process, uses that input to render a predictable output. In each stage of its operation, the machine's process is visible to humans – either directly or by using tools (such as the microscope and telescope) – and, for this reason, is something related to the scale of the human. This latter means that the human is able to take action – either by operating the machine or by intervening to repair, adapt, or improve it.

On the other hand, with electronic power, the operation of the device (for example, a computer) is not "visible" – indeed, it can only be imaged through specialised apparatuses such as screens and other interfaces and is, consequently, of a more theoretical nature. The interface does not provide us with an imprint or an analogue reproduction and has no particular relation to what it represents, being a virtual capacity (within the particular interface's parameters of operation) to constitute any image at all (e.g. from pixels). Unlike a photograph or a painting, the interface does not share the medium of light with the human eye. Instead, it produces an arrangement on the basis of code, by which its operations can be presented in a way meaningful to humans (such as an image). In this sense, visibility is not something crucial to computers (for example) but is an add on or application to allow humans to interact with them in particular ways. In essence, if our understanding of visibility is referenced to the human eye, then information is not visible.

The director, Leos Carax, has been explicit about this as a concern of the film,[15] making the interesting point that machines can be turned on and off, but a computer is always on. This indicates that any given computer is, in fact, only a terminal – that is, a discrete interface – for a global network that never sleeps and enacts protocols and operations according to its own algorithmic priorities (such as updating itself). I think it would be wrong to say that Carax wishes to critique this difference so much as he takes note of it and, particularly, of how this change impacts the ideas we have of ourselves as humans.

The central character, M. Oscar (played by Denis Lavant), is chauffeur driven around Paris in a stretch limousine. The film takes place over the course of a day, during which Oscar has a number of assignments or appointments. Unusually, each appointment requires Oscar to act out a specific character, for which he is heavily made up and briefed on characteristics and lifestyle. These characters include a beggar woman, a motion-capture actor, a somewhat monstrous individual who disrupts a fashion shoot, a father collecting his daughter, and a businessman. Without wishing to ascribe my views to Carax, I speculate that, with these wildly diverse roles and performances, something is being said in the film about "our place" in a milieu of electronic technology. How is the human – a holy motor in its engine-powered car – to

15 In an interview included as an extra on the DVD *Holy Motors* (Directed by Leos Carax, Artificial Eye 2013).

fit into this "new world" of dividuality? The limousine is a sort of bubble through which the "real" M. Oscar travels, disconnected from the outside world which he only ever enters (it seems) in character, with a role to play. These roles are, in the main, recognisable "types" – shady businessman, concerned father, gangster hitman, etc. – that are well familiar from film and also literature. What is the connection between electronic technology and these character types?

Here, I think we need to consider information technologies in particular: the types are informational assemblages or statistical combinations (manner of hair style, having glasses or a scar, wearing rags or a business suit, etc.) that help us recognise (in most cases) the sort of character involved. Are we, in our day-to-day lives, doing a similar thing? Of course, the person has always been a mask (persona), but I think the film is making a point about the speed and flexibility with which we now change masks. To use a Heideggerian term, perhaps we humans have become a sort of standing reserve to ourselves: we try to adopt the most efficient character for the task at hand (getting a grant or job, impressing a potential partner, making a friend envious, etc.). Such characters are not merely a means to facilitate social discourse because the informational "type" always takes itself as being engaged in a specific project.[16] It is always a dividual or entrepreneur of itself. In other words, the film suggests that the subject has become a kind of open platform, to be filled temporarily (from project to project) with the appropriate informational content[17] – that is, an interface.

Visibilities

M. Oscar briefly encounters, in his limousine, someone who appears to be his boss, played by Michel Piccoli. In their exchange, Oscar complains that his performances now take place in front of cameras that are too small to see. His boss chides him, telling him he should relish the "beauty of the act"; Oscar replies, "But what if there is no beholder anymore?" That is, no beholder capable of seeing the "beauty" of the act. At the end of the film, the limousines themselves complain that humanity no longer wants "visible machines" nor action. Oscar's performances don't amount to spectacle because no one appears to be watching him. Yet, almost ironically, this very absence of an audience (or, more specifically, the seeming invisibility of the interfaces which give access to the performance) demands the utmost rigour and perfection in

16 The self as entrepreneurial project has, arguably, displaced the modernist notion of a biography. With various co-authors, Luc Boltanski has been at the forefront of tracking the neoliberal modulations of the subject. See, for example, the recent book by Luc Boltanski and Arnaud Esquerre, *Enrichment: A Critique of Commodities* (Catherine Porter tr, Polity 2020).

17 On the theory of platforms, see Nick Snicek, *Platform Capitalism* (Polity 2012); Benjamin H Bratton, *The Stack: On Software and Sovereignty* (MIT Press 2016).

the execution of the characters. This is Oscar's responsibility both to himself (as a performer) and to his boss (as his "agency"). The spectacle has absorbed its own status as spectacle, leaving a play of mirrors as Oscar (and the other performers) fail to encounter each other but, instead, operate in parallel, occasionally giving rise to an illusion that they are together in the same space and time. The more perfect the character, the more alone they are, performing only for themselves and for reasons which remain obscure. Perhaps the point is to "play" with the statistical requirements of each character for them to be recognisable as such or, better, for them to be informational.

More generally, by becoming our own projects, we have internalised the camera or, more to the point, internalised a certain mode of surveillance that is, in many respects, quite different to the disciplinary type set out by Foucault. That, after all, was still a matter of training bodies, to make them efficient and compliant. Now, the focus is elsewhere: not so much a training of the soul (which would be nothing new) but a training of intentions and, I think, perceptions. What am I able to perceive and why? How do I process what I perceive? What obligation does perception place me under? What do I intend to achieve as a result, and does the intention match the desired outcome? Disciplinary surveillance was a question of convergence, of conforming to a relevant norm; now, there is more of a pressure towards divergence or, at least, a more flexible distribution of the self, which is to be constantly self-monitored and assessed. The disciplined body could sometimes rest, but, under control, the work never ends.

In this light, the film can indeed be read as problematising its own framing, making the viewer question how it is that we frame our senses (how we perceive). De-naturalising perception obviously means that a technique is involved, and, where there is technique, there is probably an intention: a choice is being made; a particular aim is being pursued. Yet, to the extent that information and communications technologies must also take account of their own framing (Luhmann refers to this as the difference between the utterance and the information relayed by the utterance[18]), our perceptions (and intentions) are folded back on themselves: we perceive a need to problematise our own perceptions and intentions. So this obviously creates a feedback loop which, as mentioned, will not allow us any rest. It is a disorientation we cannot escape; at the same time, it is a disorientation we must find a way of addressing. (Trying to return to a Newtonian universe won't do it!)

If we have to ask questions about our own perceptions, inevitably, we also have to ask them of others. This is an unavoidable condition for us, but it can quickly spiral into conspiracy theories if we consider that there is nothing shared between us and another. The conspiracy theory is something like

18 Niklas Luhmann, *Social Systems* (John Bednarz and Dick Baecker trs, Standford UP 1966) 151.

the unconscious of information and communication technologies. However, *Holy Motors* is not explicit about this theme, but, as watchers, we are not sure of what we are seeing – certainly, the film shows that, at least on occasion, actors are interacting with other actors (e.g. the deathbed scene drawn from Henry James and Oscar's encounter with Kylie Minogue's character Eva/Jean). Yet the status of these interactions is never clear. The sequence with Eva/Jean implies a history between her and Oscar and the possibility that they had a child together. Given what we have already seen in the film, there is no reason to believe this is a "real" encounter. The apparent intimacy of their encounter, with the implication of a tragic past, is possibly just as staged as everything else. There is no outside to the performances, and one is never not in character. Eva/Jean and Oscar's brief encounter is presented as an accident, but Eva/Jean already seems made up for the meeting, wearing a wig that she will remove on resuming the performance that was apparently interrupted by Oscar.

As inheritors of Quattrocento perspective, visibility implies distance. The film suggests that such a vision is no longer possible because there are no longer fixed points of view and no "outside" from which what is happening can be assessed or evaluated. The loss of spectacle is an implosion of perspectives. This is implied early on in the film, when Carax himself appears as a guest in an airport hotel. The room has a window through which an airport at night is visible. On the table is a computer with a screensaver showing birds, the sound of which can be heard on the soundtrack. What looks like a framed picture of a zeppelin hangs on the wall. Everything implies flight and movement, but the room is akin to a cell. One side is covered with wallpaper depicting tree trunks, as if the room opened out into a forest. Carax finds a hidden door in this wall, but it leads only to that most enclosed of spaces, a cinema theatre, where the audience sits with eyes closed or asleep. It seems as if the transit spaces of the cinema – the hotel, the airport, and the ship (heard on the soundtrack and then echoed in the design of the house in the following scene) – will not, in fact, lead anywhere, and there is no way out.

This collapse of space demands a new notion of visibility; the confined spaces of discipline have become immanent to themselves, as if a labyrinth had been spliced with a moebius strip. The clue to this, I think, is the manner by which Carax discovers the hidden door. He first sees a keyhole and opens it, using a key which seems to be fused with one of the fingers of his right hand. This recalls Kafka's parable *Before the Law*, in which the man from the country waits outside of the entrance to the law – an entrance unique to him – without ever being able to enter. The centre of the law, its secret and origin, are unapproachable, hidden at a remove which it is impossible to traverse. For Carax, it is different. Not only can he open and pass through the door, but the key is also part of him. Like the man from the country, this door seems to be just for him, but, on passing through, he finds another enclosure. This is the space of control: enclosures within enclosures, where the obligation is to keep moving from one to the other: constant traversal. All apparent exits and transits are, in fact, interfaces: not three-dimensional volumes, but flat informational zones. Like one of M. Oscar's assignments, movement and encounters are only data to be captured and translated. The ubiquity of the screen is such that, in the limousine, Celine,[19] the chauffeur, warms Oscar by turning on the moving image of a fireplace. Contra Wiener, it seems that information has indeed become energy.

Law

Law is not addressed as an explicit subject in the film. Nevertheless, there are allusions. For example, the apparent employment contract is evident in some of the set-ups, particularly in the exchange with the Piccoli character and when Celine pays Oscar at the end of the shift. To that extent, the film points to a certain ambiguity in the employer-employee relationship that, by itself, is fairly commonplace. Who is hiring Oscar, and who is (presumably) paying the agency for him to perform? It seems there is a service being provided, but there is no direct relation between Oscar and the consumer. It suggests some sort of mediation which echoes the film's concern with digital technology. We humans might seem to be together, interacting with each other but, in fact, our relations are heavily mediated, going by way of communications and outsourcing. There are invisible, virtual forces shaping our physical interactions in some mysterious way (because they are non-visible and often difficult to conceptualise). But as Kafka's parable implies, law has always done this – it is never fully present – so it is a question of how things change under a regime of control.

Any legal system is concerned with organising how humans can (and should) live together. Some may argue that human society does not need law, and a legal system is always parasitic upon some more fundamental human sociality. In practice, I am doubtful of this for at least two reasons. First, law allows for certain things to be taken for granted, such that we don't need to organise our relations with others from the ground up every time. In this sense, law provides an abstract context within which we can operate with a more particular focus on the specific interaction to hand. This is part of a human tendency to abstract generally. Of course, this has dangers, but to dismiss law as a whole (or in part) provides little in terms of pragmatic solutions. Second, I think the idea of human society without law – without some systematisation of consequential differences – rests on an overly optimistic

19 Celine is played by Edith Scob who, at the end of the film, dons the mask she famously wore in *Eyes Without a Face* (directed by Georges Franju 1960). In that film, the mask hid her disfigurement, but now, in *Holy Motors*, it hides nothing. It is just another face, another persona. Indeed, its very blankness might make it the most efficient and flexible of all faces.

notion of what humans are: that they are "naturally" benevolent, rational, reasonable, etc. Intuitively, I am not convinced by this and prefer the view expressed by Nietzsche in *The Genealogy of Morals*: humans have to be made benevolent, rational, etc. Law – in spite of all its problems and shortcomings – is an important system for achieving this.

What does *Holy Motors* suggest about this? For me, it is that the idea of a social contract as the presumed organising basis upon which human interaction takes place, is no longer sufficient. In short, the image of contractual exchange is no longer convincing in light of digital technologies. Why not?

1 Digital technologies do not operate by exchange. Rather, in the context of big data, they look for patterns and derive consequential interactions on that basis. So too with the governance of populations, as Foucault argued.[20]
2 The contract presupposes an individual as being a discrete, self-motivated entity, who knows what is in their best self-interest. The world in which that model of the individual was relevant is on the decline. *Holy Motors* suggests that the discrete individual is being replaced by discrete roles – but, as noted, who is the (in)dividual behind these roles? It might be that we need to think differently about this: rather than a true individual "behind" the role, the roles suggest a more distributed individual, better thought of (perhaps) as a series of patterns.
3 The Hobbesian notion of sovereignty is outdated; the idea of the social contract involving an exchange of freedom for protection has not disappeared but has become marginalised. Protection, as it were, has been outsourced and is (increasingly) a personalised matter. The broader point is that the type of sovereignty the Hobbesian contract suggests (centralised, hierarchical) is an incomplete notion: sovereignty is also distributed and more horizontal. (For example, something like an algorithm has the potential to exercise a sovereign function to the extent that it decides on something.)
4 Contract also implies "free" choice. Freedom to choose is an important part of being an individual, but how does it change if it occurs without reference to some centralised social contract, such as in Hobbes? Ian MacNeil argued that we should consider a more diffuse network of social contracts in which each individual chooses the particular contracts they wish to enter. However, I wonder about this vision of a "new social contract" (as he called it)[21] as it seems to find its proper articulation in practices such

20 See, generally Michel Foucault, *Security, Territory, Population: Lectures at the Collége de France 1977–78* (Graham Burchell tr, Palgrave Macmillan 2007); Michel Foucault, *The Birth of Biopolitics: Lectures at the Collége de France 1978–79* (Graham Burchell tr, Palgrave Macmillan 2010).

21 Ian MacNeil, *The New Social Contract: An Inquiry into Modern Contractual Relations* (Yale UP 1981).

as "uber-isation", precarity, and zero-hour contracts. If an individual is called upon to constantly decide about everything in any social interaction, it becomes very difficult for that individual to maintain its integrity – too much energy is required to formulate the necessary contractual terms (and foster the underlying trust) of each and every interaction. Increasingly, contracts hide an imbalance of power; the choice is often "take it or leave it". In a sense, M. Oscar has to begin each appointment anew – this is only mitigated by the fact that the role has been pre-determined for him, but, even then, he is exhausted at the end of the day. Moving from role to role – perhaps this is a consequence of too much choice?

5 Within the framework of Giorgio Agamben's thinking, the important issues involve the relationship between *zoë* and *bios*. In his *Homo Sacer* series, Agamben sees this as the central question of law and sovereignty, and similar points seem evident in *Holy Motors*: what is an authentically meaningful human life? To what extent does that depend on interaction with others? How might such interactions be organised? Famously, Agamben sees the Western tradition as increasingly concerned to remove *bios* – the specificity of the person – to reveal the bare, almost animalistic life of *zoë* beneath.[22] Is the difference between M. Oscar and the roles he plays this difference: between his bare life in the back of the limousine and the specific characters he becomes? If everything becomes informational, it seems that specific forms of life cannot be maintained because one must always be willing to discard what one is in response to the next project or "opportunity".

6 How are we to think of "individual" obligation and responsibility in a world mediated by digital technologies? What is responsibility if our interactions are being shaped, to some extent, by the dispersed pattern making and decision taking of algorithms?[23] This has already been an issue, of course, in relation to racial bias in the writing and performance of certain algorithms, but this is a consequence that is (relatively speaking) fairly visible. What about less visible and harder to conceptualise consequences that result from such technologies?[24] These are, to an extent, out of the frame,

22 See, generally, Giorgio Agamben, *Homo Sacer: Sovereign Power and Bare Life* (Daniel Heller-Roazen tr, Standford UP 1998).

23 See, for example, Mireille Hildebrandt, *Smart Technologies and the End(s) of Law* (Edward Elgar Publishing 2015).

24 For example, the prosecution of post office managers in England when inadequate software "showed" that the managers had been stealing money out of the till. (They had not, but many were imprisoned and fined as a result of what the computer systems indicated to be the case.) See *Hamilton & Others v Post Office Limited* (EWCA Civ 577); Chris Baynes, 'Hundreds of Post Office Workers "Vindicated" by High Court Ruling Over Faulty IT System That Left Them Bankrupt and in Prison' *Independent* (17 December 2019); *(Hamilton & Others v Post Office Limited)* accessed 22 January 2024.

and I think this is why *Holy Motors* remains necessarily silent about what is "really" going on. Once we move beyond the mechanical and human scale, how are we to discern "what is going on" and our responsibilities relative to it? (This also leads back, of course, to conspiracy theories.) The Kylie Minogue episode typifies this confusion – is there an authentic past relationship here, or is this just another performance?[25]

Conclusion

Of course, there is much more to say about *Holy Motors*. Each of the episodes merits at least a chapter in its own right. However, to conclude this chapter, I would like to come back to the notion of exposure, touched on earlier. The disciplined world of the machine was one in which human activity prevailed: "man" could make both "himself" and the world around "him". In such a world, the rights and responsibilities of the human were developed in light of *homo faber*,[26] and "man" was property owning and exchanging. The human individual was responsible for its choices and actions. Society was a matrix held together by tacit yet common obligations and standards.

In contrast, the world of information is one which displaces the centrality of the human. The human no longer makes itself but responds to statistical forecasts and – always retroactively, of course – unforeseen events. It no longer shapes its world so much as it "learns from past mistakes". Because information is the difference that makes a difference, such differences have to be constantly produced: innovation, aspiration, creativity, and so on are the appropriate values. In such a context, humanity prioritises its ongoing confrontation with its own uncertain futures: this is the notion of exposure. Humanity is exposed to uncertainty, risk, and contingency. It no longer acts in a visible world but manages fluxes of data. This is not a lament but an observation.

At the end of the film, the limousines rest in their garage. One of the neon lights has stopped working, so we see "Holy Mot rs". Perhaps this is the holy word, the thing which humanity thought was special to it but which the film suggests is increasingly the preserve of networks and communications technologies.[27] Or perhaps "Holy Motors" is an oxymoron. "Holy" implies whole, complete, and self-identical. A motor is differentiated in its parts and

25 On this theme, as to the status of truth and its performance, a connection could be made between *Holy Motors* and Donald Cammell and Nicolas Roeg's film *Performance* (1970) and Antonini's *Blow Up* (1966).

26 See Arendt (n 12) 12; Hans Blumenberg, *History, Metaphors, Fables: A Hans Blumenberg Reader* (Hannes Bajohr, Florian Fuchs and Joe Paul Froll trs, Cornell UP 2022) Ch 12.

27 Many thanks to Alexia Katsiginis for pointing this out to me.

works by resistance and friction. The human problem is, perhaps, to be unavoidably caught between these two functions.

Reference List

Agamben G, *Homo Sacer: Sovereign Power and Bare Life* (D Heller-Roazen tr, Standford UP 1998)
Arendt H, *The Human Condition* (U of Chicago P 2018)
Ascher I, *Portfolio Society: On the Capitalist Mode of Production* (Zone Books 2016)
Bateson G, 'Form, Substance, and Difference' in *Steps to an Ecology of Mind* (U of Chicago P 2000)
Baynes C, 'Hundreds of Post Office Workers "Vindicated" by High Court Ruling Over Faulty IT System That Left Them Bankrupt and in Prison' *Independent* (17 December 2019); *(Hamilton & Others v Post Office Limited)* accessed 22 January 2024
Blow Up (Directed by Michelangelo Antonioni 1966)
Blumenberg H, *History, Metaphors, Fabels: A Hans Blumenberg Reader* (H Bajohr, F Fuchs and JP Froll trs, Cornell UP 2022)
Boltanski L and Esquerre A, *Enrichment: A Critique of Commodities* (C Porter tr, Polity 2020)
Bratton BH, *The Stack: On Software and Sovereignty* (MIT Press 2016)
Deleuze G, *Negotiations 1972–90* (M Joughin tr, Columbia UP 1997)
Eyes Without a Face (Directed by Georges Franju 1960)
Flusser V, *Into the Universe of Technical Images* (Nancy Ann Roth tr, U of Minnesota P 2011)
Foucault M, *Security, Territory, Population: Lectures at the Collége de France 1977–78* (G Burchell tr, Palgrave Macmillan 2007)
Foucault M, *The Birth of Biopolitics: Lectures at the Collége de France 1978–79* (G Burchell tr, Palgrave Macmillan 2010)
Haggerty KD and Ericson RV, 'The Surveillant Assemblage' (2000) 51 The British Journal of Sociology 605
Hamilton & Others v Post Office Limited (EWCA Civ 577)
Hardt M and Negri T, *Multitude: War and Democracy in the Age of Empire* (The Paragon Press 2004)
Hildebrandt M, *Smart Technologies and the End(s) of Law* (Edward Elgar Publishing 2015)
Holy Motors (Directed by Leos Carax, Artificial Eye 2013)
Janich P, *What Is Information?* (E Hayot and L Pao trs, U of Minnesota P 2018)
Lash D, *The Cinema of Disorientation: Inviting Confusions* (Edinburgh UP 2020)
Luhmann N, *Social Systems* (J Bednarz and D Baecker trs, Standford UP 1966)
MacNeil I, *The New Social Contract: An Inquiry into Modern Contractual Relations* (Yale UP 1981)
Maturana HR and Varela FJ, *Autopoiesis and Cognition: The Realization of the Living* (D Reidel Publishing Company 1980)
Performance (Directed by Donald Cammell and Nicolas Roeg 1970)
Snicek N, *Platform Capitalism* (Polity 2012)
Terranova T, *Network Culture: Politics for the Information Age* (Pluto Press 2004)

Chapter 8

Kafka in the Balkans

Before the Law, Nihilism, and Crisis in Cristi Puiu's *Aurora*

Camil Ungureanu

Introduction

What is the significance of the legal system in the post-communist democracy transitioning from a totalitarian communist Leviathan? How is the relationship between the individual, authority, and the law re-articulated in the post-communist periphery of Europe?[1] Such concerns are at the core of the cinematic oeuvre of Cristi Puiu, the initiator of the "unexpected miracle"[2] of the Romanian new wave[3] and the most representative of what has been generally interpreted as a cinematic neo-realism, often portraying the disillusionments of the post-communist democracy at Europe's margins.[4] In particular,

1 See Manuela Boatcă, 'Coloniality of Labor in the Global Periphery: Latin America and Eastern Europe in the World-System' (2013) 36 Review (Fernand Braudel Center) 287–314.

2 Dominique Nasta, *Contemporary Romanian Cinema: The History of an Unexpected Miracle* (Wallflower 2013). See also Nick Roddick, 'Eastern Promise' (October 2007) 17(10) Sight & Sound 36–39.

3 This phrase was coined by Anthony Oliver Scott, 'New Wave on the Black Sea' *The New York Times Magazine* (2008). In an interview with Mihai Fulger, Puiu argues that there is neither a "new wave" nor a "new cinema" in post-socialist Romania, since this would imply there is a certain "recycling" of old themes (Mihai Fulger, *The "New Wave" in the Romanian Cinema* (Art 2006).

4 For discussions of the new Romanian wave as neo-realism, see Nasta (n 2); Andrei Gorzo, *Things That Cannot Be Said Otherwise: A Way of Thinking About Cinema, from André Bazin to Cristi Puiu* (Bucharest: Humanitas, 2012); Andrei Gorzo and Andrei State (eds), *Politics of Cinema: Contributions to the Interpretation of Contemporary Romanian Cinema* (Tact Publishing House 2014); Monica Filimon, *Cristi Puiu* (U of Illinois P 2017); Doru Pop, *Romanian New Wave Cinema: An Introduction* (McFarland 2014); Christian Ferenz-Flatz, *Phenomenological Explorations in the New Romanian Cinema* (Tact 2015); Bogdan Popa, *The Sex and the Capital: A Theory of the Romanian Film* (Tracus Arte 2017); Claudiu Turcus, *Against Memory: From the Socialist Aestheticism to the New Romanian Cinema* (Editura EIKON 2017); Claudiu Turcus, 'The Reception of the New Romanian Cinema and Cristi Puiu's *Aurora*' in Andrei Gorzo and Andrei State (eds), *Politics of Cinema: Contributions to the Interpretation of Contemporary Romanian Cinema* (Tact 2014) 111–34; Bogdan Popa, 'What's Wrong with the Romanian New Wave? Auteur Cinema, the Communist and the Production of the Violent Working Class' (2018) 9(1) Studies in Eastern European Cinema 89–102.

DOI: 10.4324/9781003461180-8

I focus on Puiu's *Aurora* (2010),[5] which I interpret contextually and against the backdrop of Franz Kafka's parable *Before the Law*. Puiu's representation of the man before the law in *Aurora* displays, I argue, relevant similarities to Kafka's parable. Kafka's enigmatic story *Before the Law* is built on unsolved paradoxes: first, law appears accessible and functioning, yet it is never realised. Second, law is seemingly general or universal, yet access to it turns out to be singular. In the parable, the "countryman" seeking justice arrives in the city driven by the belief that "the Law should be accessible at all times and to everyone". Nonetheless, while standing before the law, the countryman finds many unexpected "difficulties". The law's custodians are either "monstrous" or invisible: the gatekeeper or guardian of law possesses a fearsome and outlandish appearance that is intimidating. This figure of the gatekeeper representing authority echoes Thomas Hobbes's Leviathan. ("But take note: I am powerful. And I am only the least of all doorkeepers", he declares.) Furthermore, even if "the gate to the law stands open", the judges, who interpret and give voice to the law, are unreachable and unseen. However, the commoner still regards law as understandable and something worth believing in. The law's fulfillment is, for him, worth waiting for throughout one's life.

However, only at the end of his life does the guardian reveal a key insight about accessing the law. The gatekeeper sees that the man is already dying and tells him, "No one else could ever be admitted here, since this gate was made only for you. I'm now going to shut it". Thus, by the end of the man's life in waiting, neither the general nor the singular "moment" of law is fully realised: justice never comes although individual life is shaped by its call.

Unsurprisingly, Jacques Derrida deconstructed Kafka's parable by converting it into the expression of a "quasi-ontology"[6] of law and justice. Derrida's reading dramatises and exalts law's paradoxes: law is caught in the unresolvable aporia between universalisation and specific interpretations in concrete situations, the call for unconditional justice and the force and violence inscribed in specific applications and decisions.[7] Since justice is never completely known and never fully comes, the "doorkeeper . . . keeps nothing", and the door remains "open onto nothing".[8] Nevertheless, while Kafka's parable maintains its irreducibly enigmatic and paradoxical essence as it juxtaposes a countryman against a legal Leviathan, it also serves as a biting socio-political commentary on the intricate interplay between the

5 Director: Cristi Puiu; Script: Cristi Puiu; leading actor: Cristi Puiu (as the engineer Viorel).

6 Derrida uses "quasi-ontological" to signal his distance from foundationalism. See Jacques Derrida, 'Force of Law' in Drucilla Cornell, Michael Rosenfeld and David Gray Carlson (eds), *Deconstruction and the Possibility of Justice* (Routledge 1992a) 3–37; Camil Ungureanu, 'Derrida's Tense Bow' (2013) 18(6) The European Legacy 727–39.

7 Derrida, 'Force of Law' (n 6). For a critical analysis, Ungureanu, 'Derrida's Tense Bow' (n 6).

8 Derrida, 'Force of Law' (n 6) 206.

individual, authority, and law in the decadent Habsburg Empire, a milieu Kafka himself experienced. The countryman seeks legal justice, only to confront a labyrinthine bureaucratic and monstrously frightening power structure that is disconnected from society.[9]

Puiu's equally enigmatic representation of the man before the law in *Aurora* displays relevant similarities to Kafka's parable: the protagonist looking for the fulfillment of the law faces a bureaucratic state apparatus – the "post-communist Leviathan". The law and legal authority appear accessible and functional, yet they are not realised, even if the individual protagonist accepts the general legitimacy of the law and seeks legal justice. However, there is also a notable displacement in Puiu's scenario rooted in the specific context of the ongoing crisis of the post-communist state and society. Notably, while Kafka constructs the parable on the opposition between the innocence of the justice-seeker who still believes in the law and the state apparatus, in Puiu's cinematic sociology of a society in ruins, this straightforward dichotomy disappears. In *Aurora*, there is no inherent conflict between the ostensibly good countryman and the evil bureaucracy or between society or its people and Leviathan. The countryman is not an innocent seeking for justice in the capital city – the locus of the alienating and frightening bureaucracy – but a middle-aged, educated, bourgeois urban male in crisis who turns violent and commits a multiple murder, targeting his ex-wife's parents and seemingly new partner.[10] Likewise, the state bureaucracy, while alienating, is not "monstrous" and transcendent but banal and immanent. Moreover, whereas the countryman as murderer and the law's guardian are on opposite sides their relationship to the law, it is equally devoid of ethical content and significance. Kafka's ominous transcendence of the state and legal apparatus is flattened, not without comic effects, to a routinised legal machinery. In Puiu's vision, the enigmatic dialectic between the general and the singular moment of the law is thus emptied of ethical life (*Sittlichkeit*): in

9 See Julien Preece (ed), *The Cambridge Companion to Kafka* (CUP 2002).

10 On masculinity and its crises, see esp. Raewyn Connell, 'Masculinities in Global Perspective: Hegemony, Contestation, and Changing Structures of Power' (2016) 45(4) Theory and Society 303–18; Raewyn Connell and James W Messerschmidt, 'Hegemonic Masculinity: Rethinking the Concept' (2005) 19(6) Gender and Society 829–59. For the evolving image of women in Romanian cinema, see Florentina Andreescu, 'The Changing Face of the Sacrificial Romanian Woman in Cinematographic Discourses' (2011) 11(4) Studia Politica: Romanian Political Science Review 661–74; Florentina Andreescu and Michael Shapiro (eds), *Genre and the (Post-)Communist Woman: Analyzing Transformations of the Central and Eastern European Female Ideal* (Routledge 2015); Camil Ungureanu, 'Socialist Cinema, Gender, and the Robot Revolution: Ion Popescu Gopo's *Galax, the Doll-Man* (1984) Beyond Utopia and Dystopia' (2023) 4 Studies in European Cinema 98–112; Mihaela Petrescu, 'New Romanian Cinema, Women's Self-Empowerment, and Hegemonic Masculinity: Female Figures in Cristian Mungiu's *Occident* (2002) and Radu Muntean's *Boogie* (2008)' (2020) 17(1) Studies in European Cinema 51–65.

a post-communist society in crisis, the individual, the guardians, and the law become part of an empty comedic form.[11]

*

In the following, to substantiate this interpretation, I introduce first the post-communist backdrop of Puiu's film and key elements of his portrayal of a middle-aged male in crisis who is preparing for committing a multiple murder. Second, I deal with the significance of his crime and surrender to the police, reflecting on the parallelism and differences with Kafka's *Before the Law*. I argue that both the realist and postmodern or anti-realist interpretations of Puiu's film (either as capturing reality or being purely self-referential)[12] are one sided: the movie expresses the dialectical tension between the unveiling of the post-communist reality and its dissolution. *Aurora* is built on the unresolved dialectic between a cinematic-sociological radiography of a society in ruins and an all-dissolving nihilism that empties law of any system of belief. This dissolution or loss is self-reflective as it involves problematising the directorial belief in his capacity to represent, criticise, or unveil reality as such. *Aurora* is, thus, the clinical observation of an alienated male gaze into a crisis that is individual, societal, and directorial: Puiu's "cinematic sociology"; the director portrays the key protagonist (called Viorel), playing out his alienation and crisis. As Puiu states, "*Viorel, c'est moi!*"[13]

Breaking the Law: Anticlimactic Preparations

The fall of communism in 1989 sparked the great expectation that Romania would gradually align with "consolidated" democracies in the West based on the rule of law. However, the anticipated convergence of post-communist countries and liberal democracies turned out to be a myth. Neoliberalism's "going local"[14] strategy in a relatively small nation at Europe's margins failed to produce equal freedom, shared economic prosperity, and the rule of law. In practice, the fall of communism generated a rearrangement of the world system and the integration of ex-communist countries in the global capitalist

11 For the comedic in Puiu, see esp. Alina Haliliuc, 'What Is So Funny About the Death of Mr. Lazarescu?' (2015) 48(1) Journal of Popular Culture 154–67.

12 Gorzo, *Things That Cannot Be Said Otherwise* (n 4); Filimon (n 4) speaks of "epiphanies of reality". In contrast, Turcus analyzes *Aurora* as an exercise in self-referentiality which would mark the end of the Romanian new wave as neo-realism. See later for a partial critique of these two interpretations. See Claudiu Turcus, 'The Reception of the New Romanian Cinema and Cristi Puiu's *Aurora*' in Andrei Gorzo and Andrei State (eds), *Politics of Cinema: Contributions to the Interpretation of Contemporary Romanian Cinema* (Tact 2014) 111–34.

13 Cristi Puiu, 'I Wanted This Character to Be Me – "Viorel, c'est moi!"' Interview by Adam Popescu, Evenimentul Zilei (2000) <https://evz.ro/am-vrut-ca-personajul-asta-sa-fiu-eu-viorel-cest-moi-895031.html> accessed 12 April 2024.

14 Cornel Ban, *Ruling Ideas: How Global Neoliberalism Goes Local* (OUP 2016).

order.[15] Transitioning from a semi-peripheral position within the communist constellation dominated by the Soviet Union, with very limited autonomy, Romania evolved into a semi-peripheral and semi-autonomous actor in the global capitalist system. This transformation was marked by a reliance on a new extractivist logic concerning the country's natural and human resources.[16] Structural inequality, poverty, and systemic corruption have led to political polarisation and contributed to mass emigration. Combined with low natality, emigration has led to a severe population decline and a radical sense of alienation and social precariousness.[17]

Despite the initial "great expectations" after the Romanian revolution, the passage from communist totalitarianism to post-communist democracy has been marked by an unexpected continuity. The opposition between the communist and neo-liberal democratic discourses has relentlessly sapped the social bonds leading to atomisation, alienation, and the destruction of community. In the apt title of Lucian Georgescu, the new Romanian cinema reflected this abrupt passage from "great expectations to great despair".[18] A sense of disempowerment acutely perceived amongst the male population has fed the emergence of a gendered mix of conservatism and nationalism that has been capitalised on by far-right parties: the Great Romania Party and, most recently, the Alliance for the Union of Romanians.[19]

In this context, *Aurora* can be interpreted as a cinematic sociological radiography of the pathologies of post-communist democracy, namely atomisation, disintegration of social bonds, and the crisis of masculinity. Thereby, Puiu pursues this concern, which is at the core of his previous film, *The Death of Mr. Lazarescu* (2005). In *The Death of Mr. Lazarescu*, a dying man gradually loses the elements of his communal existence – his home, community, family, and even his ability to communicate – as he becomes entangled in the bureaucratic maze of the Bucharest hospital system and finally passes away. Whereas *Aurora* documents a parallel process of estrangement,[20] this

15 Immanuel Wallerstein, *World-Systems Analysis: An Introduction* (Duke UP 2004); Immanuel Wallerstein, *European Universalism: The Rhetoric of Power* (The New Press 2006).

16 Cfm Boatcă (n 1); Corina Tulbure, 'Mobility and Post-Socialism: Cross-Border Shaming and Un-Belonging in a White Europe' (2022) 11(1) State Crime Journal 110–27.

17 Since 1989, Romania has lost 16.4% of its population (3.8 million people). By 2050, projections climb to 35%. Cfm. Tim Judah, 'Romania's Demographic Tailspin Heralds Social Change' *Balkan Insight* (2019) <https://balkaninsight.com/2019/11/28/romanias-demographic-tailspin-heralds-social-change/>.

18 Lucian Georgescu, 'The Point of No Return: From Great Expectations to Great Desperation in New Romanian Cinema' in Michael Gott and Todd Herzog (eds), *East, West and Centre: Reframing Post-1989 European Cinema* (Edinburgh UP 2015) 147–58.

19 Mihaela Mihai and Camil Ungureanu, 'Far-right Ecology and Geopolitical Resentment at Europe's Periphery: The Case of Romania's "Conservative Revolution"' (2024) Geoforum Volume 156, November 2024, 104122.

20 Puiu purposefully aimed at continuities between these two movies. Gina, Viorel's lover, who is giving him Xanax, is "one of the doctors in *The Death of Mr. Lazarescu* – it's the same

time, Puiu portrays a divorced middle-aged man in crisis who "gives death". More specifically, *Aurora* documents 36 hours in the life of an engineer called Viorel, played by Puiu himself. This day and a half seem like any other, filled with banal activities and routines. And yet, Puiu's camera observes Viorel's actions at an extremely slow pace before the murder of his ex-wife's presumed lover, a public notary, alongside an unknown woman accompanying him[21] – ordinary daily activities, initial preparations (such manufacturing bullets) – to the concluding scene, where he surrenders to the police and stands "before the law".

The storyline aligns with that of a crime thriller, yet Puiu deliberately deviates from the conventions typically associated with this genre. Through extended and deliberately protracted scenes, with the film spanning 182 minutes, Puiu dissects each gesture and movement of the impending assassin.[22] The preparations for the murder and the abrupt crime itself happen against the background of meticulously detailing "just another dull day" in the life of the protagonist. The director's cinematic male gaze is cold, dispassionate, observational – a self-reflective instance of alienation.[23] Crafted with "impassible" long and often fixed shots conveying a sense of eerie alienation and numbness, Puiu's anti-thriller positions a Bresson-like, blank-faced character at its core.[24] Viorel conducts himself emotionlessly and without a discernible rationale throughout the film. The movie's extremely slow pacing and aesthetics of banality produce a numbing effect, emptying moral consciousness, meaningful communication, and law of their substance.

Aurora opens with a noisy scene in a post-communist Romanian factory that seems half in ruins. Preceding the opening credits, the camera tracks the protagonist at work, alone, against a derelict landscape. After a while, he strokes a stray dog – a symbolic alter ego. The protagonist looks aimlessly

---

Gina from that film. And Pusa's [Viorel's mother] next-door neighbor is the nurse from the ambulance in *Lazarescu*. It's not just the same actress. (And I wanted this nurse to have her own Mr. Lazarescu at home – the old man who offers Viorel the drink)". In Puiu, *apud* Rob White, 'Cristi Puiu Discusses Aurora' (2010) 64(2) Film Quarterly 5.

21 Later, Viorel would also murder his ex-wives parents in their house.

22 There is a certain resemblance to Chantal Akerman's meticulous rendition of banal life interrupted by a murder in *Jeanne Dielman, 23 quai du Commerce, 1080 Bruxelles*. However, in Puiu's oeuvre, the female victim remains voiceless. This cinematic omission could be scrutinised from a gender standpoint, considering that the woman is doubly "sacrificed": she is both murdered and visually absent from the film. Nonetheless, we find this criticism unconvincing: Puiu's emphasis lies in portraying a crisis of masculinity in a larger social context.

23 For a non-essentialist approach to the differences between the male and female gaze, see Lisa French, *The Female Gaze in Documentary Film* (Palgrave Macmillan 2021). In my view, Puiu's "male gaze" is programmatically assumed to convey an experience of alienation and dispossession.

24 In Bresson, this anti-dramatic acting makes space for a divine or spiritual force directing the "human comedy". In Puiu, this style of acting points to a dissolution of individuality. See also Ferencz-Flatz (n 4).

around and starts walking in silence. Recently divorced, Viorel has a dispassionate relationship with a woman called Gina. He also endeavors to renovate his apartment. Puiu's camera chronicles his routine, capturing long takes of him overseeing the painting of his home, taking a lengthy shower,[25] and strolling through a desolate and grey city.[26] Shot in low lighting and grey and saturated tones, the city landscape is a metaphor for the protagonist's crisis and his subjectivity in ruins. The movie is shot in excruciatingly long takes in Bucharest and its periphery.[27] The city landscape is derelict, desert-like, and inhabited by industrial skeletons; likewise, family, social, and work relationships are broken and fragmentary. The day seems to be like any other: grey, repetitive, dull. There is no momentum that builds up: in dissonance with its theme, Puiu constructs an anti-thriller. He gets manufactured bullets for a rifle and makes a call, but there is no answer.

Viorel's family has disintegrated for unclear reasons. We don't get to know his wife, her life, her reasons, or her entourage. Critics may argue that this cinematic ellipsis that eliminates the future victim (his ex-wife) and her entourage from the cinematic representation is objectionable from a gender perspective: the victims, their lives, desires, and dreams are also cinematographically "sacrificed". But Puiu's choice does not implicitly condone a hegemonic masculinity;[28] his focus is on representing/revealing a crisis of male subjectivity against the background of a broader social crisis.

Viorel is also estranged from his presumed mother, Pușa, and maintains a cold, impersonal, and occasionally verbally violent relationship with her partner, Mr. Stoian. He is equally alienated from work and the workplace, having quit his job for unknown reasons. In the post-communist capitalist society, the social fabric that once provided coherence to Viorel's identity

25 Paul Arthur highlights Puiu's meticulous attention to bodily realism in his examination of *The Death of Mr. Lazarescu*. This focus on physicality extends to scenes in *Aurora*, such as the shower sequence and the consumption of pie post-murder. However, rather than reinforcing reality, these instances paradoxically contribute to a sense of reality's dissolution. (Paul Arthur, 'Habeas Corpus: A Meditation on the Death of Mister Lăzărescu and Corporeal Cinema' [May–June 2006] Film Comment 44–49.)

26 See also Ferenz-Flatz (n 4).

27 In Pier Paolo Pasolini's *Accattone* (1961) and *Mamma Roma* (1962), the urban periphery serves as a backdrop of decay, atomisation, and the unpredictable emergence of salvation. Epiphanies manifest in the most unexpected of places and moments (Costica Bradatan and Camil Ungureanu (eds), *Cinema and Sacrifice* (Routledge 2016). However, Puiu deliberately mutes the potential for such epiphanies.

28 Puiu actually acknowledges the "fascistic" dimension of his violent male protagonist. See note 45. For the question of the representation of gender in communist and post-communist cinema, see Florentina Andreescu and Michael Shapiro (eds), *Genre and the (Post-)Communist Woman: Analyzing Transformations of the Central and Eastern European Female Ideal* (Routledge 2015); Petrescu (n 10) 51–65; Popa, *The Sex and the Capital* (n 4); Bogdan Popa, *Queer De-Centering Queer Theory Communist Sexuality in the Flow During and After the Cold War* (Manchester UP 2021).

and substance to social and legal norms has been dismantled. His interactions with other members of society, whether in shops, at his daughter's school, or with the police officers, lack substance; they are grounded in distrust and occasional verbal aggressiveness. For instance, Viorel tells Pușa that he doesn't like Mr. Stoian at all and describes his humour as disturbing. Addressing Mr. Stoian, he forthrightly warns him against donning his father's coat or venturing into his childhood room. The protagonist is cold yet also confused, mocking, and verbally aggressive. Viorel openly points out that his aversion to Mr. Stoian is "chemical and epidermal". In another disconcerting scene, Viorel enters a clothing store looking for Andreea (presumably, one of his ex-wife's friends). He interrogates the saleswomen in the shop in a way that's both menacing and confused: "Do you hear, Mrs. Raluca? But ladies' underwear, why don't you sell it? How is it? You saw that you don't have any reply at all?"

Similarly, without notice Viorel enters a classroom where a rehearsal is being held by children. He is determined to take his daughter home. Under the confused looks of the pupils and the teacher, the father converses with the teacher with a muted aggressiveness:

Teacher: What are you doing? Are you taking her?
Viorel: I say so. What do you think?
Teacher: We are rehearsing for the celebration.
Viorel: For the celebration? Are you preparing for August 23, comrades?[29]
Teacher: Can't you leave her a little longer?
Viorel: Madam Sofronea, if I tell you that I have cancer in a terminal phase, do you think that is enough?
Teacher: Are you serious?
Viorel: But are you serious?

For a while, the engineer is not physically violent. His attitude is cold, confusing, and absurd. Yet to anybody familiar with life in Bucharest, this social atmosphere of mistrust, petty conflictiveness, and (gendered) micro-aggressions is not an uncommon experience. Apart from these sporadic encounters and ephemeral half conflicts, though, numbness is the predominant "mood" of Puiu's film.

Before the Law: From Awe to Deflationary Humor

The absence of an emotionally and narratively conventional crescendo renders Viorel's first crimes even more startling: they takes place in a subterranean

29 Viorel's bitter irony is underscored by his reference to the dictator's annual celebrations on 23 August, the Independence Day under communism.

parking lot, abruptly disrupting the drowsy monotony of the movie. The violent and shattering sound of the rifle reverberates through the enclosed space, amplifying its impact. The victims' dramatic deaths are not depicted in any detail; rather, the focus remains on the male gaze and experience.

Puzzingly, after committing the first crimes, he carries on the placid routines of his life, which are interrupted by the cold-blooded killing of his ex-wife's parents. Not long afterwards, the engineer is depicted slowly eating a pie. In a long, still shot, we observe him seated on the sidewalk, his expression blank and emotionless. Eating is a purely physiological act, akin to fulfilling a basic need. There's a notable absence of affect, nervousness, or pleasure. Viorel could have felt horror and fear upon realising the gravity of his actions and the imminent police pursuit. Alternatively, he might have experienced a sense of satisfaction from reclaiming his masculinity by retaliating against his "unfaithful" wife. However, there's no discernible hint of vindictive fear, pleasure, or anxiety in his demeanor.

Upon finishing the pie, he stands up, his face equally inexpressive, and enters the police headquarters. Once again, the unfolding of the events is anticlimactic: i.e. at odds with all the conventions of a crime thriller. There is no emotional intensification, suspense, or fast pacing. As in Kafka's parable, the door to the law is open and accessible. Yet the police headquarters have no dark or threatening mystery about them, nor are the law's gatekeepers fearful – they are indifferent and matter of fact.[30] There is no sense of mystery or transcendence of the law as found in Kafka's work or, on a more optimistic note, as depicted in Derrida's impassioned philosophical appeal – a justice that dramatically calls on us, yet it is never realised.

The engineer's confession that he has committed four murders does not disturb the routine of the police officers. There is no drama, no emotional reaction inside the police station: Puiu's impersonal camera registers in long, static takes banal actions and interactions between the law's gatekeepers and the protagonist.[31] The stationary camera strategically assumes a peripheral position, reminiscent of a fly-on-the-wall documentary, capturing the mundane activities and background hum occurring in various rooms in the police headquarters.[32] However, the effect of this camera technique doesn't draw us

30 For a comparison with a Cristian Porumboiu's *Police, Adjective*, see Gheorghe Gheorghe, 'The Powers of the False in Romanian Cinema: The Case of *Police, Adjective* and *Aurora*' (2022) 27(1) Ekphrasis (2067–631X). See also Christian Ferencz-Flatz, '*Aurora*: Elements from an Analysis of Misunderstanding' (2013) 1(1) Close Up 32–43.

31 It is worth noting that women also serve as custodians of the law at the police station, although ultimately, interrogations may be conducted by men. In Puiu's portrayal, the law is predominantly perceived as a domain of men.

32 As Anna Batori observes, Puiu constructs a panoptic gaze in *Aurora*, giving the sense of a claustrophobic space (Anna Batori, *Space in Romanian and Hungarian Cinema* (Palgrave Macmillan 2018) 94–98.

closer to the characters and their lives. Instead, it imparts a sense of distance and alienation, stemming from the dissonance between the gravity of a murderer's presence and the triviality of their concerns.

Furthermore, a subtle comedic element imbues this final scene, arising from the contrast between the gravity of the protagonist's murders and the unexpectedly mundane reactions in the police station. After Viorel confesses, he is left alone in the room for a while. Contrary to expectations, he is not closely monitored, despite admitting to multiple murders. Viorel could easily escape; nobody pays him much attention, leaving him vaguely confused. The comedic effect is characterised by dry, understated, and absurd humour – an effect that doesn't provoke hearty laughter but rather discomfort, confusion, and disconcert.

While the murderer waits patiently in the chair, the others in the police station go about their business as if nothing has happened: one policeman speaks enthusiastically about a machine that takes seeds out of sour cherries; others converse about coffee making or car repairing in the foreground while we see the murderer waiting in an adjacent room. Through a series of inversions whereby the dramatic becomes trivial and comedic, the atrocious murder is emptied of its ethical significance.[33]

A critical voice may point out that this comedic mood aestheticises the gendered violence common in a patriarchal society like Romania.[34] But the humourless comedic touch draws attention to the radical alienation of the characters: both the protagonists and the guardians of the law have lost contact with the very moral substance of the law.[35] In contrast to Kafka's parable, the law is, in this vision, a societal artifact, not an element of a separated, labyrinthine state.[36] The murderer and the guardians of the law mirror each other while the judges (the interpreters and makers of law) are nowhere in view to pass judgment and implement the law.

In the foreground, the murderer (he is seated on a chair, slightly out of focus) starts detailing the crime to the police officers; we barely hear him – instead, we see the other police officers moving around and talking as if nothing had happened. The police officers register the facts in a process that is impersonal and machine-like. Significantly, the policemen repeat the same question as if

33 Puiu himself argues that the movie is interpretable as a comedy. This is, however, an overstatement: only the last scene has a comedic dimension.

34 Bogdan Popa also raises the question of class, arguing that proletarians are represented as violent in the Romanian new wave (Popa, 'What's Wrong with the Romanian New Wave?' (n 5). For a critical discussion, see Andrei Gorzo, 'Making Sense of the New Romanian Cinema: Tree Perspectives' (2018) 2(1) Close Up: Film and Media Studies 27–42). It is noteworthy that, in *Aurora*, the violent male is an urban and educated bourgeois individual.

35 This comment can be made more generally about formalism, including the Kantian view of formal law that prioritises form over the content. In a situation of crisis, the emptiness of law or norm is unveiled most clearly, with equally comedic and dramatic effects.

36 However, in both visions, law and justice are devoid of ethical life.

they have not understood. Viorel diligently repeats the victims' names three times. The repetitions and Victor's misplaced earnestness, out of tune with his condition as a murderer, generate a discreet, absurd, humorous effect yet, at the same time, unveil the social interaction's mechanical, dehumanising, and estranged nature.

A policeman seems to break the monotony of detailing the identity and the addresses of the victims by asking a crucial question: "Why did you kill them?" Viorel's answer is symptomatic: "I realize that what I am saying has no equivalent. But . . . since I suppose you'll have statements and reports to fill in, I will try to be as precise as possible". Viorel is not driven by a moral sense of guilt but by an automatic sense of duty to fill out bureaucratic forms. Still, instead of a precise explanation for the public files, he impassively divagates without saying anything conclusive about his inner life, rationale, or motivations:

> Yes. Amalia (Viorel's wife) is careless like a child. And it is very easy to believe what certain people say. . . . I did not end up with this divorce because I wanted to end up with a divorce. Did you understand? And when you divorce a person, it is as if you are separating from just one person. *I couldn't leave things like that.*

Viorel fails to clarify his rationale; his experience and actions are opaque to himself, yet he conveys the lack of acceptance of a change in his personal life and a yearning for a lost "order". He confusedly and hesitantly observes, "I don't know what you think, but I personally believe that justice does not have access to the level of complexity that my wife and I had". But the appeal to complexity or the singularity of his experience remains unsubstantiated; only evanescent echoes and shadows of his lost individuality remain. It's the vague trace or remembrance of a lost singularity.

The first policeman interrupts him abruptly, bringing him back to the bureaucratic details of the declaration, displaying no interest in actually getting a proper answer or understanding the crimes. The significance of the crimes is reduced to a bureaucratic procedure conveying a sense of personal and social alienation:

Policeman: Who is Amalia?
The criminal: Amalia is my wife. My strong wife. Now her name is Livinski. . . .
Policeman: What do you do, Mr. Ghenghea?
The criminal: I am a specialised metallurgical engineer at the heavy equipment plant. . . .
The Policeman: And the domicile?

Once again, repetitions emphasise the reduction of public authority and services to their mechanical-formal dimension. Public authorities show no comprehension of or interest in understanding the significance of the assassin's atrocious murder. As Puiu comments after his immersive preparatory research into criminal procedures:

> The justice system does not seek to restore any truth nor to do justice. The role of justice is to protect the social body. They threw him behind bars, and that's all that matters. That was a small revelation of mine, everything started from there.

The movie ends with a characteristic exchange between the policeman and the murderer. The latter is asked to write down his testimony, so he asks for a pen:

The criminal:	Would you give me a pen?
The policeman (proud):	Look . . . a pen with Steaua [the football team]. . . . I'm going to the toilet.[37]

The criminal and the representative of justice have equally lost contact with the moral significance of their acts and the demand for legal justice: the gravity of a dramatic situation is substituted by comic incongruity and small emotions stirred by trifling details like the logo on a pen.

Puiu's troubling rendition of Viorel's multiple murders has been interpreted as a neo-realist representation of post-communist realities or, at the opposite extreme, as a solipsistic exercise rooted in the disbelief in the possibility of accessing reality and people's real motivations. In this latter reading, Puiu's *Aurora* would represent the finale of the new Romanian wave and its neo-realist agenda.[38] But these opposed interpretations are, as I've suggested, one sided. First, *Autora* does away with various realist conventions. Puiu's vision is marked by anti-realist elements: there are no explanatory causes, motivations, or driving affects that propel one either to break the law or to obey it. Likewise, there are no safe objective realities or criteria that can help us perceive and evaluate the social pathologies represented in *Aurora*.

37 However, Viorel also invokes, albeit confusedly, his singularity. His last words are: "Do not take this the wrong way. I have listened to you, and I have seen how you think that you have understood and have closely listened to what I just told you. And this makes me really scared". Yet he does not look really scared, but just confused. Once again, these are traces or echoes of a lost individuality or singularity.

38 Filimon (n 4), for instance, argues that Puiu's art is concerned with epiphanies of reality. More interestingly, Gorzo's hermeneutics is based on the view that Puiu echoes a Bazinian realist aesthetics (*Things That Cannot Be Said Otherwise*, n 4). In his view, in Puiu, "the investment in the anteriority of the real is in tension with an increasingly acute, but still not inescapable, awareness of the representational nature of cinema. . . . Puiu's art is a very evolved art, but it is a very evolved expression of an old-school essentialism" (217–18).

As Puiu notes, "Usually when you're delivering your story and you're honest with yourself, your message can't be clear".[39]

Second, in *Aurora*, reality is not, as Turcus claims, completely dissolved into self-referentiality.[40] In Puiu's words, "Cinema is an instrument for investigating the real, for investigating life".[41] Puiu's vision is, to an important degree, interpretable as a cinematic urban sociology. He documents different social spaces – shops, the school, the factory, the city center and periphery, the life in apartment buildings. It portrays a societal and urban crisis.

In contrast to these opposite interpretations, I submit that *Aurora* is built on an unsolved dialectic or hesitancy[42] between social radiography and nihilism. Turcus convincingly posits, drawing from Puiu's own reflections, this crisis is compounded by a profound self-doubt regarding our ability to grasp objective reality or the inner workings of others' minds. Puiu argues about the motivation to make *Aurora*:

> [W]e are condemned to remain imprisoned in our own mind. Yet, desiring to break free. The driving force [behind *Aurora*] has been the fear of the abyss that yawns in my mind when I close my eyes, cover my ears, and cease to be deceived by the illusion of communicating with the other.[43]

Puiu's film self-reflectively comments on this relationship between director, camera, and reality: cinema is integrated into this particular social existence rather than standing apart to dominate, control, or comment from an external viewpoint. However, while the film portrays a personal crisis, it does so against the backdrop of a broader socio-political and legal undoing. Both individual and collective lives are portrayed in disarray: as reality unfolds, it remains simultaneously unstable and opaque. Questions abound: Why does the protagonist commit the crimes? What compels him to surrender to the authorities? Why does urban society appear in ruins? And why do the guardians of the law treat it as a meaningless bureaucratic process? In *Aurora*, we are provided

39 He continues: "I'm the author of the film, I'm telling the story, but I'm also trying to understand this story. I have some facts only and the right way for me to understand something about what I'm doing – and about life itself – is to accept that to some extent I don't know. But it's very difficult because most people are looking for answers". Puiu *apud* White (n 20) 6.

40 Turcus (n 12).

41 Puiu apud White (n 20) 5.

42 Although I prefer to speak of a dialectic between different and overlapping "voices" or gazes, an analogy can be made with Strauss's usage of the concept of hesitancy. See László Strausz, *Hesitant Histories on the Romanian Screen* (Palgrave Macmillan 2017). For a critical appraisal of Strauss' argument, see Gorzo, 'Making Sense of the New Romanian Cinema' (n 34).

43 Cristi Puiu, 'After the Experience with "Aurora," I Can Confront Death' Interview with Mihai Chirilov, Evenimentul Zilei (2011) <https://evz.ro/cristi-puiu-dupa-experienta-cu-aurora-pot-infrunta-moartea-923687.html> accessed 12 April 2024.

insight into the realities of post-communist society; however, concurrently, the depicted reality and the one who unveils it appear to be slipping into a void.

Conclusion

In Puiu's portrayal, akin to Kafka's parable, the law is effective yet inaccessible. However, Kafka's ominous sense of the Leviathan's transcendence and its overwhelming weight on the individual dissipates in Puiu's work, replaced by dry, nihilistic comedic effects. While Kafka's countryman maintains a belief in legal justice, resiliently expecting it from the Leviathan, Puiu's portrayal presents the protagonist and the custodians of the law as embodying distinct facets of a society in decay, disillusioned by the unfulfilled promises of communism and the subsequent post-communist neoliberal democracy. Puiu's cinematic construction is interpretable as a socio-existential comment on the relationship between the male individual, the law, and authority and illustrates a specific disenchanted perspective on the post-communist condition. The director's perspective is imperceptibly split between a critical radiography of neoliberal post-communism and a radical absence of belief. Given the structural "ambivalence" between Puiu's sociological and nihilist gazes, I've argued that neither a realist nor a postmodern interpretation of the movie is fully sustainable.

In Puiu's vision, law is neither the instrument of capitalist exploitation, as explored by Marx, nor is it political, as argued by critical legal studies. In contrast, in *Aurora*, law, regarded as a social relationship endowed with moral and political significance, transforms into an empty shell and a mechanical routine when lacking an underlying belief system to sustain it. In Puiu's scenario, a Derridean interpretative injunctions that the "doorkeeper keeps nothing" and the "door [is] open onto nothing" needs to be interpreted literally and not as gesturing towards a call for unconditional justice that cannot be fully represented. At best, law is an automatism that has merely the function of preserving the social order.

In this context, Viorel's act of violence is ultimately aimless, the last gesture of a (self-) destructive male subjectivity in crisis, dispossessed of its ties to the world – to his family, work, and social environment. The protagonist's gendered violence is a gesture of impotence and not the reaffirmation of mastery or being in control. Yet, at the same time, it is a symptom of the denial of change and the impossible desire to restore a lost order: nihilism, the yearning for a lost order, and a violent masculinity are key ingredients of Puiu's cinematic vision, which is premonitory of the current conservative revolution.[44] Fueled by resentment and anger, this masculinity currently channels its sense

44 In a presaging passage, Puiu underscores this violent-fascistic dimension of his protagonist: "All the heroes we take as models are uncompromising and this is the fascist dimension of the thing. Viorel is like this. He's the one who's going to impose his philosophy on the world without negotiation. To live inside a community, you have to make compromises and concede things". In Puiu *apud* White (n 20) 6.

of dispossession and meaninglessness towards macho salvationist populists who promise the restoration of the old order and hierarchies.

The threat of this dissolution of (male) subjectivity is self-reflective: the filmic experience is traversed by the ghost of nihilism – the loss of belief in stable moral criteria of assessing reality and having access to any cognoscible reality per se. Kafka in the Balkans navigates a society in ruins, oscillating between social critique, comedy, and lack of belief.

Acknowledgements

This chapter was written as part of the project Screening Social Transformations (Project Leader: Constantin Parvulescu). Research for this chapter was supported by a grant of the Ministry of Research, Innovation and Digitization, CNCS-UEFISCDI, project number PN-III-P4-PCE-2021-0141, within PNCDI III. I thank Bogdan Popa for discussions on a previous version of this chapter as well as the editors of this book.

Reference List

Andreescu F, 'The Changing Face of the Sacrificial Romanian Woman in Cinematographic Discourses' (2011) 11(4) Studia Politica: Romanian Political Science Review 66

Andreescu F and Shapiro M (eds), *Genre and the (Post-)Communist Woman: Analyzing Transformations of the Central and Eastern European Female Ideal* (Routledge 2015)

Arthur P, 'Habeas Corpus: A Meditation on the Death of Mister Lăzărescu and Corporeal Cinema' [May–June 2006] Film Comment 44–49

Ban C, *Ruling Ideas: How Global Neoliberalism Goes Local* (OUP 2016)

Batori A, *Space in Romanian and Hungarian Cinema* (Palgrave Macmillan 2018)

Boatcă M, 'Coloniality of Labor in the Global Periphery: Latin America and Eastern Europe in the World-System' (2013) 36 Review (Fernand Braudel Center) 287–314

Bradatan C and Ungureanu C (eds), *Cinema and Sacrifice* (Routledge 2016)

Connell R, 'Masculinities in Global Perspective: Hegemony, Contestation, and Changing Structures of Power' (2016) 45(4) Theory and Society 303–18

Connell R and Messerschmidt JW, 'Hegemonic Masculinity: Rethinking the Concept' (2005) 19(6) Gender and Society 829–59

Derrida J, 'Force of Law' in D Cornell, M Rosenfeld and D Gray Carlson (eds), *Deconstruction and the Possibility of Justice* (Routledge 1992a) 3–37.

Derrida J, 'Before the Law' in D Attridge (ed), *Acts of Literature* (Routledge 1992b)

Ferencz-Flatz C, '*Aurora*: Elements from an Analysis of Misunderstanding' (2013) 1(1) Close Up 32–43

Ferencz-Flatz C, *Phenomenological Explorations in the New Romanian Cinema* (Tact 2015)

Filimon M, *Cristi Puiu* (U of Illinois P 2017)

French F, *The Female Gaze in Documentary Film* (Palgrave Macmillan 2021)

Fulger M, *The "New Wave" in the Romanian Cinema* (Art 2006)

Georgescu L, 'The Point of No Return: From Great Expectations to Great Desperation in New Romanian Cinema' in M Gott and T Herzog (eds), *East, West and Centre: Reframing Post-1989 European Cinema* (Edinburgh UP 2015) 147–58

Gheorghe G, 'The Powers of the False in Romanian Cinema: The Case of *Police, Adjective* and *Aurora*' (2022) 27(1) Ekphrasis

Gorzo A, *Things That Cannot Be Said Otherwise: A Way of Thinking About Cinema, from André Bazin to Cristi Puiu* (Humanitas 2012)

Gorzo A, 'Making Sense of the New Romanian Cinema: Three Perspectives' (2018) 2(1) Close Up: Film and Media Studies 27–42

Gorzo A and State A (eds), *Politics of Cinema: Contributions to the Interpretation of Contemporary Romanian Cinema* (Tact Publishing House 2014)

Haliliuc A, 'What Is so Funny About the Death of Mr. Lazarescu?' (2015) 48(1) Journal of Popular Culture 154–67

Judah T, 'Romania's Demographic Tailspin Heralds Social Change' *Balkan Insight* (2019) <https://balkaninsight.com/2019/11/28/romanias-demographic-tailspin-heralds-social-change/> accessed 20 March 2024

Mihai M and Ungureanu C, 'Far-right Ecology and Geopolitical Resentment at Europe's Periphery: The Case of Romania's "Conservative Revolution" (2024) Geoforum Volume 156, November 2024, 104122.

Nasta D, *Contemporary Romanian Cinema: The History of an Unexpected Miracle* (Wallflower 2013)

Petrescu M, 'New Romanian Cinema, Women's Self-Empowerment, and Hegemonic Masculinity: Female Figures in Cristian Mungiu's *Occident* (2002) and Radu Muntean's *Boogie* (2008)' (2020) 17(1) Studies in European Cinema 51–65

Pop D, *Romanian New Wave Cinema: An Introduction* (McFarland 2014)

Popa B, *The Sex and the Capital: A Theory of the Romanian Film* (Tracus Arte 2017)

Popa B, 'What's Wrong with the Romanian New Wave? Auteur Cinema, the Communist and the Production of the Violent Working Class' (2018) 9(1) Studies in Eastern European Cinema 89–102

Popa B, *Queer De-Centering Queer Theory Communist Sexuality in the Flow During and After the Cold War* (Manchester UP 2021)

Preece J (ed), *The Cambridge Companion to Kafka* (CUP 2002)

Puiu C, 'I Wanted This Character to Be Me – "Viorel, c'est moi!"' Interview by Adam Popescu, Evenimentul Zilei (2000) <https://evz.ro/am-vrut-ca-personajul-asta-sa-fiu-eu-viorel-cest-moi-895031.html> accessed 12 April 2024

Roddick N, 'Eastern Promise' (October 2007) 17(10) Sight & Sound 36–39

Scott AO, 'New Wave on the Black Sea' *The New York Times Magazine* (2008) accessed 21 January 2024

Tulbure C, 'Mobility and Post-Socialism: Cross-Border Shaming and Un-Belonging in a White Europe' (2022) 11(1) State Crime Journal 110–27

Turcus C, 'The Reception of the New Romanian Cinema and Cristi Puiu's *Aurora*' in A Gorzo and A State (eds), *Politics of Cinema: Contributions to the Interpretation of Contemporary Romanian Cinema* (Tact 2014) 111–34

Turcus C, *Against Memory: From the Socialist Aestheticism to the New Romanian Cinema* (Editura EIKON 2017)

Ungureanu C, 'Socialist Cinema, Gender, and the Robot Revolution: Ion Popescu Gopo's *Galax, the Doll-Man* (1984) Beyond Utopia and Dystopia' (2023) 4 Studies in European Cinema 98–112

Ungureanu C, 'Derrida's Tense Bow' (2013) 18(6) *The European Legacy* 727–39

Wallerstein I, *World-Systems Analysis: An Introduction* (Duke UP 2004) and *European Universalism: The Rhetoric of Power* (The New Press 2006)

White R, 'Cristi Puiu Discusses Aurora' (2010) 64(2) Film Quarterly 5–7

Chapter 9

Revitalising the Law

An Existentialist Take on Law and Film

Louis Hill

Introduction

It has become increasingly common in legal academia to turn to films and series.[1] There are plenty of good reasons a legal academic may do so: it could be to better grasp and criticise the collective legal consciousness[2] which is embedded and diffused in and through movies, to illustrate a legal concept

1 In France, for instance, a significant number of law and cinema books were published between 2017 and 2023: see, e.g., Fabrice Defferard (ed), *Le droit saisi par la Science-Fiction* (Mare & Martin 2017); Arnaud Coutant, *Les lois d'Alfred Hitchcock* (Mare & Martin 2018); Valère Ndior and Nicolas Rousseau (eds), *Le droit dans la saga Harry Potter* (Enrick B. Editions 2019); Quentin Le Pluard and Peran Plouhinec, *Du droit dans Game of Thrones* (Mare & Martin 2019); Fabrice Defferrard, *La pensée juridique de Sheldon Cooper: Ou Comment faire du droit avec the Big Bang Theory* (Mare & Martin 2019); Magalie Flores-Lonjou, Estelle Épinoux and Vincent Lefebvre, *Frontière(s) au cinéma* (Mare & Martin 2019); Quentin Le Pluard and Marion Talbot (dir), *Du droit dans Disney* (Mare & Martin 2020) Raphaël Maurel (ed), *Le droit dans la saga Jurassic Park* (Enrick B. Editions 2021); Alexandre Ciaudo, Yannick Lécuyer and Anne-Laure Mosbrucker (eds), *Le droit contre-attaque: L'univers Star Wars au prisme du droit* (Presses Universitaires de Franche-Comté 2021); Fabrice Defferard, *Les lois de Michel Audiard: Liberté, Fraternité, Égalité* (Mare & Martin 2021); Caroline Cornella, Pauline de Bilbao and Rosalie Le Moing (eds), 'The Handmaid's Tale et le Droit International Public' (2023) 3 Les Cahiers de l'IEDEC <http://ediec.univ-lyon3.fr/fileadmin/medias/Documents_EDIEC/Publications/Cahiers_de_l_EDIEC/Actes_colloque_THT_et_DIP_Cahier_3_01.pdf> accessed 1 February 2024; Raphaël Maurel, *Le droit dans le seigneur des anneaux* (Enrick B. Editions 2023).

2 See, e.g., Marie-Anne Frison-Roche, 'Droit et cinéma. Livret de séminaire' (2015) MAFR <https://mafr.fr/en/article/droit-et-cinema-livret-de-seminaire-printemps-2015> accessed 1 February 2024: "Reprenant l'affirmation de Savigny . . . selon laquelle le droit exprime l'esprit d'un peuple, on peut songer qu'il en est de même des représentations que les cinémas nationaux font du droit, exprimant à travers celui leur propre esprit juridique, plus ou moins conscient" ("As Savigny asserted . . . that the law expresses the spirit of the people, so too do national cinemas' représentations of law express their own, more or less conscious, legal spirit") (author's translation); see also Maurel, *Le droit dans la saga Jurassic Park* (n 1) 24.

DOI: 10.4324/9781003461180-9

or principle when teaching or writing,[3] to fish for new ideas related to law (by thinking of new legal technologies, utopias, or dystopias, for instance),[4] or to better understand some legal phenomena by shedding new light on them.[5] These goals are well known and all seem worth undertaking. However, the turn to cinema is therein treated as a question of methods, rather than as a question of existence. Yet it is not uncommon for lawyers to claim that resorting to movies brings a little fun into the "daily lives of lawyers".[6] But this claim is not taken seriously. It is formulated as a mere biographical anecdote. In this chapter, I would like to take it more seriously. The idea is to situate the discussion on law and film at a more intimate level: What is it in films that captivates lawyers? Or we could take a more provocative perspective and ask what it is about law that makes lawyers look away from it.[7] The aim of this chapter is to provide the beginning of an answer to this question.

Emotions do matter in legal scholarship. Jean d'Aspremont has shown how the centrality of international organisations (IOs) stems from the feeling of "love" experienced by international legal scholars towards such IOs.[8] Likewise, in a conference held at the University of Aix-Marseille, Loïc Azoulai argued that the crisis of legitimacy that the European Union is currently facing can be studied and answered from an existential perspective. By that, he means that it is necessary to understand not only what European law does institutionally, but also how it is experienced existentially, by citizens but also by civil servants, lawyers, and legal scholars. In fact, he begins the

3 See, e.g., Olivier Lasmoles, *Le droit pénal fait son cinéma: Le droit pénal français en 62 films analysés et commentés* (LexisNexis 2022); see also See Jean-Christophe Roda, 'Propos Introductifs' in Ndior and Rousseau (n 1) 10; Maurel, *Le droit dans la saga Jurassic Park* (n 1) 22–23.

4 This is very much the approach of Fabrice Defferard: see Defferard, *Le droit saisi par la Science-Fiction* (n 1). On the critical aspects of law and cinema, see Maurel, *Le droit dans la saga Jurassic Park* (n 1) 24.

5 See, e.g., Conor Casey and David Kenny, 'How Liberty Dies in a Galaxy Far, Far Away: Star Wars, Democratic Decay, and Weak Executives' (2021) 35 Law & Literature 221. Conor Casey and David Kenny argue that three lessons related to contemporary constitutional issues may be inferred from the Star Wars saga; see also Arthur Thévenet, 'Les relations entre le gouvernement des États-Unis et la République de Gilead, un État à deux "têtes" en droit International Public' in Cornella, de Bilbabo and Le Moing (n 1) 73–91, 73: "L'oeuvre de *The Handmaid's Tale* nous rappelle combine les normes internationales sont peu efficientes lorsqu'un système interne décide de rompre avec l'État de droit et les autres valeurs contenues dans la Charte de l'ONU" ("*The Handmaid's Tale* reminds us the extent to which international rules are inefficient when a domestic legal system decides to break with the rule of law and the value contained in the UN Charter") (author's translation).

6 Roda (n 3) 9; Maurel, *Le droit dans la saga Jurassic Park* (n 1) 22.

7 Élie Aslanoff argues that what is interesting about law is its outside: see Élie Aslanoff in this volume.

8 Jean d'Aspremont, 'The Love for International Organizations' (2023) 20 International Organizations Law Review 111.

conference by asking, "What does European law do to the life of those who study and teach it?"[9] In a similar fashion, I would like to ask, "How does cinema affect the lives of those who use it in legal academia?" The governing idea is that the turn to cinema affects the way legal scholars live their own existence as legal scholars. Understanding the use of cinema by legal scholars means understanding how it affects their existence. To do so, I would like to take an existentialist perspective.

The terms "existentialist" and "existential" are used in philosophy to refer to the thought of various thinkers, such as Soren Kierkegaard, Friedrich Nietzsche, Martin Heidegger, Jean-Paul Sartre, Albert Camus, Karl Jaspers, and Maurice Merleau-Ponty.[10] What these thinkers have in common is that they endorse an approach "that takes as its starting point the individual's existence".[11] That means the existentialist will tend to seize reality not as an object that can be known but as something that affects and transforms the subject.[12] In other words, existentialists do not accept the distinction between the object and the subject. They thus strive to understand what human existence is by elucidating its meaning,[13] its temporality,[14] and its absurdity.[15] These may seem like traditional themes, but they are dealt with in a very fresh manner; existentialists take into account the subjective components that shape one's perception of reality. For instance, Karl Jasper believes that the task of philosophy is to "catch sight of reality at its origin and to grasp it through the way in which I, in thought, deal with myself".[16] Existentialism, in the wide sense explored here, focuses on the attitudes, emotions, and perspectives that shape the way the subject constitutes or deals with reality. As Albert Camus writes: "Great feelings take with them their own universe, splendid or abject. They light up with their passion an exclusive world in which they recognize their climate". Camus adds that there is thus "a universe of jealousy, of ambition, of selfishness or of generosity".[17] In life,

9 Loïc Azoulai, 'Le droit de l'Union européenne comme mode de vie' (2017) Aix-Marseille <https://amupod.univ-amu.fr/video/0646-conference-cejm-le-droit-de-lunion-europeenne-comme-mode-de-vie-pr-loic-azoulai/> accessed 28 September 2023.

10 Steven Earnshaw, *Existentialism: A Guide for the Perplexed* (Continuum 2006) 1; Richard Gravil, *Existentialism* (Humanities-Ebooks 2007); Jack Reynolds, *Understanding Existentialism* (Routledge 2006) 1–2.

11 Earnshaw (n 10) 1; André Lalande, *Vocabulaire technique et critique de la philosophie* (4th edn, vol. 1, Presses Universitaires de France 1997) 319.

12 Lalande, ibid 320.

13 See how Jean Grondin, one of the main commentators on Hans-Georg Gadamer, has applied the latter's philosophy to investigating the meaning of human existence: see Jean Grondin, *Du sens de la vie* (Bellarmin 2003).

14 See, e.g., Martin Heidegger, *Being and Time* (Harper Perennial Modern Classics 2008).

15 See, e.g., Albert Camus, *The Myth of Sisyphus* (Penguin 2005; 2nd edn, Justin O'Brien tr).

16 Karl Jaspers, *Philosophy of Existence* (U of Pennsylvania P 1971) 3.

17 Camus (n 15) 9.

it is true that our emotions, feelings, values, and wishes affect how we, as human beings, experience the universe around us. As Ralph Waldo Emerson argues, "Nature always wears the colours of the spirit"'.[18] For the person who has lost a friend, "the sky is less grand as it shuts down over less worth in the population".[19] This echoes Camus's idea, according to which every feeling generates its own universe. The universe Camus attempts to unveil and discuss in *The Myth of Sisyphus* is that of the absurd. He engages with the absurdity of life as a subjective experience. Camus focuses on the universe of the one who feels existence as absurd, and part of his task at the beginning of the book is to share this feeling with the reader. This move from objective reality to subjective reality is shared by other existentialists, although in various forms and concerning various topics. Existentialist literature is sometimes very difficult to read as it presents an inherently intuitive, literary, sometimes poetic style. It is this style, based on the refusal to separate the object's being from the subject's existence, which define the existentialist outlook in the wide sense used here.

In this chapter, I will investigate, from an existentialist perspective, what resorting to cinema does to the life of legal scholars. The piece is not to be understood as a historical, sociological, or anthropological study. I have not conducted interviews, nor have I analysed legal discourses in an attempt to give an account of how legal scholars understand their own use of cinema.[20] I build on my own experience to understand what cinema does to the existence of legal scholars.[21] More precisely, I will argue that it is a revitalisation factor. The chapter begins by defining what is meant by "revitalisation". It literally means giving new life to something. But what does it mean to give new life to legal scholarship by resorting to cinema? After answering this question, I will defend the main claim of this chapter: resorting to cinema revitalises the existence of legal scholars. The chapter ends with concluding remarks on the importance of revitalising legal scholarship. I argue that it is not just a matter of doing research happily but also of thinking critically.

18 Ralph Waldo Emerson, *Nature* (James Munroe and Company 1836) 14.
19 Ralph Waldo Emerson, *Nature* (James Munroe and Company 1836) 14.
20 In that sense, what I am doing is a little different from what Jean d'Aspremont or Loïc Azoulai are doing in international and European law. They analyse legal discourses to give an account of what legal scholars actually feel. For instance, Loïc Azoulai explicitly builds from the work of the American anthropologist Clifford Geertz: see Azoulai (n 9).
21 The overarching framework belongs to the field of phenomenology. For an example of how phenomenology can be used in legal scholarship, see Duncan Kennedy, 'Freedom and Constraint in Adjudication: A Critical Phenomenology' (1986) 36 Journal of Legal Education 518: "This paper attempts to describe the process of legal reasoning as I imagine I might do it if I were a judge". On the critical potential of phenomenology, see Vincent Forray and Sébastien Pimont, *Décrire le droit . . . et le transformer: Essai sur la décriture du droit* (Dalloz 2017) 92–105.

Defining Revitalisation

Revitalisation literally means to give new life to something or someone. But what is the meaning of the word "life"? I borrow the concept from Friedrich Nietzsche. In his essay *On the Use and Abuse of History for Life*,[22] originally published in 1874, he uses the notion of "life" to criticise German historicism, which was highly influential at the time. According to Nietzsche, the excessive use of history tended to disconnect Germans from life. He does not explicitly state what he means by "life", although he does attempt to loosely clarify the notion by describing it as "the dim driving force that insatiably desires . . . itself".[23] This sentence is not very helpful in understanding what Nietzsche means by "life". It is thus necessary to look into his reasoning.[24]

In this essay, he argues that, although history can be of great service to life, its abuse disconnects men from life. According to him, history is useful when human beings direct it towards the present, its needs, and its impulses. More precisely, Nietzsche discusses three services that history can provide to life. It can provide examples of heroes and models who may inspire humans ("monumental history", as Nietzsche calls it); it can serve a critical purpose by showing the contingency in history and enable free individuals to break from tradition ("critical history"); it may promote a sense of familiarity in the world by leading individuals to understand the present as the result of historical processes that bind a community as a whole as one spirit ("conservative history"). For Nietzsche, each of these uses of history is correct and useful. But they may also, each in its own way, disconnect human beings from the present. Such a disconnection is the main object of Nietzsche's essay. He argues that history, as the term was used in Germany in the middle of the nineteenth century, tends to disconnect individuals from "life". Historical knowledge had become, according to him, an end in itself. Historical facts were accumulated in a constant flux of books, encyclopaedias, articles, etc.

22 Friedrich Nietzsche, *On the Use and Abuse of History for Life* (Grapevine India Publishers 2022).

23 Friedrich Nietzsche, *On the Use and Abuse of History for Life* (Grapevine India Publishers 2022) 23.

24 Nietzsche does use the concept later in *Human, All too Human* (Helen Zimmern tr, Prometheus 2008), *The Dawn of Day* (John McFarland Kennedy tr, CreateSpace Independent Publishing Platform 2017), and *The Gay Science* (Thomas Common tr, Dover Publications 2006). But, in these books, he seems to refer to a struggle between all things (cells, thoughts, impulses). See Dorian Astor (ed), *Dictionnaire Nietzsche* (Robert Laffont 2017) 929. This meaning of "life" is present in the essay *On the Use and Abuse of History for Life*; he describes great men who make good use of history as "fighter[s]" while weak men get the feeling, when confronted by history, that to know is to be as detached as possible and thus lose sight of their own legend: see Nietzsche (n 22) 46. But this definition of life as struggle is not dominant in this essay. It remains necessary to explore its meaning by dwelling on Nietzsche's reasoning.

However, this knowledge can never be "digested",[25] in the sense that it can never inspire new impulses, wishes, needs, actions, or events. This reminds me of the main character in *Everything, Everywhere, All at Once*,[26] who gains knowledge of everything in every possible universe but who initially is discouraged, disenchanted, and depressed, rather than inspired by this omniscient view of the world. According to Nietzsche, individuals often accumulate facts without being transformed by the knowledge being acquired.[27] The facts remain dead, and the historian becomes a mere accumulator. As a result, knowledge and action separate. This, according to Nietzsche, has dramatic consequences for modern culture. One of these consequences is the separation that modern individuals make between their interior lives (the realm of thought) and their exterior lives (the realm of action). According to Nietzsche, such a separation creates a lifeless exterior. Individuals conform to habit and social conventions rather than living according to their own inner impulses and wishes. The excess of history also creates a futile interior life: inner beliefs and desires are without consequences in the sense they do not inspire action. Nietzsche writes:

> It seems impossible for a strong full chord to be prolonged, however powerfully strings are swept: it dies away again the next moment in the soft and strengthless echo of history. . . . One may bring the greatest and most marvellous thing to perfection; it must yet go down to Orcus unhonoured and unsung. For art flies away when you are roofing your deeds with the historical awning.[28]

With the abuse of history vanishes the very possibility that an event can be transformative. As soon as it occurs, it is turned into history, that is as a mere fact that can be accumulated and exchanged between lifeless individuals, who have become "wandering encyclopaedias".[29] Nietzsche's reasoning

25 Nietzsche does use the concept later in *Human, All too Human* (Helen Zimmern tr, Prometheus 2008), *The Dawn of Day* (John McFarland Kennedy tr, CreateSpace Independent Publishing Platform 2017), and *The Gay Science* (Thomas Common tr, Dover Publications 2006). But, in these books, he seems to refer to a struggle between all things (cells, thoughts, impulses). See Dorian Astor (ed), *Dictionnaire Nietzsche* (Robert Laffont 2017) 929. This meaning of "life" is present in the essay *On the Use and Abuse of History for Life*; he describes great men who make good use of history as "fighter[s]" while weak men get the feeling, when confronted by history, that to know is to be as detached as possible and thus lose sight of their own legend: see Nietzsche (n 22) 46. But this definition of life as struggle is not dominant in this essay. It remains necessary to explore its meaning by dwelling on Nietzsche's reasoning 26–27.

26 Daniel Kwan and Daniel Scheinert, *Everything, Everywhere, All at Once* (139 minutes, AGBO 2022).

27 Nietzsche (n 22) 26.

28 Nietzsche (n 22) 31–32.

29 Nietzsche (n 22) 27.

provides us with a good definition of "life": it refers to action but not any kind of action. Nietzsche seems to praise the authentic action: that is, an action produced by the impulses, instincts, and will of the individual who is fully committed to it. He thus denounces the cynicism of his contemporaries who view everything as a contingent fact that can be studied but never as something that matters.

Nietzsche's critique of historical thought provides us with a good view of how (historical) knowledge may devitalise instead of revitalising the historian. History has become an obstacle for action, for transformative events that come from and affect authentic beings; in other words, beings who are capable of dominating their own life instead of simply enduring it. What I mean by "revitalisation" is thus the process by which something repairs the bridge between knowledge and life, as defined earlier.

The Need to Revitalise Legal Scholarship

The reason I insist on the revitalising aspects of the law and cinema movement is that legal scholarship often finds itself in need of revitalisation. If we follow the Nietzschean definition outlined earlier, this means that law as a discipline does not foster authentic action: that is, an action that stems from the inner beliefs and impulses of an individual who is fully committed to it. In other words, it can be uninspiring. Two aspects of legal scholarship may explain this.

First, legal scholarship can be devitalising, because of its historical nature. By "historical", I do not mean to refer to the use of the historical method in legal scholarship.[30] Legal scholarship has a historical character, whether we use the historical method, analogical reasoning, or the sociological method.[31] Legal scholarship can be thought of as a tradition. The notion of "legal tradition" is frequently used in comparative law[32] and history[33] to describe a set of beliefs, practices, institutions, and methods passed on through generations of lawyers. On a more concrete level, legal traditions manifest themselves through the intergenerational interpretation of inherited (authoritative)[34]

30 For an overview, see Geoffrey Samuel, *Rethinking Historical Jurisprudence* (Edward Elgard 2022); Harold J Berman, 'The Origins of Historical Jurisprudence: Coke, Selden, Hale' (1994) 103 The Yale Law Journal 1651.

31 For an overview of each method and how judges use them, see Benjamin N Cardozo, *The Nature of the Judicial Process* (Yale UP 1921).

32 See, e.g., Patrick Glenn, *Legal Traditions of the World* (4th edn, OUP 2010); Duncan Fairgrieve and Horatia Muir Watt, *Common law et tradition civiliste: Convergence ou divergence* (Presses Universitaires de France 2006); John H Baker, *The Common Law Tradition: Lawyers, Books, and the Law* (Hambledon 2000).

33 Harold J Berman, *Law and Revolution: The Formation of the Western Legal Tradition* (Harvard UP 1990); Donald Kelley, *The Human Measure: Social Thought in the Western Legal Tradition* (Harvard UP 1990).

34 See Geoffrey Samuel, 'Interdisciplinarity and the Authority Paradigm: Should Law Be Taken Seriously by Scientists and Social Scientists?' (2009) 36 Journal of Law and Society 431.

texts, such as the *Corpus Iuris Civilis* for the glossators, the post glossators, and the humanists; the Civil Code for modern French lawyers; or old precedents in the common law systems. In law, these texts even have authority, in the sense that they may be studied, criticised, and interpreted, but they can never be disregarded. They are the starting point of most legal operations. The authority of tradition is, of course, not specific to law. In fact, in legal scholarship as in academia in general, students are told to continue a conversation. It is even a methodological requirement that dissertations begin with a literature review, in which the relevance of the project is shown. In academia, learning how to think like a lawyer means learning how to continue an intergenerational conversation about old texts. It is technical in the sense that it requires knowledge of the past and recognising which texts are important (which are authorities),[35] whether they are formal sources of law, like the French civil code; doctrinal authorities, such as the *Corpus Iuris Civilis*; or books of reference, such as Blackstone's commentaries[36] in English law.

This traditional character of legal scholarship creates a strong risk of devitalisation. The relevance of a given research project is, above all, evaluated in light of its ability to contribute to an ongoing conversation. This must be celebrated, in the sense that it makes the accumulation of knowledge possible and gives a social aspect to research by enabling discussions, collective projects, etc. Nonetheless, it gives priority to the past over the present and may therefore distract lawyers from life. As Nietzsche wrote about the use of history: "There is always the danger here, that everything ancient will be regarded as equally venerable, and everything without this respect for antiquity, like a new spirit, rejected as an enemy".[37] Undoubtedly, this risk is strong in legal scholarship because of its traditionalism, although this aspect is not unique to legal studies.[38] The reification of some legal categories has therefore frequently been denounced in legal scholarship. Some lawyers have, for instance, been accused of treating given legal concepts as natural things that cannot be thought otherwise or remade.[39] This shows that respect for antiquity can lead to a petrified science, as Nietzsche meant it. It also shows that this conservative attitude can, and often is, resisted in legal studies.

35 On the importance of authorities in traditions, see Hans-Georg Gadamer, 'The Rehabilitation of Authority and Tradition' in Hans-Georg Gadamer (ed), *Truth and Method* (2nd edn, Joel Weinsheimer and Donald G. Marshal trs, Continuum 2004) 277–84.

36 William Blackstone, *Commentaries on the Laws of England* (Lippincott [1765] 1893).

37 Nietzsche (n 22) 21–22.

38 Roscoe Pound, *Fashions in Juristic Thinking* (Holdsworth Club of the U of Birmingham 1937) 1: "But fashions in thought are as exacting, and sometimes as arbitrary, as fashion in dress".

39 See in particular the critique of abstraction made by François Gény and Raymond Saleilles; see Marie-Claire Belleau, 'Les juristes inquiets: Classicisme juridique et critique du droit au début du XXe siècle en France' (1999) 40 Les Cahiers de droit 507.

But legal scholarship can be devitalising in a second way. It can be excessively technical. The feeling that law is, because of its technical nature, uninspiring is, of course, widespread. In fact, the first encounter with law as an academic discipline is, for that reason, usually not a happy one, even for those who will later become great admirers of the law. In an address at Brown University in 1897, Oliver Wendell Holmes described his years at Harvard Law School as difficult years: "One found oneself plunged in a thick fog of details. . . . One doubted oneself how it could be worthy of the interest of an intelligent mind".[40] Although Holmes was later seduced, inspired, and even amazed by the functioning of the law,[41] sometimes calling it his "mistress",[42] he started his law education in a state of disenchantment.[43] Similarly, Benjamin Cardozo, who also spoke passionately[44] about the judicial process,[45] acknowledged that legal education can sometimes be uninspiring: "To the lips of eager youth comes at times the halting doubt whether law in its study and its profession can fill the need for what is highest in the yearnings of the

40 Oliver Wendell Holmes, 'Brown University – Commencement 1897' in Oliver Wendell Holmes (ed), *The Collected Legal Papers* (Dover Publications 2007) 164.

41 See, e.g., Oliver Wendell Holmes, 'Law in Science and Science in Law' (1899) 12 Harvard Law Review 443, 446–47: "[The development of the law of torts] is like the niggardly uninventiveness of nature in its other manifestations, with its few smells or colors or types, its short list of elements, working along in the same slow way from compound to compound until the dramatic impressiveness of the most intricate compositions, which we call organic life, makes them seem different in kind from the elements out of which they are made, when set opposite to them in direct contrast".

42 Oliver Wendell Holmes, 'The Law' in Oliver Wendell Holmes (ed), *Collected Legal Papers* (n 40) 26: "[T]his abstraction called the Law, wherein, as in a magic mirror, we see reflected, not only our own lives, but the lives of all men that have been! When I think on this majestic theme my eyes dazzle. If we are to speak of the law as our mistress, we who are here know that she is a mistress only to be wooed with sustained and lonely passion – only to be won by straining all the faculties by which man is likest to a god".

43 It is interesting to note that although Holmes, as one of the forerunners of American realism, often reduced legal rules to instruments of public policy, he still had a very enchanted perspective on the common law tradition. He thus predates the divide between "thinkers who adhere to a disenchanted, instrumentalist, and secularized view of the law and theoreticians who try to reenchant it by reintroducing a degree of magic, sacredness, and mystery into the law". See Yishai Blank, 'The Reenchantment of Law' (2011) 96 Cornell Law Review 633–34.

44 Benjamin N Cardozo, 'Our Lady of the Common Law (An Address Delivered in 1928 by the Late Justice Benjamin N. Cardozo)' (1939) 13 St. John's Law Review 231.

45 Benjamin N. Cardozo, 'The Game of the Law and Its Prizes' in Margaret E Hall (ed), *Selected Writings of Benjamin Nathan Cardozo: The Choice of Tycho Brahe* (Fallon Publications 1947) 414, 417: "It is in truth a fascinating process, baffling, elusive, infinite in the variety of its aspects, and yet infinite also in its appeal to the heart and mind and spirit of generous and ambitious youth".

human spirit".[46] Law often presents itself, at least to the first-year law student, as something a little "dry".[47] Because of this dryness, law can be uninspiring.

To see how legal technicalities can make legal scholarship uninspiring, it is necessary to better understand what we mean when we say that law is "technical". It is first and foremost because of its odd language. Undoubtedly, lawyers use words that differ in and of themselves or in their use from ordinary language. This has been studied[48] and often criticised.[49] Legal language is, to a great extent, different from ordinary language. This difference has been admirably portrayed in a Netflix series called *Maid*.[50] It tells the story of a young mother who attempts to escape a situation of domestic violence. In her quest for freedom, she is repeatedly confronted with legal language: for instance, when she applies to live in a women's shelter and when she is sued by her husband for full custody of her child. In these instances, filmed from the subjective viewpoint of the young mother, the sentences uttered by those who speak legalese are replaced by sentences solely formed by the word "legal" to underline the inaccessibility of legal language to the "man [or woman] on the underground".[51]

This disconnection between legal language and ordinary language stems not only from the development and continued existence of a special cast of individuals in charge of studying, interpreting, and teaching the law[52] but also, and foremost, from the fact that they use a strange language. To understand how legal technique can devitalise legal scholarship, it is, therefore,

46 Benjamin Cardozo, 'Mr. Justice Holmes' in Hall (n 47) 77.

47 The term is, for instance, used by the French comparatist Édouard Lambert to describe the comparative study of legislation when it is taught in an ahistorical manner: see Édouard Lambert, 'Une réforme necessaire des études de droit civil' (1900) 40 Revue internationale de l'enseignement 216, 243: "It is impossible, indeed, to reduce this teaching to a dry analysis of the principles of common legislation". ("Il est impossible en effet de réduire cet enseignement à une sèche analyse des principes du *droit commun législatif*") (author's translation).

48 On the issue of legal language's technicality, see, e.g., Peter Tiersma, *Legal Language* (The U of Chicago P 1999); James Boyd White, *Justice as Translation* (The U of Chicago P 1994); Frederick Schauer, 'Is Law a Technical Language' [2015] San Diego Law Review 501; Elisabeth Mertz, *The Language of Law School: Learning to 'Think Like a Lawyer'* (OUP 2007).

49 See, e.g., Jeremy Bentham, 'Thirteenth Device: Fiction' in Jeremy Bentham (ed), *Rationale of Judicial Evidence* (Fred B. Rothman & Co [1927] 1995); David Melinkoff, *The Language of the Law* (Brown and Company 1963). For a study on the mystification effect of legal grammar, see Robert P Charrow and Veda R Charrox, 'Making Legal Language Understandable: A Psycholinguistic Study of Jury Instructions' (1979) 79 Columbia Law Review 1306; Christopher Williams, 'Legal English and Plain Language: An Introduction' (2004) 1 ESP Across Cultures 111.

50 Molly Smith Metzler, *Maid* (Netflix 2021).

51 See *Woodland v Swimming Teachers Association* [2014] AC 537, 586.

52 Friedrich Carl von Savigny, *Of the Vocation of Our Age for Legislation and Jurisprudence* (Abraham Hayward tr, The Lawbook Exchange [1831] 2002) 28: "Law is henceforth more artificial and complex, since it has a twofold life; first, as part of the aggregate existence of the community, which it does not cease to be; and, secondly, as a distinction branch of knowledge in the hand of the jurists".

necessary to specify how legal language, as a technical language, comes to differ from ordinary language. One way to look at it is to see law as a mere code: that is, a set of linguistic conventions that are themselves expressed in ordinary language.[53] According to this view, learning legal language means learning definitions and not, as is the case of natural language, using words in social contexts.[54]

This devitalises law in the sense that it is intended to make legal concepts univocal. Of course, this is an impossible task since definitions use terms that must, in turn, be defined.[55] Making legal language unambiguous is infinite and, thus, impossible. Nonetheless, by providing formal definitions and attempting to reduce linguistic complexity – for instance, by using quantitative objectives and standards[56] – the attention of legal actors is redirected. Instead of focusing on the ethical, political, philosophical, and cultural determinants of one's ordinary understanding of a given term, which may need to be criticised, lawyers are led to ignore these determinants by focusing instead on the long list of items that are supposed to define a given concept. It is not that the definition succeeds in lifting ambiguity but that the very fact of providing a formal definition tends to lead lawyers to adopt a conventional understanding of a given word, concept, or rule. This devitalises legal thinking to the extent that it leads the lawyer to interpret the law not according to the necessities of the present but according to mathematical beauty.[57] The law is then "dealt with as if it contained only the axioms and corollaries of a book of mathematics".[58]

The trouble is not that law in itself does not resonate with life. After all, law as a discipline and a social practice is full of life. Disputes are very lively,[59] and the interpretation of legal rules, which are to be applied to the facts, has a strong cultural and ideological dimension.[60] Legal reasoning is,

53 See, e.g., Peter Tiersma, 'Some Myths About Legal Language' (2006) 2 Culture and the Humanities 29, 48: "In sum, it would be a gross mischaracterization to suggest that lawyers have a language of their own".

54 On the idea that meaning is established in context, see Stanley Cavell's interpretation of Wittgenstein's philosophy: Stanley Cavell, *The Claim of Reason: Wittgenstein, Skepticism, Morality, and Tragedy* (OUP 1999).

55 See Forray and Pimont (n 21), 215–16.

56 On the rise of a new kind of governance based on an imaginary of calculus, see Alain Supiot, *Governance by Numbers: The Making of a Legal Model of Allegiance* (Hart 2017).

57 This would go against the pragmatism of common law thinking: see Geoffrey Samuel and Pierre Legrand, *Introduction au Common Law* (La Découverte 2008) 75–76.

58 Oliver Wendell Holmes, *The Common Law* (Harvard UP [1881] 2009) 3.

59 Rudolph von Jhering, *The Struggle for Law* (John J Lalor tr, The Lawbook Exchange 1997) 28–29: "It is not a mere money-interest which urges the person whose rights have been infringed to institute legal proceedings, but moral pain at the wrong which has been endured. He is not concerned simply with recovering the object. . . . An inner voice tells him that he should not retreat, that it is not the worthless object that is at stake but his own personality, his feeling of legal right, his self-respect".

60 On the ideological dimension of learning legal language, see Mertz (n 48) 73.

to a great extent, about framing facts, giving narratives,[61] exchanging policy arguments,[62] and imagining hypothetical, sometimes even counterfactual, situations.[63] In that sense, legal reasoning requires the lawyer to be imaginative, engaged, committed: that is, alive in the Nietzschean sense of life outlined earlier. However, in treating legal language as a code, the attention of the lawyer shifts away from the lively aspects of legal reasoning. This statement echoes Savigny's critique of the adoption of a civil code in Germany in 1814. Savigny argues:

> For the code, by its novelty, its connection with the prevailing notions of the age, and its external influence, will infallibly attract all attention to itself, away from the real law-authority; so that the latter, left in darkness and obscurity, will derive no assistance from the moral energies of the nation, by which alone it can attain to a satisfactory state.[64]

In a similar fashion, by treating legal language as a code, lawyers are pushed to repress their own subjective "moral energies" – that is, their personal feelings, emotions, images, memories, beliefs, wishes, preferences – that a legal concept may provoke or summon. The code separates the subjective from the objective, the personal from the impersonal. Lawyers cease to see their activity as an extension of their inner life. Furthermore, when one's attention is focused on the mastery of a code, one ceases to be open to something transformative. A good way to explain this idea is to think of a dialogue. It is common to think of a dialogue as a transformative experience, in which one's openness is rewarded by a change of perception. This is only possible when one focuses on what is new, odd, or unsettling. *A contrario*, a narrow-minded attitude will prevent the subject from being changed by the dialogue. In fact, in these instances, we barely speak of a dialogue at all. This narrow-minded attitude is present when one is speaking through a code. As mentioned previously, the code distracts the mind from what is unsettling, misunderstood, ambiguous. As Habermas writes about the codified languages of natural sciences: "Language is separated out of its embeddedness in interactions and attains monologic

61 Geoffrey Samuel, *A Short Introduction to Judging and to Legal Reasoning* (Edward Elgard 2018) 87–90.

62 See, e.g., Ronald Dworkin, *Taking Rights Seriously* (2nd edn, Harvard UP 1978) 82–83; Peter Cane, 'Consequences in Judicial Reasoning' in Jeremy Horder (ed), *Oxford Essays in Jurisprudence* (4th edn, OUP 2000). For a good example, see *McLoughlin v O'Brian* [1983] 1 AC 410.

63 Maksymilian Del Mar, *Artefacts of Legal Inquiry: The Value of Imagination in Adjudication* (Hart 2020).

64 See Savigny (n 52) 39.

closure".[65] In other words, speaking through a code is not a dialogue but a monologue. It is thus devitalising, in a Nietzschean sense: just like the abuse of history prevents the historian from being transformed by an event, which is immediately reduced to a fact,[66] the lawyer's jargon, when reduced to a code, is used to make complex and unsettling facts fit into petrified categories.

The Revitalisation of Legal Scholarship Through Films

In light of this, I would argue that the reason lawyers turn to films, beyond the methodological (instrumental) goal being pursued, is because movies are impressive. By impressive, I do not mean to refer to *Game of Thrones*' dragons, or *Jurassic Park*'s dinosaurs; rather, I mean that movies impress images on us that we cannot escape. The only way to escape a scary or horrific scene may be to put our hands in front of our eyes. That is because movies are incredibly immersive. I would like to argue that this can be used by lawyers to (re)connect law and life.

The immersive nature of cinema is obvious to anyone who has ever watched a movie. The combination of images and music can trigger strong feelings. In addition, the way the film is shot (long shot, full shot, close shot, static shot, etc.) can help the spectator empathise with a given character by showing the story from the protagonist's perspective. Watching a movie is like being in someone else's body for a few hours. It is literally about changing one's point of view. Owing to this immersive character, cinema is transformative, not in a passive sense of being transformed, but in an active sense of acting on changed beliefs. It is thus full of life, in Nietzsche's sense.

Take, for instance, my personal experience with the movie *Okja*. It is the story of a young girl who lives on a farm that has been selected to take care of a genetically engineered animal that holds the middle between a large pig and a hippopotamus. The animal, called *Okja*,[67] is taken away from the little girl by the corporation that made it. In one of the film's more disturbing scenes, a scientist cuts a bit of flesh from the animal and puts it directly in a cooking pan. The meat looks like a sausage which would, under other circumstances, make me feel hungry. But in this context, I felt instantly repelled by the meat. The movie made me see meat as a dead animal, as Martin Gisbert would say.[68] It is transformative in that it made me want to join animal rights associations and prevented me from eating meat for several months after viewing

65 Jürgen Habermas, *Knowledge and Human Interests* (Jeremy J Shapiro tr, Beacon Press 1971) 193.

66 See n 28.

67 Bong Joon Ho, *Okja* (118 minutes, Netflix 2020).

68 Martin Gibert, *Voir son steak comme un animal mort* (Lux 2015).

the movie. The experience allowed me to align my ethical (theoretical) commitments with my inner desires, goals, and impulses.

By turning to cinema, lawyers may (re)connect law and life. This is true whatever move they are attempting to make: whether cinema is used to exemplify, to illustrate, to experiment, to analyse, or to inspire a legal idea. In any case, a legal idea is linked to something that not only exists outside the realm of legal studies ("life" in a large sense) but may also be worth living for ("life" in the Nietzschean sense outlined earlier). Such a link is to be cherished. It revitalises legal studies by giving legal ideas "consequences", as Nietzsche would put it. For instance, when teaching tort law, especially when teaching the legal rules and informal schemes[69] that govern the award of damages in France, students sometimes have the impression of learning something arid, highly technical, which will not transform them or provide meaning to existence. Yet without understanding the stakes of such rules, students may have a hard time learning, remembering, interpreting, and applying them. To highlight the importance of such rules, I often refer to *Worth*.[70] In this movie, Michael Keaton is a lawyer who is put in charge of the 9/11 victim compensation fund and has to develop a legal formula defining what is compensable damage and who can benefit from the fund. The movie shows the complexity but also the importance of the legal work being carried out by Michael Keaton. It sheds light on the values that underpin the compensation rules being established and underlines the many affects and emotions involved in the process. In other words, it provides a thick description of damage assessment. By connecting tort law to this movie, which relates to a specific compensation fund, my wish is that students will understand, not only from a theoretical viewpoint but also, more generally, from an emotional standpoint, why these rules matter – why they, for instance, would be worth fighting for.

To be clear, I am not arguing that movies enable lawyers to reconnect with real life. Obviously, lawyers have a real life of their own (most of them, at least). What I am arguing here is that movies are livelier, in a Nietzschean sense, than real life. That is because they reconnect something foreign, such as an idea, a story, an issue, a historical fact, or another point of view on reality, to the intimate: that is, one's own feelings, emotions, perspectives, preferences, etc. A good way to understand this is to think of how movies can end cognitive dissonance. Knowing something in the abstract and being ready to act on it are two different things. The historian Paul Veyne gives the example of the Dorze people, who believe that leopards are Christian

69 In France, judges use the *nomenclature Dintilhac* to calculate the amount of damages that should be awarded. It is based on a doctrinal report, written by judges and law professors. Formally, it is not legally binding.

70 Sara Colangelo, *Worth* (Anonymous Content 2020).

animals who respect the fasts imposed by the Coptic Church. Nonetheless, they still protect their cattle from leopards on fasting days. They believe two things at the same time. Similarly, Veyne argues that kids believe in Father Christmas while also believing that their parents bought their presents.[71] The point is that it is possible to believe in something while not believing in it too much. I may be fully convinced that climate change will cause famines, wars, and natural disasters, but will continue living my life without any sense of panic, even making long-term plans (buying a house by the sea, having kids, etc.). What would happen if I started to actually believe in climate change? Not as a theoretical thing that I know but as a thing that I live with. Would I build a "private apocalypse bunker"[72] like Mark Zuckerberg? In this context, watching an apocalyptic series such as *L'effondrement*[73] might be helpful. It will reconnect my abstract knowledge to my subjective life. After all, watching *Okja*[74] made me realise what I already knew: that meat is made of dead animals. Movies thus reconnect what one knows in the abstract with how one sees and lives in reality. Consequently, by resorting to movies, lawyers do more than just connecting the "law in the books" to the "law in action".[75] (Movies are probably not even the best way to do that; sociology seems more adequate.) They reconnect legal knowledge to subjective life: that is, the set of inner desires, beliefs, and attitudes one lives with and acts on. They transform abstract beliefs into beliefs that command action. They are thus revitalising in the Nietzschean sense, outlined earlier.

Concluding Remarks

Movies are often described by lawyers as tools. They help lawyers teach, study, and fish for new ideas. Nonetheless, resorting to movies in legal scholarship does more than that. As I hope to have shown, it revitalises the law by connecting abstract (legal) knowledge to subjective life. Because of the historical and technical character of legal thinking, lawyers sometimes become, like Nietzsche's historians, "wandering encyclopaedias".[76] They acquire and produce knowledge that fails to inspire and transform them. In this context, movies can be liberating. They reconnect abstract legal knowledge to "life", in a Nietzschean sense. By "life", I do not mean to refer to the "law in

71 Paul Veyne, *Les Grecs ont-ils cru à leurs mythes?* (Seuil 1983) 11.

72 Hamilton Nolan, 'Why Is Mark Zuckerberg Building a Private Apocalypse Bunker in Hawaii?' *The Guardian* (21 December 2023) <www.theguardian.com/commentisfree/2023/dec/21/mark-zuckerberg-apocalypse-bunker-hawaii> accessed 1 February 2024.

73 Guillaume Desjardins, Jérémy Bernard and Bastien Ughetto, *L'effondrement* (Canal + 2019).

74 See n 67 and accompanying text.

75 Roscoe Pound, 'Law in Books and Law in Action (1910) 44 American Law Review 12.

76 See n 29.

action"[77] or the law in "everyday life".[78] I mean to refer to the subjective life of the individual who is moved, inspired, or changed by a new experience.

The revitalising power of movies may seem anecdotical. It may be reduced to a way of being happy and feeling alive while doing legal research. This would make it a biographical issue, rather than an epistemic one. Admittedly, I argued at the beginning of the chapter that the revitalisation of the law through films is something that happens regardless of the epistemic move that one is undertaking (resorting to movies as objects of study, pedagogical tools, etc.). I argued that it was a question of existence. Nonetheless, existential issues are not without epistemic consequences. This is a well-known fact in comparative law, in which openness to alterity is paramount.[79] Such openness cannot be equated to a method.[80] It is a way of being that must be lived. Yet it does lead to better scholarship: it helps comparative lawyers avoid projecting their own categories on foreign legal cultures. Likewise, the scholar who, through cinema, is inspired by legal knowledge may conduct better legal research.

As I hope to have shown throughout this chapter, revitalised knowledge is transformative. And what is being transformed, if not seeing things differently? And what is seeing things differently, if not being critical? Although resorting to movies cannot be reduced to an epistemic move – it is an existential one – it does have epistemic consequences. The epistemic importance of existential attitudes is, in fact, something that is well known by those who enjoy watching detective series. In these series, such as *The Mentalist*,[81] *The X-Files*,[82] or *Mindhunter*,[83] it is often curiosity, faith, enchantment, or care that enable detectives like CBI consultant Patrick Jane or Special Agents Fox Mulder and Holden Ford, to solve a murder. Their acolytes, who are usually depicted as rational, technical, disenchanted detectives, would be incapable of doing so without them. It is their irrational, even obsessive interest in the case that leads them to the truth. The subjective attitudes within them, lead to the discovery of the truth that is "out there".[84] Similarly, being inspired by legal knowledge through movies improves legal research.

77 Pound (n 75).

78 For this kind of approach, see Patricia Ewick and Susan S Silbey, *The Common Place of Law: Stories from Everyday Life* (Chicago UP 1998).

79 See Pierre Legrand, '*Entendre* l'altérité' in Pierre Legrand (ed), *Le droit comparé* (Que sais-je, Presses Universitaires de France 2016).

80 Although Gadamer argued that in the social sciences, interpretation was truthful when conducted with vigilance and openness, he argued that this was not a method, despite the misleading title of his book: see Gadamer (n 35). On the refusal to call it a method, see Jean Grondin, 'Gadamer's Basic Understanding of Understanding' in Robert J Dostal (ed), *The Cambridge Companion to Gadamer* (CUP 2006).

81 Bruno Heller, *The Mentalist* (Warner Bros Television 2008–2015).

82 Chris Carter, *The X-Files* (Ten Thirteen Productions, 20th Century Fox Television 1993–2018).

83 Joe Pendall, David Fincher, and Charlize Theron, *Mindhunter* (Netflix 2017–2019).

84 I mean to allude to the famous *X-Files* (conspiracist) motto: "The truth is out there".

Reference List

Astor D (ed), *Dictionnaire Nieztsche* (Robert Laffont 2017)
Azoulai L, 'Le droit de l'Union européenne comme mode de vie' (2017) Aix-Marseille. <https://amupod.univ-amu.fr/video/0646-conference-cejm-le-droit-de-lunion-europeenne-comme-mode-de-vie-pr-loic-azoulai/> accessed 5 June 2023
Baker JH, *The Common Law Tradition: Lawyers, Books, and the Law* (Hambledon 2000)
Belleau M-C, 'Les juristes inquiets: Classicisme juridique et critique du droit au début du XXe siècle en France' (1999) 40 Les Cahiers de droit 507
Bentham J, 'Thirteenth Device: Fiction' in J Bentham (ed), *Rationale of Judicial Evidence* (Fred B. Rothman & Co 1995)
Berman HJ, 'The Origins of Historical Jurisprudence: Coke, Selden, Hale' (1994) 103 The Yale Law Journal 1651
Blackstone W, *Commentaries on the Laws of England* (Lippincott 1893)
Blank Y, 'The Reenchantment of Law' (2011) 96 Cornell Law Review 633
Boyd White J, *Justice as Translation* (U of Chicago P 1994)
Camus A, *The Myth of Sisyphus* (2nd edn, J O'Brien tr, Penguin 2005)
Cane P, 'Consequences in Judicial Reasoning' in J Horder (ed), *Oxford Essays in Jurisprudence* (4th edn, OUP 2000)
Cardozo BN, *The Nature of the Judicial Process* (Yale UP 1921)
Cardozo BN, 'Our Lady of the Common Law (An Address Delivered in 1928 by the Late Justice Benjamin N. Cardozo)' (1939) 13 ST. John's Law Review 231
Cardozo BN, 'The Game of the Law and Its Prizes' in ME Hall (ed), *Selected Writings of Benjamin Nathan Cardozo: The Choice of Tycho Brahe* (Fallon Publications 1947)
Cardozo BN, 'Mr. Justice Holmes' in ME Hall (ed), *Selected Writings of Benjamin Nathan Cardozo: The Choice of Tycho Brahe* (Fallon Publications 1947)
Carter C, *The X-Files* (Ten Thirteen Productions, 20th Century Fox Television 1993–2018)
Casey C and Kenny D, 'How Liberty Dies in a Galaxy Far, Far Away: Star Wars, Democratic Decay, and Weak Executives' (2021) 35 Law & Literature 221
Cavell SL, *The Claim of Reason: Wittgenstein, Skepticism, Morality, and Tragedy* (OUP 1999)
Charrow R and Charrox V, 'Making Legal Language Understandable: A Psycholinguistic Study of Jury Instructions' (1979) 79 Columbia Law Review 1306
Ciaudo A, Lécuyer Y and Mosbrucker A-L (eds), *Le droit contre-attaque: L'Univers Star Wars au prisme du droit* (Presses Universitaires de Franche-Comté 2021)
Colangelo S, *Worth* (Anonymous Content 2020)
Cornella C, de Bilbao P and Le Moing R (eds), 'The Handmaid's Tale et le Droit International Public' (2023) 3 Les Cahiers de l'IEDEC <http://ediec.univ-lyon3.fr/fileadmin/medias/Documents_EDIEC/Publications/Cahiers_de_l_EDIEC/Actes_colloque_THT_et_DIP_Cahier_3_01.pdf> accessed 5 June 2024
Coutant A, *Les lois d'Alfred Hitchcock* (Mare & Martin 2018)
d'Aspremont J, 'The Love for International Organizations' (2023) 20 International Organizations Law Review 111
Defferard F (ed), *Le droit saisi par la Science-Fiction* (Mare & Martin 2017)
Defferard F (ed), *La pensée juridique de Sheldon Cooper: Ou comment faire du droit avec the Big Bang Theory* (Mare & Martin 2019)
Defferard F (ed), *Les lois de Michel Audiard: Liberté, Fraternité, Égalité* (Mare & Martin 2021)
Del Mar M, *Artefacts of Legal Inquiry: The Value of Imagination in Adjudication* (Hart 2020)
Desjardins A, Bernard J and Ughetto B, *L'effondrement* (Canal + 2019)
Dworkin R, *Taking Rights Seriously* (2nd edn, Harvard UP 1978)

Earnshaw S, *Existentialism: A Guide for the Perplexed* (Continuum 2006)
Emerson RW, *Nature* (James Munroe and Company 1836)
Ewick P and Silbey SS, *The Common Place of Law: Stories from Everyday Life* (Chicago UP 1998)
Fairgrieve D and Muir Watt H, *Common Law et Tradition Civiliste: Convergence ou Divergence* (Presses Universitaires de France 2006)
Flores-Lonjou M, Épinoux E and Lefebvre V, *Frontière(s) au cinéma* (Mare & Martin 2019)
Forray V and Pimont S, *Décrire le droit . . . et le transformer: Essai sur la décriture du droit* (Dalloz 2017)
Frison-Roche M-A, 'Droit et cinéma: Livret de séminaire' (2015) MAFR <https://mafr.fr/en/article/droit-et-cinema-livret-de-seminaire-printemps-2015> accessed 5 June 2024
Gadamer H-G, 'The Rehabilititation of Authority and Tradition' in H-G Gadamer (ed), *Truth and Method* (2nd edn, J Weinsheimer and D Marshal trs, Continuum 2004)
Gadamer H-G, *Truth and Method* (2nd edn, J Weinsheimer and D Marshal trs, Continuum 2004)
Gisbert M, *Voir son steak comme un animal mort* (Lux 2015)
Glenn PH, *Legal Traditions of the World* (4th edn, OUP 2010)
Grondin J, *Du sens de la vie* (Bellarmin 2003)
Grondin J, 'Gadamer's Basic Understanding of Understanding' in RJ Dostal (ed), *The Cambridge Companion to Gadamer* (CUP 2006)
Habermas J, *Knowledge and Human Interests* (J Shapiro tr, Beacon Press 1971)
Heidegger M, *Being and Time* (Harper Perennial Modern Classics 2008)
Heller B, *The Mentalist* (Warner Bros Television 2008–2015)
Holmes OW, 'Law in Science and Science in Law' (1899) 12 Harvard Law Review 443
Holmes OW, 'Brown University – Commencement 1897' in OW Holmes (ed), *The Collected Legal Papers* (Dover Publications 2007)
Holmes OW, 'The Law' in O Wendell Holmes (ed), *Collected Legal Papers* (Dover Publications 2007)
Holmes OW, *Collected Legal Papers* (Dover Publications 2007)
Holmes OW, *The Common Law* (Harvard UP 2009)
Jaspers K, *Philosophy of Existence* (U of Pennsylvania P 1971)
Jhering R, *The Struggle for Law* (JH Lalor tr, The Lawbook Exchange 1997)
Joon Ho B, *Okja* (118 Minutes, Netflix 2020)
Kelley D, *The Human Measure: Social Thought in the Western Legal Tradition* (Harvard UP 1990)
Kennedy D, 'Freedom and Constraint in Adjudication: A Critical Phenomenology' (1986) 36 Journal of Legal Education 518
Kwan D and Scheinert D, *Everything, Everywhere, All at Once* (139 Minutes, AGBO 2022)
Lalande A, *Vocabulaire technique et critique de la philosophie* (4th edn, vol. 1, Presses Universitaires de France 1997)
Lambert É, 'Une réforme necessaire des études de droit civil' (1900) 40 Revue internationale de l'enseignement 216
Lasmoles O, *Le droit pénal fait son cinéma: Le droit pénal français en 62 films analysés et commentés* (LexisNexis 2022)
Legrand P, '*Entendre* l'altérité' in P Legrand (ed), *Le droit comparé* (Presses Universitaires de France 2016)
Le Pluard Q and Plouhinec P, *Du droit dans Game of Thrones* (Mare & Martin 2019)
Le Pluard Q and Talbot M (eds), *Du droit dans Disney* (Mare & Martin 2020)
Maurel R (ed), *Le droit dans la saga Jurassic Park* (Enrick B. Editions 2021)

Maurel R (ed), *Le droit dans le seigneur des anneaux* (Enrick B. Editions 2023)
McLoughlin v O'Brian [1983] 1 AC 410
Melinkoff D, *The Language of the Law* (Brown and Company 1963)
Mertz E, *The Language of Law School: Learning to 'Think like a Lawyer'* (OUP 2007)
Metzler MS, *Maid* (Netflix 2021)
Ndior V and Rousseau N (eds), *Le droit dans la saga Harry Potter* (Enrick B. Editions 2019)
Nieztsche F, *The Gay Science* (T Common tr, Dover Publications 2006)
Nieztsche F, *Human, All too Human* (H Zimmern tr, Prometheus 2008)
Nieztsche F, *The Dawn of Day* (JM Kennedy tr, CreateSpace Independent Publishing Platform 2017)
Nieztsche F, *On the Use and Abuse of History for Life* (Grapevine India Publishers 2022)
NolanH, 'Why Is Mark Zuckerberg Building a Private Apocalypse Bunker in Hawaii?' *The Guardian* (21 December 2023) <www.theguardian.com/commentisfree/2023/dec/21/mark-zuckerberg-apocalypse-bunker-hawaii> accessed 5 June 2024
Pendall J, Fincher D and Theron C, *Mindhuter* (Netflix 2017–2019)
Pound R, 'Law in Books and Law in Action' (1910) 44 American Law Review 12
Pound R, *Fashions in Juristic Thinking* (Holdsworth Club of the U of Birmingham 1937)
Roda J-C, 'Propos Introductifs' in V Ndior and N Rousseau (eds), *Le droit dans la saga Harry Potter* (Enrick B. Editions 2019)
Samuel G, 'Interdisciplinarity and the Authority Paradigm: Should Law Be Taken Seriously by Scientists and Social Scientists?' (2009) 36 Journal of Law and Society 431
Samuel G, *A Short Introduction to Judging and to Legal Reasoning* (Edward Elgard 2018)
Samuel G, *Rethinking Historical Jurisprudence* (Edward Elgard 2022)
Samuel G and Legrand P, *Introduction au Common Law* (La Découverte 2008)
Savigny FC, *Of the Vocation of Our Age for Legislation and Jurisprudence* (A Hayward tr, The Lawbook Exchange 2002)
Schauer F, 'Is Law a Technical Language' [2015] San Diego Law Review 501
Thévenet A, 'Les relations entre le gouvernement des États-Unis et la République de Gilead, un État à deux "têtes" en droit International Public' in C Cornella, P de Bilbabo and R Le Moing (eds), 'The Handmaid's Tale et le Droit international public' (2023) 3 Les Cahiers de l'IEDEC <http://ediec.univ-lyon3.fr/fileadmin/medias/Documents_EDIEC/Publications/Cahiers_de_l_EDIEC/Actes_colloque_THT_et_DIP_Cahier_3_01.pdf>accessed 5 June 2024
Tiersma P, *Legal Language* (U of Chicago P 1999)
Tiersma P, 'Some Myths About Legal Language' (2006) 2 Culture and the Humanities 29
Veyne P, *Les Grecs ont-ils cru à leurs mythes?* (Seuil 1983)
Williams C, 'Legal English and Plain Language: An Introduction' (2004) 1 ESP Across Cultures 111
Woodland v Swimming Teachers Association [2014] AC 537

Chapter 10

Lost Horizons, or How to Lose More Slowly

Geoffrey Samuel

Introduction: Welcome to LA (Losers Anonymous)

There are many ways to classify films. Two of the most dominant are by author – considered to be the director – and by genre, this latter by definition being very general in its employment of categories like the Western, the musical, *film noir*, and so on. Another standard approach is cinema by country. The late and great (but still largely ignored by those who write often rather unoriginal books on the "philosophy" or "theory" of cinema) Raymond Durgnat (1932–2002), before anyone else, brought a whole new taxonomical dimension to cinema studies.[1] He sometimes took a standard generic category such as *film noir* and broke it down into a range of different, often socially orientated species, and sometimes he employed a completely new category such as populism. He never got round to classifying films around losers, but it might have been a focal point that would have interested him (or particular kinds of losers might have been of interest). One can certainly imagine him writing on this topic in one of his *Films and Filming* or *Film Comment* articles. (He mostly kept clear of *Sight & Sound*.) This present chapter, then, is offered in the spirit of Durgnat, although it comes nowhere near to capturing his extraordinarily insightful, free-thinking, and pioneering contribution to cinema studies.[2]

Professor Pierre Legrand has suggested that anyone who is serious about pursuing comparative law – or better, comparative legal studies – is doomed

1 On Raymond Durgnat, see Henry Miller (ed), *The Essential Raymond Durgnat* (Palgrave Macmillan & British Film Institute 2014).

2 See, e.g., Raymond Durgnat, *A Mirror for England* (Faber & Faber 1970) (Reprinted as a 2nd edn with a Forward by Kevin Gough-Yates); Raymond Durgnat, *A Mirror for England* (BFI/Palgrave Macmillan 2011); Raymond Durgnat, *Sexual Alienation in the Cinema* (Studio Vista 1972); Raymond Durgnat, *The Strange Case of Alfred Hitchcock* (Faber & Faber 1974); Raymond Durgnat, 'Genre: Populism and Social Realism' (1975) 11(4) Film Comment. This is just a short selection from his many publications.

DOI: 10.4324/9781003461180-10

to fail.[3] Can she or he ever really know the law of the other? His point is this: a comparative lawyer formed within one legal culture can only come to another legal culture through the mentality of their own legal mentality. One can try hard, guided by the utmost good faith, to step outside of this home culture and mentality, but, in the end, one can only make sense of the other by reference to one's own understanding of law. Referencing Samuel Beckett, one is talking about the "unfailing failure to understand".[4] And so "one must resign oneself to one's cognitive limits"; one must learn to "fail better".[5] Indeed, moving beyond comparative law itself, is not every thesis, article, and monograph on legal theory or in defence of this or that aspect of legal scholarship simply an example of work doomed to fail? Theorists are model builders, and models are nothing but frameworks to interpret data. Moreover "all models are wrong", and they are wrong "precisely because they are not reality".[6] Consequently, there is no universally accepted or "true" theory of law because such a theory belongs to the world of fiction. No theory covers the whole gambit of legal knowledge. All one can hope to achieve, at least as far as comparative law is concerned, again according to Legrand, is to fail better.[7] Can the comparatist and the jurist find relief, then, eating popcorn in the cinema, watching some of the classic movies about losing? Probably not. But films about losers, if they have depth, might at least provoke interpretative reflection.

The world of cinema narrative is full of losers. There are movie winners, of course, but the cynical lawyer might say that most of these films are best left to non-lawyers since the lawyer knows that no one wins in law, even when they do. Cheap lawyers are cheap because they usually lose while expensive lawyers just present their clients with unimaginably high bills. An exaggerated view, no doubt, yet there are real technological threats to lawyers and jurists. As for the rich, they can buy the best lawyers, but *Citizen Kane* (1940, director Orson Welles) reminds us that even billionaires lose in the end. As for the rich lawyers themselves, they are about to become losers as their work will increasingly be taken over by artificial intelligence (AI) algorithms.[8] "Is there a way to win?" asks Kathy Moffit in *Out of the Past* (1947, director Jacques Tourneur); no, replies Jeff, there is only a "way to lose more slowly". Thanks to AI, all

3 Pierre Legrand, *Negative Comparative Law: A Strong Programme for Weak Thought* (CUP 2022).
4 Pierre Legrand, *Negative Comparative Law: A Strong Programme for Weak Thought* (CUP 2022) 35.
5 Pierre Legrand, *Negative Comparative Law: A Strong Programme for Weak Thought* (CUP 2022) 36.
6 Erica Thompson, *Escape from Model Land: How Mathematical Models Can Lead Us Astray and What We Can Do About It* (Basic Books 2022) 25.
7 Legrand (n 3) 1–46.
8 Cf Simon Deakin and Cristopher Markou (eds), *Is Law Computable? Critical Perspectives on Law and Artificial Intelligence* (Hart Publishing 2020).

lawyers and jurists, even if they do not yet know it, are slow losers. They are like those in Australia in *On the Beach* (1959, director Stanley Kramer): they are waiting for the end. Perhaps cinema, or some films at least, can help these doomed people to "fail better". Or, at least, they can ease the pain as the best of popular art can and should do. Failing that, some films show how time is often a fundamental element in the tragic journey of the loser. Has the past, with its dream of the law computer, come to reclaim the future?

A Taxonomy of Losing

How, then, might the cinema of losers help ease the pain of losing? Perhaps the main response to this question is a simple one: it is always satisfying to know that there are "good" people in worse losing positions than oneself. So, are there films about lawyers as losers? One immediately thinks of *The File on Thelma Jordan* (1950, director Robert Siodmak) or *Party Girl* (1958, director Nicholas Ray), but the moment one takes law as a thematic focal point in cinema taxonomy, one comes up against, seemingly, two problems. The first is that there are not that many films, relatively speaking, within this classification, and secondly, a good many of them are not really about losers (the present theme) as such. *Jordan* is a particular exception here, and what is also of interest is that the film falls within the classic category of post-war *film noir*. Now, if there is one generic category about losers it must surely be *films noirs*. As the UK critic Raymond Durgnat wrote in one of the leading articles on the subject, "In 1946 French critics, having missed Hollywood films for five years, saw suddenly, sharply, a darkening tone, darkest around the crime film".[9] Durgnat famously produced a taxonomy – a scientific endeavour so loved by many jurists – of *film noir* movies, but it does not include a category of losers since most of the central characters in this genre of films would fall into this class. Nevertheless, it does provide the reader with a whole range of largely empirical labels in which one can distribute the losers.

One could choose many from this family tree. However, given the loser theme, three films stand out as worth examining in detail in this genre (if it is a genre, which Durgnat disputes) of *film noir*. First, because they are all about interesting losers in their ambiguity. In *Out of the Past* (1947, director Jacques Tourneur), Jeff, the private eye, has been described as a sad and laconic dick,[10] and in *Kiss Me Deadly* (1955, director Robert Aldrich) – a film championed by Durgnat – the private eye is written off by the police in the film as a sad bedroom dick. In *The Killers* (1964, director Don Siegel), Johnny North is drawn into crime not just because of the *femme fatale* but

9 Raymond Durgnat, 'Paint It Black: The Family Tree of Film Noir' (1970) 6–7 Cinema 48–49; Raymond Durgnat, 'The Family Tree of Film Noir' (1974) 10(6) Film Comment 6.
10 Raymond Durgnat, *Films and Feelings* (Faber & Faber 1967) 144.

equally because he is a washed-up racing driver reduced to working at local stock-car racetracks.

Secondly, however, because they all take place in what might be called a totally negative legal space. One is talking here of a context in which the rule of law is absent. Or, at least, what is absent is the kind of law in the mind of the standard legal theorists (usually white, male Oxbridge or Ivy league: the "usual suspects", as one leading French jurist has wonderfully described them). A recent United Kingdom Supreme Court case has cast these people who live "outside" the law – in this case, people who want nothing to do with it – as "persons unknown".[11] Of course, in many crime films, one might observe that the law (as envisaged by the usual suspects) is often largely missing, yet it usually intrudes at some point – the police, public prosecutor, and/or prison authorities are involved at various times, or the whole narrative may involve a cop. In *Out of the Past*, *Kiss Me Deadly*, and *The Killers* the context is largely a world outside the law – people English judges would cast as "persons unknown" – although the police do have something of a presence in two of the films: a negative one in the 1947 film (a smug bore) and a useful one in the 1955 movie (helping paint the private eye as an utterly negative character). The setting of these films is one in which the world of crime and corruption is separate from "normal" life – such life wonderfully portrayed by the upstanding family menaced by robber thugs or assassins in films like *Violent Saturday* (1955, director Richard Fleischer) – and yet equally integrated into the institutions of society. They are in society, but as "persons unknown" to any legal regime, save as potential defendants in criminal proceedings. Yet one gets the impression, in these three films at least, that at some point in American society, the worlds of politics and crime are more or less one and the same (a point, of course, that comes to fruition in *The Godfather* (1972) and *The Godfather Part II* (1974), both directed by Francis Ford Coppola).

A third reason is that three films notably use the image – that is to say, the settings (racetracks, gyms, nightclubs), the architecture, the consumer goods, and so on – as an integral part of the "resonance". The protagonists might be "persons unknown", but their surroundings are by no means unfamiliar in an iconic way. Durgnat explained this of notion of resonance as follows:

> This resonance can be discussed only in moral-emotional terms. Its frame of reference is to a body of overt and covert feelings, assumptions, value-judgments, which an artist expects his spectators to share, through which he can appeal to them. Not only can he express his feelings to them, he can express their feelings for them, stimulate questions, affirmations, negations.[12]

11 *Wolverhampton City Council v London Gypsies and Travellers* [2023] UKSC 47.
12 Durgnat (n 10) 173.

Might not these three films have resonance for lawyers and jurists? Think of the image of a law library: all those books and journal articles lining the shelves and gathering dust. But who reads them now? Who reads the articles contained in the 1967 editions of the *Cambridge Law Journal*? Who reads all those old published doctoral theses to be found on the *rayons* of *la bibliothèque*? If ever there was an exercise in losing, it is writing academic law pieces. Publish or perish is the *regula iuris* compelling law academics to engage in an activity that many know is for short-term gain only. One thinks of *The Trial* (1962, director Orson Welles) set not in "the studio construction it may seem, but the derelict Gare d'Orsay".[13] What a fine image setting for the law library with its derelict books containing words now long forgotten or unconsciously recycled by each new generation of young academics hoping to make the grade. Durgnat described the setting in *The Trial* as an "elaborate nowhere".[14] What resonance, what an image for the law library, one might say.

There is a fourth reason why these three films are worthy of attention. All three are works of popular art. There is not just the resonance point; these films are classic examples of what can be created when scriptwriters, cinematographers, actors, and directors all come together in an act of cooperative talent. *Kiss Me Deadly* would not be the same film if there had been a different cinematographer or a different scriptwriter or different actors; in *The Killers*, the interaction of Lee Marvin, Clu Gulager, Angie Dickinson, and Ronald Reagan is enough to endow this nihilistic film with its criminal intensity, which itself is represented as a dichotomy between a violent class of thugs, professional contract killers (in sharp suits and dark glasses), small-time crooks, and psychopaths (Clu Gulager) on the one hand and "respectable", well-off white collar criminals (pretending, for the most part, not to be) on the other. These are subversive films, all the more powerful given the iconic actors. *The Killers* became more subversive, of course, in that one of its key characters – Jack Browning – was played by Ronald Reagan, who was soon after to enter politics and end up as US president. It was also in 1963 that a US President was assassinated, some believe by the American mafia. As Serge Chauvin observes, Browning was a loathsome hypocrite who claimed to abhor violence but was happy to kill (or try to kill) Johnny North (John Cassavetes) and the two contract killers.[15] He was seemingly handy with handgun and rifle, although not handy enough (one reason he also became a serious loser). In *Out of the Past*, Kirk Douglas is at ease in being all charm and warmth until he is not, while Ralph Meeker in *Kiss Me Deadly* seems

13 Durgnat (n 10) 103.

14 Durgnat (n 10) 32.

15 Serge Chauvin, *Les Trois Vies des* Tueurs*: Siodmak, Siegel et la fiction* (Rouge Profond 2010) 127.

the perfect choice as the amoral and arrogantly dim loser moving around in a chrome-like landscape fit for Ayn Rand. As Durgnat said, it "is the stark, abstract style of writer (AI Bezzerides), cameraman (Ernest Laszlo) and director [Robert Aldrich] which spans the space dividing the 'mere' detective story from the pure, intense, violent nightmare mood".[16]

A fifth reason why these three films are notable is that they represent the full gambit of the original *film noir* cycle. Lawrence Alloway saw the period between 1946 and 1964 as one "that can be regarded as a continuation of the traditional movies" and in which the films "for all their adaptions to the new crises, found forms in which to maintain the impact and confidence of earlier movies even as a shift in mass communications was modifying Hollywood's authority".[17] Alloway was not talking specifically about the *films noirs* – his emphasis was on violence in the cinema – but he made the point that this was "the period of the fall guy", mentioning, along with some other films of the late 1940s, *Out of the Past*.[18] Johnny North (John Cassavetes) in *The Killers* (1964), the film that closes the period emphasised by Alloway, is a classic fall guy, just as Swede (Burt Lancaster) was in the first version of *The Killers* (1946, director Robert Siodmak), a film that opens the Alloway period. What is also interesting about the two films (the 1946 and the 1947 ones) that open the period and the one that closes the cycle (1964) is that it is the past that destroys the fall guys. In *Kiss Me Deadly* (1955), it is, one might say, the future.

Kathie Comes Home

One of the major causes of the often slow (losing more slowly) destruction of the *film noir* "hero" and/or "heroine" is the past, represented by one of Hollywood's finest private eye movies. *Out of the Past* (1947) (a.k.a. *Build My Gallows High*) belongs to the classic detective *film noir* tradition made famous by earlier films such as *The Maltese Falcon* (1940, director John Huston) and *The Big Sleep* (1946, director Howard Hawks), these latter two having Humphrey Bogart as the iconic private eye. *Out of the Past* is in many ways a much darker film but one whose imagery, script, plotting, and characterisations are superior to the Bogart movies, as excellent as those two might be. It was directed by Jacques Tourneur, who had already made his name as one of the European émigrés who brought to Hollywood the rich expressionist monochrome style that was one of the defining characteristics of the 40s *film noir*.[19]

16 Raymond Durgnat, *Eros in the Cinema* (Calder & Boyers 1966) 94.
17 Lawrence Alloway, *Violent America: The Movies 1946–1964* (Museum of Modern Art 1971) 21.
18 Lawrence Alloway, *Violent America: The Movies 1946–1964* (Museum of Modern Art 1971) 26.
19 Tourneur directed some of the classic Val Lewton films: see Joel Siegal, *Val Lewton: The Reality of Terror* (Secker & Walburg 1972).

The film opens with the camera placed in a car which arrives in a small Californian town to pull into Jeff Bailey's garage. This is the past coming to reclaim Bailey (Robert Mitchum). As the journey into the past begins, Bailey finally tells the truth to his girlfriend (Virginia Huston), one of two people devoted to Jeff, that he is not Bailey but Markham, an ex–private eye who had betrayed a client – a gang boss called Whit Sterling (Kirk Douglas) – by falling in love with the boss's lover, Kathie Moffat (Jane Greer), who had run away with a large sum of Whit's money. Whit had hired Jeff to find her, which he did, but the couple then tried to make their own life together, which finally collapsed when Jeff's ex-partner saw them together at the racecourse. Jeff does his best to throw off his ex-partner (a good "gumshoe"), but to no avail – he had followed her, not him – and the situation is only resolved (so to speak) when Kathie cold-bloodedly kills the ex-partner and disappears, leaving Jeff to bury the body and to try to find a new life. It is Whit who claws Jeff back into the past by hiring him to steal back some tax records which are being used to blackmail Whit; Jeff, riddled with guilt about how he had betrayed the "big op" (gang boss), agrees, only to find that Whit and Kathie (now back with Whit) are setting him up as the murderer of the blackmailer. I'm in a frame, says Jeff at one point, but all I can see is the frame. Jeff manages to escape from this complex frame-up, only to find himself back under the control of Kathie after she once again cold-bloodedly kills another obstacle to her ambition: namely, Whit himself. Jeff once more seemingly runs away with Kathie, but, as a final phone call made by Jeff while Kathie is packing indicates, Jeff has had enough. He has betrayed too many people: not just Whit, his ex-partner, and his devoted girlfriend but equally himself.

Jeff's small-town girlfriend, Ann, was not the only person devoted to him. His young garage assistant, the Kid (Dickie Moore), who is deaf and mute but no fool or coward (he saves Jeff's life at one point by killing Whit's unpleasant "heavy"), is more than just a faithful employee; in Jeff, he finds some escape from his isolated world and seems intuitively to "know" about Jeff and his past. The Kid is in many ways central to the structure of the complex plot in that he is the messenger who, through his sign language to Jeff at the beginning of the film about the mystery visitor to the garage (Jeff was in the mountains with his girlfriend, fishing), warns us that the past is about to revisit and not in a positive way. "Trouble?" asks his girlfriend; "Maybe not", Jeff replies pessimistically. The Kid is there at the end of the film as well: first, to indicate to Jeff's grieving girlfriend that, yes, Jeff was running off with Kathie (but how could he have known?) and then to gesture with affection to the sign displaying Jeff's name over the garage. It is only as we leave the cinema do we realise just how much the Kid's life, together with Ann's, has been ruined by Jeff. Ann seemingly must now turn to the "decent" but actually smug and boring local law officer who has always been devoted to her, and the Kid has nothing to look forward to without the one person who cared for him.

Kathie Moffat is usually portrayed as the paradigm *femme fatale*. "Kathie exploits and betrays the men", says one male film writer; another writer describes her as "lethal" and a "corrupt woman".[20] Well, one might ask, what about the men in the film? Most of them appear lethal and corrupt, and the more one thinks about Jeff's past, the more corrupt he appears. Why should Kathie not be like the men who form the social context and background in which she lives and works (and was possibly brought up)? She is far more intelligent than most of them (including Jeff), and rather than being just "lethal" and "corrupt", she is actually trying to get ahead of the game, so to speak. Some might respond by pointing to the fact that she kills Jeff's partner in "cold blood": (to quote several film writers) and later kills Whit. But she knows Jeff's partner was nothing but a cheap blackmailer who would ruin their lives and Whit a violent and tiresome bully. Her cultural upbringing would "rightly" tell her that this is the only way to deal with such people. In fact, this is basically what she tells Jeff. Whit and his associates, of course, would have done the same thing in the same circumstances, but somehow, film writers would not be describing them with the same distain they reserve for the *femmes fatales*. If Jeff had not "betrayed" her, she would have given him a reasonable life. After all, she had been pretty faithful when they had run away together, and he had been the lowest of low detectives to keep them in, presumably, meagre bread. But what Jeff could not face, in the end, was that she would be the one in charge. Jacques Tourneur and his scriptwriter, Daniel Mainwaring, produced a film that is perhaps more nuanced than some film writers have appreciated.

Here, then, is an interesting point for reflection for the lawyer eating his or her popcorn. Is not the vilification of Kathie a failure to appreciate the cultural context in which she exists? Once one appreciates this context and then applies an ethical interpretation, Kathie emerges in rather a different light. One is not saying she is some kind of moral figure. Indeed, quite the opposite as, of course, she would be the first to admit. But *Out of the Past* is not really interested in moral characters – save to the extent of portraying some of them as insufferably stuffy and boring. (One can only feel sorry for poor Ann, now stuck with the law-and-order man.) It is essentially portraying a culture that operates outside the law; it is about the non-law side of society. So, when judged in these terms, Kathie proves to be far more ambiguous. Indeed, had Jeff not betrayed her and himself, she might well have found space to look after the Kid as well. She had that potential.

Reaganomics, or Où Est le Grisbi?

This same non-law (or negative law) culture forms the context of another, later film about time, losers, and a *femme fatale*. Don Siegel's remake of *The Killers* (1964) certainly presents a different visual image from the traditional *film noir*, even if it is no less bleak in its characters and narrative. The first

20 See, e.g., William Luhr, *Film Noir* (Wiley-Blackwell 2012) 100–22.

version (*The Killers*, 1946), which took its cue from a short story by Ernest Hemmingway, was a traditional 1940s *film noir* with the usual *femme fatale* and underworld characters. It was directed by Robert Siodmak and starred Burt Lancaster as the doomed central character, with a minor role for Albert Dekker (who, as will be seen, played Dr Soberin in *Kiss Me Deadly*), and it is a fine film, up there with all the other 1940s Hollywood crime movies. In fact, it is far more expressionist than *Out of the Past*, with its night and long shadows (chiaroscuro effect). Moreover, it is again set largely in a world in which the law has no part. But Siegel's version is a rather different product in that it opens the way to a new kind of crime movie – a new kind of "*film noir*" – set against the corporate landscape of modern office blocks and sharp suits, the weather being largely bright and sunny (rather than dark, wet, and rainy, as in the traditional *films noirs*). Yet this landscape, instead of ameliorating the menace of violence, only exacerbates it.

The film opens with a credit sequence appearing against the background of frozen red-and-black images of two men in dark glasses, the image unfreezing at the end of the credits with the live face of Lee (Clu Gulager) who, together with his senior partner, Charlie Strom (Lee Marvin), is about to carry out a contract killing on Johnny North (John Cassavetes). As they enter an institute for the blind (where North teaches car mechanics) to carry out the contract, it soon becomes evident that these two killers are capable of extreme violence. This is not graphically shown, as might be the case today; it is definitively established, in some ways almost offscreen, when Lee Marvin deals with the secretary. From that moment on, one knows what he is capable of doing, and there is no longer a need to repeat such actions, save for some moments near and at the end of the film. As for Lee, it later appears that not only is he equally capable of highly professional violence – he is continually exercising his hand muscles and, on one occasion, is doing press ups as well as drinking only carrot juice as it is "good for the eyes" – but he is also something of a playful psychopath with sadistic tendencies. These two killers are frightening, yet Siegel establishes this more by image and action suggestion than by graphic scenes.

Like *Out of the Past*, this is a narrative told in flashback. Charlie, breaking a long-held principle, decides to investigate why Johnny North did not try to escape, even though he had had warning of the men's arrival. The two killers follow a menacing journey (for others, rather than for them), which leads to Jack Browning, the Whit-type gangster magnificently portrayed by a very sinister Ronald Reagan (his last film before moving into politics and a role he very much regretted accepting). What they gradually discover is a heist and two double-crosses, with the bait being, of course, a *femme fatale* (named Sheila Farr), portrayed by the '60s icon Angie Dickinson.[21] As Charlie says,

21 On her '60s life, see <www.foxnews.com/entertainment/50s-star-angie-dickinson-frank-sinatra-why-never-married-love-life>.

on discovering Sheila Farr's betrayal of Johnny, "You didn't need us" for you "killed him four years ago".

Actually Sheila Farr, like Kathie Moffat in *Out of the Past*, turns out to be one of the more nuanced and complex characters in the movie. As with the 1947 film, she moves uniquely in a world inhabited by rich corporate criminals and enjoys the luxuries that such a life brings, but her relationship with Johnny North – indeed, with more ordinary people as we learn bits about her past – is always ambiguous. Did Kathy love Jeff, despite the fact that she was part of a plan to frame him in the 1947 film? Did Sheila love Johnny North, despite her deadly double-cross? The two characters offer an interesting exercise for a comparatist, although perhaps Farr will come off worse in some ways. What makes *The Killers* somewhat bleaker than *Out of the Past* is that there are few if any morally worthwhile characters; the whole narrative is situated amongst classes of people who largely live outside the law. Is this a precursor to the Trump era? Perhaps less Trump and more the financial rottenness of the pre-crash days, for some have described Jack Browning as a dodgy financier rather than a gangster. He resorts to crime to raise some extra capital, although he turns out to be quite handy, though, as we have said, not handy enough (to his and Sheila's detriment) with a rifle.

Given this nihilism, why should these two films be worthy of note and discussion? Perhaps it is appropriate here to draw an analogy with legal studies. In his works on legal epistemology, the late French Professor Christian Atias (1947–2015)) talked in terms of methodological sedimentation.[22] The methods and habits of thought of lawyers have been slowly built up by way of sedimentation over the centuries since Roman times. One might say the same of the Hollywood crime film and its European imitations (see especially the work of Jean-Pierre Melville). Those who watch the first version of *The Killers* (1946) and, of course, *Out of the Past* (1947) as well, followed, as will be seen, by *Kiss Me Deadly* and then Siegel's *The Killers* will soon appreciate, when they watch more contemporary thrillers, how these films are the *répéres* in a sedimentation process which now finds its expression in crime film technique. Some later films directly reference one or more of these *répéres*. For example, John Boorman's *Point Blank* (1967) openly refers to Siegel's film not just in its gangster plot, which reunites Lee Marvin with Angie Dickenson, but in its title as well; Siegel's *The Killers* was entitled *À Bout Portant* in France.

However, it is later films such as John Flynn's *The Outfit* (1973) in which one can truly appreciate the important influences of the *répéres*. Based on the book by Richard Stark (actually Donald Westlake), it employs the same kind of very tight direction that Siegel used to great effect in *The Killers* while

22 See, e.g., Christian Atias, *Épistémologie juridique* (Presses Universitaires de France 1985); Christian Atias, *Épistémologie du droit* (Presses Universitaires de France 1994).

equally employing the types of scenes and characters familiar from both *Out of the Past* and *Kiss Me Deadly*. Robert Ryan holds his own with Whit and Jack Browning, even if he lacks the cultural sophistication of Dr Soberin in *Kiss Me Deadly*. (In fact, the only words he keeps saying to his female partner are "Shut up".) Flynn equally appreciates the importance of landscape and image: it always seems grey and about to rain, yet the colour photography has a cold steel-like feel. There is even a cameo by Jane Greer, and Joe Don Baker, at the end, has his Lee Marvin scene, complete with silenced revolver. Admittedly, *The Outfit* is deliberately retro – in some ways, it is out of its period (1946–1964) – but the kind of tight direction evident in Siegel's film plus the use of photographic geometry and image so carefully employed (as will be noted) in *Kiss Me Deadly* is to be seen in many contemporary thrillers. One might add that in addition to the cameo by Jane Greer, Flynn has cameos by other iconic actors from the *film noir* period. These films will not be, as has been said (trigger warning), to everybody's taste. The final scene in *The Killers*, in which a mortally wounded Charlie, using his Smith and Wesson .44 magnum with enormous silencer, finishes off both Browning and Farr in their middle-class suburban house (with nice front lawn) remains shocking. ("Lady, I don't have the time".) But they are both important landmarks in the history of the Hollywood crime movie, and their influence is felt in many subsequent crime films. These are losers, as the face of Jack Browning before his demise so clearly expresses. No wonder Ronald Reagan wanted the film suppressed.

Blow Me a Kiss

Kiss Me Deadly (1955) is another private eye film but featuring, this time, a much less sympathetic central character than Jeff in *Out of the Past*. He is Mickey Spillane's Mike Hammer (Ralph Meeker), a violent and sadistic private detective who specialises in sleazy divorce cases ("He's a bedroom dick", says one policeman.) Spillane (1918–2006) was no literary figure, but his books sold millions of copies, and if he were alive today, he would no doubt be an ardent Trump supporter while one imagines, if Trump ever read novels, that Spillane might well be high on his list. Robert Aldrich, who directed the film, loathed the Spillaine books, and perhaps it was this loathing that goaded him, along with his cinematographer, Ernest Laszlo, and scriptwriter Albert Bezzerides, into creating one of the most extraordinary crime films ever to come out of Hollywood.

You, the viewer, are in the passenger seat of a smart 1950s sports car – "Va-va-vroom", says Hammer's *garagiste* later in the movie – and it is in the middle of a *film noir* (steely monochrome) night on a lonely road. The driver switches on the radio, which announces Nat King Cole's "I'd Rather Have the Blues", which sets the mood while the credits roll (backwards!). Suddenly, in front, a barefooted women dressed only in a trench coat is running down the middle lane towards the car. Hammer, narrowly avoiding her, picks her up – she has escaped from the local "laughing house" (as Hammer sensitively puts it) – and smuggles her past a police roadblock set up, seemingly, to recapture her. They stop for petrol; she goes to the toilet and later comes out with the words "Remember me", the first of several literary (and time) allusions in this movie. They are intercepted, and Hammer wakes up to see and hear the woman being tortured to death (originally excised by the British censor). Hammer finally escapes, and the hunt starts for the "the Great Whatsit", a nuclear Pandora's box: "Listen to me as if I was Cerberus barking with all his heads at the gates of hell", says the culturally sophisticated but psychopathic criminal Dr Soberin (Albert Dekker). "I will tell you where to take it but don't . . . don't open the box". (She does.)

The plot is complex and the characters, on the surface, one dimensional but actually more nuanced in often rather unpleasant ways. What is striking, as Durgnat explained, is the visual feel of the film: it is in a cold-as-steel monochrome style which brings out all the 1950s icons from cars and apartment blocks to (the then) state-of-the-art telephone recorders and clothes. Hammer is a genuine anti-hero of a type (nasty) that does not become common until a couple of decades later. He thinks he is smart. Remember "Remember me"? Well, he does, goes to the morgue, and finds the key which will lead him to the Great Whatsit, having already rescued someone he believes to be the dead woman's ex-flatmate, who claimed she was being hunted down by the mafia ("they") in the search for information. (She is, in fact, a plant to lead "them" to the Great Whatsit). As Hammer's secretary says, "First, you find a little thread, the little thread leads you to a string, and the string leads you to a rope, and from the rope you hang by the neck".

"Remember me" is just one of the literary allusions thrown into this nihilistic mix, which is, perhaps, nothing more than a modern retelling of Pandora's box. Bezzerides claimed that Spillane hated what he had done to his book, no doubt recoiling at the idea that his beloved Mike Hammer would be forced to read Christina Rossetti. But the dialogue is wonderful. When Hammer tries to bribe information from a boxer – "Okay, how much did they give you? I'll top it" – the latter replies: "You can't top this; they said they'd let me breathe". Not long after, it becomes apparent that our anti-hero is really not so smart. One is reminded of the dialogue right at the beginning of the film with the woman he picked up (whom he now knows to have been a nuclear scientist called Christina Bailey):

Woman (Christina Bailey):	You have only one real lasting love.
Hammer:	Now who could that be?
Woman:	You. You're one of those self-indulgent males who thinks about nothing but his clothes, his car, himself. Bet you do push-ups every morning just to keep your belly hard.

Indeed, in a controversial ending (it was changed and then restored in the DVD version), he might even have, as one might say today, "done a Trump". Va-va-vroom!

The dialogue, the photography, the consumer icons, the plot, the literary allusions, and the like all help create a film that was well in advance of its time. Indeed, one still has a feeling that this is a contemporary piece of cinema set in the 1950s, a bit like Roman Polanski's *Chinatown* (1974) is a sophisticated recreation of 1930s California. It heralded the end of the traditional *film noir* by being both backward – one thinks of the strong black shadows and the many night scenes – and forward looking. From now on, the crime film would be different in terms of both its style and its characters. The action is now largely on location and out of the enclosed world of the studio (as, of course, is the situation in Siegel's *The Killers*). As for the gangsters, one can certainly compare Dr Soberin to Whit in *Out of the Past*, but Soberin is clearly a different kind of high-class criminal with, it would seem, sinister international connections in addition to his local power base whose tentacles reach into every social class. As for Hammer, he has few if any ethical or moral dimensions, making him a different kind of central private eye than the Jeff Bailey in Tourneur's film.

Hammer is not just a loser. He succeeds in rescuing his kidnapped secretary but only after the supposed ex-flatmate – in fact, Soberin's mistress, whose name is Lily – has opened the Great Whatsit box after learning that Soberin is going to abandon her. Indeed, like Kathie Moffat, she shoots her crime boss lover. Here, the film has a link not just to *Out of the Past* but also to the recent *Oppenheimer* (2023, director Christopher Nolan): the Great Whatsit box is, as the police detective had earlier hinted to Hammer, something stolen from the Manhattan Project. As Raymond Durgnat put it, the "private eye is out of his depth in this brave new world of Communist agents and atomic fission".[23] Opened, the Great Whatsit is about to destroy quite possibly more than the beach house where Soberin, Lily, Hammer, and his secretary have all found themselves for the literally (atomic) explosive ending. The future has come to destroy the world, all partly thanks to a self-obsessed loser whom the police view with utter contempt.

M for Menace, Music, and the Mundane

A couple of other interesting points are worth noting with regard to *The Killers* and *Kiss Me Deadly*. They are worth noting for lawyers because small details matter. They can make or break resonance, just as small factual details can sometimes determine an outcome in a common law case. One feature

23 Durgnat (n 16) 92.

common to both films is the cabaret or nightclub singer. In the bar where Hammer is drowning his sorrows the *noir* atmosphere is once again emphasised with the female jazz singer redoing "I'd Rather Have the Blues" live (magnificently) while in *The Killers*, it is Nancy Wilson's cameo singing "Too Little Time". Both of these songs reflect the moods of the respective films, time being a continual motif in *The Killers* from the racetrack stopwatches to the need for speed if the heist (one of the narrative sub-plots) is to succeed. And, of course, there are Charlie Strom's final words to Sheila Farr: "Lady, I don't have the time". Never has sunny tranquil suburbia felt so appropriately menacing for a bunch of smartly dressed losers. Time, of course, matters to lawyers. A typical loser lawyer is one who fails to adhere to strict procedural or limitation time periods – and these losers are not so few and far between.

Another rather fascinating aspect is the odd mundane detail in *The Killers*: Strom washing his shirt in the hotel room while Lee does his press-ups and the Hitchcock-type street setup – disorientating in many ways – before a jolting shooting scene. There is a continual dialectic between the mundane and the violent. The three films also share another mundane versus menace feature – one noted by William Luhr. "Cocktail lounges, night clubs and hotels", he says, "tended to be spaces of glamour and sophistication in the movies of the 1930s". Yet a decade later, in the *films noirs*, "they tend to be impersonal, decadent, and dangerous".[24] In *Out of the Past* and *The Killers*, the scenes set in a hotel most certainly conform to this observation – "It's a long way down", says Lee to Charlie as he threatens to eject Sheila Farr from a hotel window – while the cocktail bar in *Kiss Me Deadly* is anything but glamorous, despite the cabaret performance of the blues song. Also, in *Kiss Me Deadly*, this mundane and violence are found in the dialogue when the two seem to sit side by side. "Do me a favour, will you?" says Hammer's secretary. "Keep away from the windows. Someone might blow you a kiss".

The Cabinet of Dr Savigny

So what is the lawyer to make of these films? Perhaps the most striking point for the jurist is the role of Germany. In legal thought and legal education, the influence of German 19th-century Pandectist thought has been dominating, even although the common law is said to be different from the civilian tradition. An English Parliamentary Select Committee report on the state of legal education published in 1846 regretted the lack of any such education worthy of the name in England, Wales, and Ireland; it recommended looking

24 Luhr (n 20) 61.

at Germany.[25] Writing in the early 20th century, Joseph Drake, in an editorial preface to an American translation of a work by Von Jhering, wrote:

> On the other hand, we find many a Puchta among our American jurists, both on and off the bench, who apply the principles that we have worked out in the development of our Common Law as though they were "a priori" mathematical axioms and not "a posteriori" working formulae, which have to be constantly reshaped to adapt them to the ever changing requirements of a developing society.

And he continued:

> American juristic thinking at the present time needs a von Ihering. Our jurists, our legislators and our courts, both bench and bar, are still holding fast to an historical "Naturrecht" built up on the precedents of the Common Law, which has many analogies to the type of juristic thinking in vogue in Germany during the first half of the nineteenth century. . . . The public is crying out against our crystallized and inelastic theory and practice of law. The proper application of the idea of law as purpose would, in many cases, loosen our legal shackles and open the way out of our legal difficulties.[26]

One would be foolish to think that this conceptual thinking has been completely abandoned.[27] In other words, the influence of German formalist thinking on law is still to be felt. It is like a stark, socially insensitive architecture of the kind that would not look out of place in *Kiss Me Deadly*.

Yet the influence of Germany is equally to be felt in the classic *films noirs*. One reason for this influence was the importation into Hollywood of German expressionist and other ideas through – or partly through – a number of émigrés escaping Nazi Germany such as Fritz Lang, William Dieterle, Robert Siodmak, and Douglas Sirk. According to Andrew Spicer:

> German expressionism is always cited as the major influence on film noir's arresting visual style and also its pessimistic mood. However, it was the influence of Weimar cinema (1919–33) as a whole, rather than just

25 Parliamentary Select Committee on Legal Education (1846), Report, 25 August 1846, House of Commons Proceedings 686.

26 Joseph Drake, 'Editorial Preface' in Rudolf von Jhering (ed), *Law As a Means to an End* (Boston Book Company 1913) xxiii.

27 See, e.g., Dan Priel, 'Two Forms of Formalism' in Andrew Roberstson and James Goudkamp (eds), *Form and Substance in the Law of Obligations* (Hart Publishing 2019) 165.

"Expressionism", that was profound, and also more complex, multifaced and indirect than is often supposed.[28]

Care must thus be taken. It is not so much individuals importing a particular style; it is more of a movement of a kind that can be visually felt rather defined. As Durgnat said, "Expressionism is as undefinable a category as 'realism'".[29] Jacques Tourneur was not one of the German refugees, but there are plenty of expressionist moments in *Out of the Past*, as there are in Aldrich's *Kiss Me Deadly*. As for the émigrés themselves, Spicer thinks their "influence was pervasive but by no means simple".[30] There certainly was an influence. "However", he says,

> rather than direct transplantation, one is looking at a process of diffusion and reappropriation where a modified Expressionism could be superimposed over existing generic conventions through a more self-conscious deployment of mise-en-scène chiaroscuro lighting, minimalist sets, mobile camerawork and the use of fractured narratives.[31]

What is particularly interesting for the comparative lawyer in Spicer's comment is his use of the word "transplant". Legal transplants are a topic that has attracted much ink and forms the basis of a debate about whether one can really talk of a rule or conceptual institution being transplanted from one legal system to another. The problem comes down to one of "science" versus "culture". Those comparatists who view law as a positivistic science think that rules and conceptual legal structures can be transplanted from one legal culture to another while those who see law as entirely the product of a particular culture argue that all that gets transferred is a meaningless form of words.[32] Can the Hollywood experience add anything to this debate? In truth, probably not that much. This said, Andrew Spicer noted that the émigrés "developed a close and detailed knowledge of their country of adoption",[33] and he concluded that the *films noirs* should be understood not as a direct transplantation of a visual style into US cinema but "as the complex synthesis of American and European cultural traditions".[34] There are similarities here with some of the German émigré jurists. For example, Otto Kahn-Freund (1900–1979) obviously brought with him to England his German learning,

28 Andrew Spicer, *Film Noir* (Routledge 2002) 11.
29 Durgnat (n 10) 87.
30 Spicer (n 28) 13–14.
31 Spicer (n 28) 14.
32 Pierre Legrand, 'What "Legal Transplants"?' in David Nelken and Johannes Feest (eds), *Adapting Legal Cultures* (Hart Publishing 2001) 55.
33 Spicer (n 28) 14.
34 Spicer (n 28) 19.

but he equally developed a close and detailed knowledge of the common law, which was to result in some major contributions to legal thought.[35] This kind of legal knowledge synthesis was true of a number of other refugees as well – indeed, one even became an English Court of Appeal judge.[36] Perhaps comparatists should talk less, therefore, about "transplants" and more about movement, influence, and cultural synthesis.

Farwell, My Loser

These three films, then, are not just representative landmarks in a key period of Hollywood crime movies (1946–1964). They are of particular interest in themselves in terms of style, acting, narrative, editing, and so on; they all have, as Durgnat would say, "resonance". They are also, of course, about losers. On this loser point, it must be stressed that there are many other Hollywood films depicting classic losers. One thinks of the great Sterling Hayden and his portrayal of crime losers in *The Asphalt Jungle* (1950, director John Huston) and *The Killing* (1956, director Stanley Kubrick). Indeed, he also comes to an unfortunate end in *The Godfather* (1972). Then there is James Stewart as the retired detective in Alfred Hitchcock's extraordinary *Vertigo* (1958): a man who loses twice in the same movie while the actual criminal, who seemingly masterminded the whole series of events, ends up a rich winner somewhere in Europe. (The studio was unhappy with this ending.) Interestingly Hitchcock wanted to make Cary Grant and Joan Fontaine two real losers in his film *Suspicion* (1941), but the studio, so Raymond Durgnat informed us, would not let him do this. This film shares with *Vertigo* the theme of a husband wanting to murder his wife and has Joan Fontaine, as a supposedly plain woman, marrying Cary Grant, a playboy, gambler, and thief who married her only for her money. She comes to believe that he wants to murder her, and towards the end of the film, Grant climbs the stairs with a glass of milk for Fontaine. Is it or is it not poisoned? As Durgnat said, the actual ending of the film is a compromise: "Hitchcock would have preferred to end with Joan Fontaine drinking the poisoned milk and lying back to die while Cary Grant, whistling unsuspectingly, posts the letter in which she has incriminated him".[37] Not only would both have been losers – although interesting ones, as Durgnat indicates in his discussion of *Suspicion* (although he does not think it is a very good film) – but the structural framework of the narrative would surely have made the film artistically notable. There are also,

35 See, e.g., Otto Kahn-Freund, 'Introduction' in Karl Renner (ed), *The Institutions of Private Law and Their Social Functions* (Routledge & Keegan Paul 1949).

36 See further Jack Beatson and Reinhard Zimmermann, *Jurists Uprooted: German-Speaking Émigré Lawyers in Twentieth-Century Britain* (OUP 2004).

37 Raymond Durgnat, *The Strange Case of Alfred Hitchcock* (Faber & Faber 1974) 178.

of course, losers in non-crime movies. Perhaps one of the most emotionally tragic is (once again) Joan Fontaine's Lisa in Max Ophüls's *Letter from an Unknown Woman* (1948), along with Stefan (Louis Jourdan), the cause of Lisa's obsession, who also ends up losing his life (probably).

Raymond Durgnat would, of course, have said many more interesting and insightful things about losers in movies, and he would have noticed connections missed by others. As Kevin Gough-Yates said in a re-publication of Durgnat's *A Mirror for England*, "[I]f you think that you have an 'original' approach to a film or a director's work . . . you generally discover that Raymond Durgnat has said it already".[38] His approach would not have appealed to many academic legal theorists since he did not profess to have a "theory". Yet he had what most academic lawyers do not have: a real sense – even if an unconscious one – of how different schemes of engagement provide different insights. Different kinds of knowledge, if you will. He once said that he did not "think that every film is political", but he did "think that every film is ideological".[39] What is so interesting about this comment is that it might now be in the process of being adopted by comparative lawyers. Two leading Italian comparatists recently made the point that methods – schemes of intelligibility such as hermeneutics, structuralism, and functionalism – "have no inherent political essence". It is "their use that determines the reactions they provoke".[40] Durgnat was criticised by many of the less perceptive film writers as being "socialist". Yet this was to miss the point. He, again perhaps unconsciously, used different schemes to highlight different reactions; he might use structuralism, functionalism, hermeneutics, dialectics, or causality to make points that could well be "political" but were often much more cultural and sociological in their assertions, often involving a stylistic analysis that was, on occasion, profound. Of course, these points, especially with respect to comparative law, need much more development, and they are made here in outline only to suggest that comparative lawyers need to be looking at the humanities as much as the social sciences.[41]

So what does all this mean for lawyers? No doubt, many jurists and lawyers will be surprised to learn they are losers, just like the protagonists in the three films discussed. Yet their insistence – or the insistence of many of them – that law is a science to be applied by "neutral" judges is to set the

38 Kevin Gough-Yates, 'Forward' in Raymond Durgnat (ed), *A Mirror for England* (British Film Institute 2011) viii. The book is described as a second edition, but it is actually just a reprinting of the original book.

39 Raymond Durgnat, 'Durgnat vs. Paul' (1978) 14(2) Film Comment 66.

40 Pier Giuseppe Monateri and Mauro Balestrieri, *Quantitative Methods in Comparative Law* (Edward Elgar 2023) 87.

41 These points are developed in much greater depth in Geoffrey Samuel, 'Can Methods from the Social and Human Sciences Be of Value in Understanding Comparative Law Methodology?' (2024) 19 Journal of Comparative Law 321.

scene in which the "neutral" judges might as well be replaced by "neutral" robots. Not that any of this machine law will actually be neutral. But the winners – the corporate bosses and their populist dictators (Reaganomics meets Donald Trump) – will hardly be concerned by such nuances. In the films, Whit, Dr Soberin, and Jack Browning did end up as losers, but one wonders if these kinds of characters are tomorrow's winners. After all, in one sense, Jack Browning really did become a US president, and a playboy and liar did once end up as a UK prime minister, even if he did not have quite the smooth attraction of a Cary Grant.

Reference List

Alloway L, *Violent America: The Movies 1946–1964* (Museum of Modern Art 1971)

Atias C, *Épistémologie juridique* (Presses Universitaires de France 1985)

Atias C, *Épistémologie du droit* (Presses Universitaires de France 1994)

Beatson J and Zimmermann R, *Jurists Uprooted: German-Speaking Émigré Lawyers in Twentieth-Century Britain* (OUP 2004)

Chauvin S, *Les Trois Vies des Tueurs: Siodmak, Siegel et la fiction* (Rouge Profond 2010)

Deakin S and Markou C (eds), *Is Law Computable? Critical Perspectives on Law and Artificial Intelligence* (Hart Publishing 2020)

Drake J, 'Editorial Preface' in R von Jhering (ed), *Law As a Means to an End* (Boston Book Company 1913)

Durgnat R, *Eros in the Cinema* (Calder & Boyers 1966)

Durgnat R, *Films and Feelings* (Faber & Faber 1967)

Durgnat R, *A Mirror for England* (Faber & Faber 1970)

Durgnat R, 'Paint It Black: The Family Tree of Film Noir' (1970) 6–7 Cinema 48–49;

Durgnat R, *Sexual Alienation in the Cinema* (Studio Vista 1972)

Durgnat R, 'The Family Tree of Film Noir' (1974) 10 (6) Film Comment

Durgnat R, *The Strange Case of Alfred Hitchcock* (Faber & Faber 1974)

Durgnat R, 'Genre: Populism and Social Realism' (1975) 11(4) Film Comment

Durgnat R, 'Durgnat vs. Paul' (1978) 14(2) Film Comment

Durgnat R, *A Mirror for England* (BFI/Palgrave Macmillan 2011)

Gough-Yates K, 'Forward' in R Durgnat (ed), *A Mirror for England* (British Film Institute 2011)

Kahn-Freund O, 'Introduction' in K Renner (ed), *The Institutions of Private Law and Their Social Functions* (Routledge & Keegan Paul 1949)

Legrand P, 'What "Legal Transplants"?' in D Nelken and J Feest (eds), *Adapting Legal Cultures* (Hart Publishing 2001)

Legrand P, *Negative Comparative Law: A Strong Programme for Weak Thought* (CUP 2022)

Luhr W, *Film Noir* (Wiley-Blackwell 2012)

Miller H (ed), *The Essential Raymond Durgnat* (Palgrave Macmillan & British Film Institute 2014)

Monateri PG and Balestrieri M, *Quantitative Methods in Comparative Law* (Edward Elgar 2023)

Parliamentary Select Committee on Legal Education (1846), Report, 25 August 1846, House of Commons Proceedings

Priel D, 'Two Forms of Formalism' in A Roberstson and J Goudkamp (eds), *Form and Substance in the Law of Obligations* (Hart Publishing 2019)

Samuel G, 'Can Methods from the Social and Human Sciences Be of Value in Understanding Comparative Law Methodology?' (2024) 19 Journal of Comparative Law
Siegal J, *Val Lewton: The Reality of Terror* (Secker & Walburg 1972)
Spicer A, *Film Noir* (Routledge 2002)
Thompson E, *Escape from Model Land: How Mathematical Models Can Lead Us Astray and What We Can Do About It* (Basic Books 2022)

Chapter 11

The Legal Spectacle

Elie Aslanoff

Translated from French to English by Irina Kronrod

Introduction

One question haunts this collection: Why should jurists talk about cinema? Why do we doctoral students at the Sciences Po Law School meet to watch and discuss films? Despite the existence of a literature in law and cinema, this activity still seems out of place. This is because lawyers, with their boring knowledge, do not seem capable of analysing such spectacular works of art. They can, of course, judge with some acuity whether or not a work of art accurately portrays a trial or a legal profession. But it has to be said that such a commentary is of limited interest. What does one gain from tracking down the traces of their trade in films? Is it the satisfaction of seeing a familiar face on the screen, rather like watching a friend on television?

Studying anomalies prompts critical thinking. Let us agree on this truism and explore cinephile jurists systematically – forming and testing hypotheses. Perhaps we will uncover some insights about the law in the process. This will be the initial phase of our work.

Without revealing the results of our investigation prematurely, we shall see that jurists turn to films because they seek life in them. They think they can break free from the formal constraints of their field of expertise by turning to another formal object: namely, film. An intriguing paradox. Behind our object of study, which seemed so narrow and limited, we discover more fundamental issues. What if there were a link between legal formalism and artistic formalism? After all, it is the same society that has empowered law and images as regulators of social practice. There is potential for exploration here, but the conventional academic form is not ideal for delving into this theme; it would compromise our purpose. Let us intentionally opt for experimentation, approaching the latter more as an art than a science. If we are merging law and art, let us fully commit to the fusion.

DOI: 10.4324/9781003461180-11

Given the issues at hand, aligning ourselves with the spirit of Guy Debord seems fitting.[1] As a political thinker, an artist, and a critical theorist of all art forms, Debord showed that the yearning to find life in films was the result of a certain organisation of society and of the state and that this yearning deserved the most scathing criticism. Drawing inspiration from him, we aim to cultivate a discourse that collectively ponders law, cinema, life, and alienation. In paying homage to Debord, let us use his own weapons. Through the practice of *détournement*, using phrases and images produced by others to build a discourse of social critique, he created his renowned work *The Society of the Spectacle*. The second part of this chapter will emulate Debord, featuring a series of appropriated quotations. Perhaps we will uncover some truths in this process. At the very least, let us hope for an entertaining exploration.

Before delving into our experiment, let us proceed to the first part and ask ourselves: Why does the lawyer speak of cinema?

Why Do Jurists Talk About Film?

Hypothesis 1: "Law Is the Most Powerful of Schools for the Imagination"

In *Du Droit dans Disney* (*Law in Disney*), one of the few French works to bring together law and cinema, we find a few elements to help us understand the approach of film-loving legal experts or "cine-jurists". The project's founders explain that jurists have an interest "in the enchanted worlds of fairy tales"[2] and recognise themselves as "the most unrepentant dreamers".[3] The "imagination of law" no longer needs proving.[4] The following contribution also states: "Since law is part of an imaginary order, it is only natural

1 Guy Debord (1931–1994), a pivotal figure and co-founder of the Situationist International, was a French theorist, writer, and filmmaker. The movement aimed to surpass conventional artistic limits by seamlessly integrating art into daily life and reshaping societal frameworks. His influential work *La Société du Spectacle* (*The Society of the Spectacle*) critiques the dominance of images in advanced capitalism. Debord extended his artistic reach through experimental films, employing the principle of *détournement* to transcend traditional art and cinema. Notably, he played an active role in the events of May 1968.

2 Quentin Le Pluard and Marion Talbot, 'Quelques mots d'introduction' in Quentin Le Pluard and Marion Talbot (eds), *Du droit dans Disney: [Actes de la VIe journée d'études des doctorants juristes de l'Université de Bretagne Occidentale et de l'Université de Bretagne Sud, le 22 mars 2019]* (Mare & Martin 2020) 13.

3 Quentin Le Pluard and Marion Talbot, 'Quelques mots d'introduction' in Quentin Le Pluard and Marion Talbot (eds), *Du droit dans Disney: [Actes de la VIe journée d'études des doctorants juristes de l'Université de Bretagne Occidentale et de l'Université de Bretagne Sud, le 22 mars 2019]* (Mare & Martin 2020).

4 Quentin Le Pluard and Marion Talbot, 'Quelques mots d'introduction' in Quentin Le Pluard and Marion Talbot (eds), *Du droit dans Disney: [Actes de la VIe journée d'études des doctorants juristes de l'Université de Bretagne Occidentale et de l'Université de Bretagne Sud, le 22 mars 2019]* (Mare & Martin 2020) 13–14.

that it should one day cross paths with fairy tales".[5] A number of similar statements can be found in academic literature.[6] Indeed, when giving their introductory courses to first-year students, civil law professors often recall Jean Giraudoux's statement, "[T]here's no better way of exercising the imagination than the study of law"[7] in order to reassure them that the law is far different from the austere image the public sometimes lends it. The strategy of cine-jurists seems to be the same as that of civil law professors. Here, we have our first hypothesis: by talking about films, jurists bring the law back into the realm of fantasy and reverie and thereby aim to dispel their public image as boring formalists.

However, there is a problem. When we link the law to fictional universes, the result is not necessarily what we would expect. Take, for example, this sentence from the article on *Bambi* in the same collection:

> The first shot is fired at around the forty-first minute by someone who is hunting in snowy weather, which might be more relevant to hunting law and environmental law since Article R. 424-2 of the French Environmental Code states that in principle, "hunting in snowy weather is prohibited".[8]

Again, the imagination of the law.

Here, the author perfectly fits the image that the public has of lawyers: rigorous, even fussy, and incapable of looking up from their law books. The effect produced by this type of article lies precisely in the discrepancy between its subject, the world of fantasy, and its language, the dull, precise expressions of legal language. Thus, the author fails to show the creative dimension of the law and instead insists on pure and simple technique at its most boring. The exercise borders self-parody and teaches us, at most, that a lawyer is first and foremost a technician, something that no one calls into question. As Bruno Latour says in *The Making of Law: An Ethnography of the Conseil d'Etat*, "Whereas fiction moves and blinds, legal fiction clams and reassures. We could of course aestheticise law, treat the legal text as a literary work – it would not prevent the two regimes of enunciation from leading in opposite

5 Quentin Le Pluard, Talbot Marion and Jean-Jacques Urvoas (eds), 'Ouverture' in *Du droit dans Disney: [Actes de la VIe journée d'études des doctorants juristes de l'Université de Bretagne Occidentale et de l'Université de Bretagne Sud, le 22 mars 2019]* (Mare & Martin 2020) 19.

6 François Ost, *Si le droit m'était conté* (Dalloz 2019) 11; François Ost, *Nouveaux contes juridiques* (Dalloz 2021) 9.

7 Jean Giraudoux, *Tiger at the Gates* (Christopher Fry tr, 2nd paperback edn, repr, Methuen 1971) 45. (The original title is *La Guerre de Troie n'aura pas lieu*, which can be translated as *The Trojan War Will Not Take Place*).

8 Quentin Le Pluard, Talbot Marion and Jean-Pierre Marguénaud (eds), 'Bambi' in *Du droit dans Disney: [Actes de la VIe journée d'études des doctorants juristes de l'Université de Bretagne Occidentale et de l'Université de Bretagne Sud, le 22 mars 2019]* (Mare & Martin 2020) 139.

directions".[9] Our first hypothesis is thus perhaps not the right one. We need to take a different tack.

Let us return to Jean Giraudoux's phrase. Professors of civil law do not generally recall the law's ironic and critical nature. They prefer to see it as a tribute to their intellectual fertility. Yet the main purpose of the sentence is to show the emptiness of the law and its reasoning. Giraudoux's phrase is uttered by Hector in *The Trojan War Will Not Take Place*, when he is talking to the jurist Busiris. At the start of the conversation, Busiris proves that the Greeks have breached the rules of international law and can therefore be attacked, citing a number of precedents. Hector asks him to argue exactly the opposite because he wants to avoid war. He then utters the famous line: "There's no better way of exercising the imagination than the study of law". And Busiris easily rearranges his arguments. The moral of the story is that the law is nothing more than a game of language, with no bearing on reality, since the Trojan War ended up taking place.

Giraudoux's text expresses the recurrent suspicion that hangs over the discourse of the jurist, accused of being useless, disconnected from reality, devoid of any real content. This leads to a new hypothesis. Do lawyers perhaps turn to film in search of social validation of their knowledge? The syllabus of a course on law and cinema offered at Sciences Po states that the course enables us to think about "law as deeply part of our social, everyday life"[10]. By pointing out that even the revered objects of popular culture talk about the law, is the lawyer seeking legitimacy?

Hypothesis 2: The Law Is Everywhere, Even in Films

Lawyers are often heard saying that "the law is everywhere", that behind the events of social life lies an order of norms and procedures that only they can perceive, and which form a secret framework.

"You do not know, little men", they say to the uninitiated,

> but at this very moment you are shackled by inextricable chains, by principles, by articles of law, by judicial precedents. You are unable to see them because you have not contemplated the sun of Justice. When you buy a loaf of bread, you believe that the truth of your act lies in the material loaf and the baker's smile. Naive illusion! Without realizing it, you've just signed a bilateral contract![11]

9 Bruno Latour, *The Making of Law: An Ethnography of the Conseil d'Etat* (Polity 2010) 265.

10 <https://syllabus.sciencespo.fr/cours/202020/177032.html>.

11 Significantly, Jurixio, one of the leading legal popularisers on YouTube France, begins his video presentation as follows: "The law is everywhere. Whether we are aware of it or not, the law punctuates our daily lives. When you pick up a loaf of bread in a bakery, you're entering into a contract. As such, you are subject to contract law". <www.youtube.com/watch?v=fuIR3L3YYp4&list=PLMo3GFNAZFt4D8SSO7DQ6v0J4HbK1yPzt>

Then, emboldened by their own words, they continue:

> The Law branches out into the tiniest corners of your lives and does not spare even your so-called leisure activities. When you are daydreaming in front of *The Big Bang Theory*, don't you notice that Sheldon Cooper is, in fact, a Kelsenian?[12] The law is everywhere, including in your books, TV series and films, which is why we lawyers control everything. We have not only invaded your world, but also your imagination. Every situation is legal, every artist is an unknowing lawyer, every word is a qualification, every perception is a code, because law is the life of the whole.

Does cinema prove the imperialism of law? The law and cinema club is the perfect laboratory for testing this hypothesis. At first glance, it seems to confirm it. The rich and varied list of films that have been screened shows that the law touches absolutely every subject. However, when we consider the discussions we've had at the cinema club, we come to different conclusions. In the cinema club, we've been able to interact, without being constrained by the dictates of the academic article. What do we talk about when we are placed in these situations?

We ask ourselves philosophical, political, sociological, and methodological questions, but rarely legal ones. We can sometimes analyse how a film represents the law, as is often the case in specialist law and cinema literature, but that's where it ends. In short, our discussions go well beyond the limits of the law. For example, one session was devoted to Pier Paolo Pasolini's film *Comizzi d'Amor*.[13] In this documentary, Pasolini asks Italians about marriage and sexuality at a time when divorce law has been relaxed and brothels reauthorised. During the post-film debate, we did not argue about legislative changes but discussed the method that Pasolini used to gather his testimonies, the sexual revolution, Pasolini's analysis of class, the family, and a host of other subjects. During another session we watched Franck Perry's *The Swimmer*[14] and talked about the mythology and symbolism of water. In these discussions, the law was not the central subject but played a background role. We could say to the cine-jurist, "If the law really is everywhere, why is it not more often on your lips when you get together in a law and cinema club? If the law is at the centre of everything, why isn't it at the centre of your debates?"

This cannot be attributed to the frivolity of the lawyers in our sample, to their guilty desire to clear their heads of the law. Although films often feature lawyers or judges, they rarely ask specifically legal questions. The most legal

12 Fabrice Defferrard, *La pensée juridique de Sheldon Cooper: Ou comment faire du droit avec the Big Bang Theory* (Mare & Martin 2019) 61.

13 *Comizi d'amore* (Directed by Pier Paolo Pasolini, Carlotta Films 1964).

14 *The Swimmer* (Directed by Franck Perry, Columbia Pictures 1968).

element brought to the screen is the trial. The camera, naturally drawn to this theatrical form, fails to see that lawyers are increasingly removed from the courtroom. The growing role of in-house lawyers in the production of law has made the trial lose its central position. Moreover, the most represented court case is the criminal one. But, in reality, criminal law is a branch that has been constantly marginalised by the development of modern law. The truly technical aspect of the law, the one that forms the subject of legal debates, is therefore generally absent. In order to really talk about the films they watch and not look for legal categories in which they do not exist, cine-jurists are forced to distance themselves from their technical preoccupations.

In the end, if we look closely, the trial and the other legal elements in the films are never more than part of the setting, a medium used to portray human passions that go much deeper than the law. In this way, cinema shows, without a doubt, that the law is to be found just about everywhere, but it also shows that the law is never at the heart of the question. It seems to be merely a gateway, a means of access to the truly important issues. Latour describes the superficiality of the law well:

> If [law] holds everything, if it makes it possible to link all people and all acts, . . . it is also because it extracts only a tiny part of their essence from all situations. Its fabric resembles that of delicately knitted lace. This is what common sense retains of its movement when it qualifies it as cold, formal, meticulous, abstract, empty. Indeed, empty it should be! It is wary of fullness, of any ballast that would slow it down, make it heavy, prevent it from linking up what it retains of the world, via its own course. It can go everywhere and make everything coherent provided that it drops almost everything. . . .
>
> Appearances are everything, the content is nothing. . . . In another case, where the judges had banned a film that had caused a scandal, the press immediately loosed its fury against a shameful act of censorship in a free country! But the judges had simply reaffirmed that one could not simultaneously say that a film consisted of a continuous sequence of shockingly violent scenes, and ban it only for people under the age of sixteen, without the Ministry having extended its powers ultra vires. Nothing else; nothing strong; nothing true; nothing sensational; nothing sentimental; nothing even fundamentally right: a reminder of a simple principle of non-contradiction, fragile and soft, always to be taken up again and reinterpreted, which prohibits, "in terms of the current laws", too much incoherence in the scattered actions of human beings – Ministries included. Nothing but surface, nothing but filaments.[15]

15 Latour (n 9) 264–66.

The law does not hide in every nook and cranny of reality; it merely covers it with a superficial film. That is why filmmakers care little about it. The law is opposed in all points to what is shown in cinema: the strong, the sensational, the sentimental, and that which passes for the very expression of the living. To my knowledge, there is only one film that shows pure law, Guy Debord's *Hurlement en Faveur de Sade*.[16] This work could be seen as a metaphor for law. When you read the film's title, you expect to see violence, morally equivocal situations, the sort of thing that first-year students might think they would find in their lectures. Then, as you enter the work, you see a completely white screen and, over it, a voice reciting a few sentences, most of which come from the civil code:

> Article 115. If a person has ceased to appear at their place of residence and nothing has been heard about them for four years, interested parties may petition the civil court to officially recognize the absence of said person.
>
> . . .
>
> Article 516. Property is either real or personal.
>
> . . .
>
> Article 488. The age of adulthood is 21 years; a person of that age is capable of all acts of civil life.
>
> . . .
>
> Article 1793. When an architect or contractor contracts with a landowner to construct a building in accordance with an agreed plan and for a specified payment, they cannot demand any increase in that payment on any grounds, whether because of an increase in the work force or materials or because of any changes or additions made to the plan, unless such changes, additions or increases have been authorised in writing and the new payment has been agreed to by the landowner.[17]

These abstruse words, floating in the void and replacing the scandalous images promised by the title, perfectly illustrate Bruno Latour's passage. Technical law, the pure law that only lawyers know and that ensures their intellectual prestige, is an empty form. It leaves out the colours of the world and has only a loose and ethereal link with reality.

A lawyer might retort: "You're taking the easy way out by making fun of the law, its technicalities and its codes! Filmmakers obviously do not dwell on legal technique. But the law is not just about technique, and all lawyers know that. The core of our profession is to ensure that films continue to show the human side of the law. That is the purpose of a cinema club for lawyers:

16 *Hurlement En Faveur de Sade* (Directed by Guy Debord 1952).

17 Guy Debord and Ken Knabb, *Complete Cinematic Works: Scripts, Stills, Documents* (AK Press 2003).

to show the law alive, in action, with its human passions and social issues. Cine-jurists are right not to limit themselves to technical issues when they debate, because doing the law right always means going beyond the law".

A new argument. A new hypothesis. Watching films allows us to see real law, the law in action, and familiarises lawyers with the real problems of the law, which are not to be found in codes and court rulings.

Hypothesis 3: Cinema Shows Life

The idea that film provides a privileged means of access to social reality and broadens the perspectives of jurists seems to underlie a part of the work in law and cinema.[18] In the introduction to a collection of articles on law and the family, Marie-Anne Frison-Roche explicitly states:

> If the law is increasingly concerned with the concrete and particular lives of people living in society, in a more sociological conception of the law, and if the cinema . . . recreates society and lets us into a thousand lives, then lawyers have something to learn from it.[19]

So lawyers watch films to see reality. It seems solid enough. It accounts for the fact that studies in the field emerged from a legal tradition, the American tradition, on which realism has had a lasting effect. It also explains the nature of the discussions in the law and cinema club.

But isn't such a statement paradoxical? Why use the cinema to observe reality? If the law is concerned with reality, why should its clerks have to look at it through this spyglass? And to which reality does cinema provide access? The everyday one, as Marie-Anne Frison-Roche suggests? The lawyer is an individual like any other, constantly immersed in reality. Are we to believe that social space is so fragmented that we have to reconstruct its image through the mirror of our cinematic experiences and are forced to project ourselves into a thousand lives? Surely the increasingly refined developments in the division of labour make this idea credible.

Marie-Anne Frison-Roche also seems to assert that the cinema gives access to the reality of the law since she cites a good number of films that depict it. But aren't lawyers supposed to know the reality of the law better than anyone else and better than a filmmaker? Do doctors have to watch *Scrubs*[20] to learn how to treat patients? Lawyers have surely become shortsighted because of their hyperspecialisation. It may also be that the pure law of the textbook, studied

18 See Louis Hill in this volume.

19 Marie-Anne Frison-Roche, 'Introduction' in Estelle Epinous and Magalie Flores-Lonjou (eds), *La famille au cinéma: Regards juridiques et esthétiques* (Mare & Martin 2016) 24.

20 *Scrubs* (2001–2010) 182 episodes.

by the student and put in order by the academic, is intrinsically alien to the law of practical life. Yet this separation is integral to law. The state can only appear as a separate body, distinct from civil society, if its official language is detached from actual social practice and creates a pseudo-world of its own.

We are changing our tone and vocabulary. We need to go further in this direction. Our answer to the first question raises another: Why is it that the lawyer looks for reality within the cinema? Or, to use Marie-Anne Frison-Roche's description, that "cinema is life"?[21] What if we added, "But this life and this cinema are equally paltry, which is why it hardly matters if one is substituted for the other"?[22] The question inevitably leads us to situationist ideas. Debord talks a lot about cinema and little about law. However, "At the root of the spectacle lies that oldest of all social divisions of labour, the specialization of *power*",[23] and "the social cleavage that the spectacle expresses is inseparable from the modern State, which, as the product of the social division of labour and the organ of class rule, is the general form of all social division".[24]

On this basis, we can construct a final hypothesis: jurists, the hyperspecialised agents of modern society, look to the cinema for an opening into social reality because their ossification into a specific function has obscured their immediate experience of the world and deprived them of any capacity for a general understanding of social relations. In the present conditions, "it is thus the most earthbound aspects of life that have become the most impenetrable and rarefied",[25] and only cinema seems capable of bringing together what social practice has separated.

There is enough here to develop a more general discourse on law and cinema by drawing on Guy Debord. Let's see where it takes us. Our last experiment.

Law as Spectacle and Representation

1

The modern mode of production is the affirmation of separation as the dominant social relationship. Incessant competition, the extreme specialisation

21 Frison-Roche (n 18) 22.

22 Debord and Knabb (n 16).

23 Guy Debord and Donald Nicholson-Smith, *The Society of the Spectacle* (Zone Books 1994) 18 <http://ebookcentral.proquest.com/lib/sciences-po/detail.action?docID=6280130> accessed 10 October 2023.

24 Guy Debord and Donald Nicholson-Smith, *The Society of the Spectacle* (Zone Books 1994) 18 <http://ebookcentral.proquest.com/lib/sciences-po/detail.action?docID=6280130> accessed 10 October 2023.

25 Guy Debord and Donald Nicholson-Smith, *The Society of the Spectacle* (Zone Books 1994) 18 <http://ebookcentral.proquest.com/lib/sciences-po/detail.action?docID=6280130> accessed 10 October 18.

of tasks, the proliferation of autonomous social spheres, and the growing individuation of cultural products have dissolved the possibility of authentic communication. Against the concrete backdrop of cities, there are now only spectres, separated from each other by the loss of any common language, a loss that forbids them the slightest dialogue, and their encounters, fortuitous and precarious, express nothing but mutual indifference. "In chancc situations we meet separated people moving randomly".[26]

2

Separation is the true product of a society of spectacle and commodities. It is rooted in commodity fetishism, which is its secret foundation.

3

In the society of myth, individual consciousness is not socially limited, and its boundaries extend to the very borders of the social world, but the low level of development of the productive forces themselves keeps society within the narrow boundaries drawn by nature. All the events of social life reach everyone's consciousness, and this common reference is the basis of the possibility of authentic communication, an appropriate language in which life senses life. Yet the authenticity of the social relationship implies a mystified relationship with the world and with nature. Since the events of social life incorporate only a tiny fraction of natural phenomena, nature appears in its pure exteriority and crystallises the images of false consciousness. Man projects his phantasmatic production onto the screen of nature, where monsters and spirits come to life, and subjectively submits to the myth because he is objectively subject to nature.

4

Historical development is nothing more than the transition from the fetishism of nature to the fetishism of society. With the invention of classes and of the state, part of the social world becomes alien to itself and posits itself as pure exteriority. The state, which has become alien to social reality, itself becomes the object of false consciousness and misguided gaze. Kings are deified, and a pantheon of anthropomorphic gods is imagined above the spirits of nature. This first split dissolves the common language of myth-based societies. The state forges its own language and its own symbols, numbers, and letters, which themselves end up becoming the objects of false consciousness. The sign, having become directly visible as a sign, becomes autonomous and

26 Debord and Knabb (n 16).

can detach itself from the immediate experience of the world. Seeing the sign unfold in isolation and no longer able to attach it to its real reference, the mystified eye invents a fictitious reference, an objectivity of its own, into which it projects its phantasmagoria, as it did with nature. This is the origin of the mysticism of numbers found in India and Greece.

5

Law is inseparable from writing. Before the emergence of writing and of the state, we see, at most, habits of behaviour, value judgments, punishments, and violence. Law, as a distinct order of reality, as a separate pseudo-world, does not exist. Just as the mathematician comes to believe in the existence of a hidden reality underlying the symbols they manipulate, the legal scholar postulates that the law reveals a higher order. At the same time, the law, as a real instrument of bureaucratic class domination, actually subjects reality to its unreal order. The law is, in fact, produced, and lived reality is materially invaded by the law. The legal order thus prefigures the spectacle.

6

Ancient societies were still based on a limited productive base, which is why the fetishism of the state did not replace the fetishism of nature but developed alongside it. With the emergence of capitalism, technical mastery made it possible to deploy social fetishism, which penetrated the whole of reality. In a mercantile society, the autonomous order of signs subjugates the whole world. Progress in the division of labour makes any unitary experience of reality impossible, and human beings can only penetrate it through a labyrinth of symbols, the walls of which maintain this distance between each individual and everyone else and give *a priori* direction to existences.

7

The social world has been completely subjugated to nature, but the individual now sees only a tiny part of the social world. Human activities, whether of production or consumption, appear as private activities, alien to each other. They are pooled by means of abstract signs – prices, contracts, laws – and can only coexist if they are mediated by these signs. Signs are the threads that integrate separate activities into a social whole, but for the individual consciousness, they have become the only social reality. Deprived of any immediate access to reality, individuals are unable to see beyond the signs that manifest it. In the false consciousness of antiquity, the separate order of reality that we thought we could detect beneath the signs conflicted with the immediate experience of reality, which had not yet been dissolved. This conflict was expressed in the opposition between the intelligible and the sensible, the celestial and the terrestrial, the divine and the human. Now that the sight of partial signs constitutes the only experience of the totality – i.e. of truth – the pseudo-world constructed by signs becomes the only effective reality.

8

The sign no longer refers to reality, which has become inaccessible; it is the referent to which people relate their actual practice. The sign no longer signifies lived reality; lived reality signifies the sign.

9

The two orders of symbols that have governed the practice of mercantile society from the outset – prices and legal categories – are matched by two castes that angrily preserve the purity of their respective pseudo-worlds and would like to compel all social forces to join their battle. For the economist, price stability is the only legitimate social goal, the only one that can be pursued by political means. For the jurist, it is legal certainty. These two fragmentary objectives – fragmentary even from the point of view of the society of spectacle and commodities – express the same false consciousness. The economist and the jurist, because they identify all reality with the social signs for which they are responsible, believe they are preserving real experience by preserving the authenticity of signs. But the sign, deprived of reference, acquires its authenticity through pure equality with itself. Formal coherence thus becomes the categorical imperative of spectacle-mercantile reason, to which the entire social world submits.

10

As social symbols become real, they themselves take on the appearance of reality. Form gives way to sensitive content and the written word to the filmed image.

11

The development of capitalism is the concrete becoming of social signs. This is how the different forms of capitalism have evolved: legal-mercantile capitalism, commodity capitalism, spectacle-bureaucratic capitalism, spectacle-reticular capitalism.

12

In the early days of capitalism, the process of dissolution of social life was a continuation of the ancient split between society and the state. As the state extended its influence, it became the mediator of social life and gradually abolished the social bodies that were foreign to it, such as corporations, guilds, and manors. Civil society was emptied of its social dimension and became the playground of the selfish while the state emerged as the social institution par excellence.

> The establishment of the political state and the dissolution of civil society into independent individuals – whose relation with one another depend on law, just as the relations of men in the system of estates and guilds depended on privilege – is accomplished by one and the same act.

The state always concentrates the abused gaze of false consciousness, and ideology is expressed in political and legal form. Class struggles are political struggles; social demands are rights; every social theory is, at the same time, a theory of the rational state. Bourgeois revolutions synthesise all of this.

13

Sovereignty is the first concept in political theory. It brings together ancient and modern ideologies of the state. Ancient ideology emphasised the separate nature of the state in order to affirm its existence as an autonomous social sphere. It is a theory of separate power, and this is also how the first theories of sovereignty are presented. But as the pseudo-world of the state unfolds within social reality, to the point of replacing it, the theory of sovereignty becomes, at the same time, a theory of society. The process culminates in bourgeois democratic ideology, in which the state explicitly asserts that it has become the social world. Rousseau, who identified the will of the state with the will of its citizens and admitted nothing between the individual and the state, revealed the truth of the modern state, which has only broken the separation between the state and social life by suppressing social life, which has built its power on the separation of individuals from one another.

14

In this first phase of capitalism, which lasted until the end of the 18th century, law was the general social symbol that ensured the cohesion of the social whole. It founded state power through sovereignty and penetrated social life through laws. At the same time, law is the very expression of the dissolution of civil society and the withdrawal of the separate individual into themselves. The legal form is based entirely on the trial: in other words, on conflict, opposing interests, and egoism. The legal relationship as a social relationship presupposes separation.

15

The rise of the market was accompanied by the rise of the modern state. But between the 16th and 18th centuries, the market did not acquire its own autonomy. Rather, it was the instrument of the mercantilist state, and its theoretical place was within political philosophy and the philosophy of law. However, the modern model of separation, in which the pseudo-world replaces social reality, contradicts the legal form, which penetrates it too superficially. Law bears the imprint of its ancient origins and is, in essence, based on the ideology of separate power. Commodities, on the other hand, once they have multiplied sufficiently, spread to every corner of material life and can mediate all forms of behaviour. From the 19th century on, the market became the dominant pseudo-world and the principle of separation between people. It was the triumph of commodity fetishism.

16

The commodification of the world is, at the same time, the commodification of writing. Like all other commodities, cultural products invaded social space, which became entirely saturated with signs. The press, which, via its regular publication, ensured a steady stream of income and, for this reason, represents the commodity form of writing, experienced its golden age. The time devoted to reading increased considerably, and the sign became part of the immediate experience. At the same time, because writing had become part of everyday life, it now described as everyday life. Signs still exist only as abstract symbols, but they already formulated a content that is much closer to immediate sensible reality, so the pseudo-world in which false consciousness objectifies itself descended from the celestial clouds to dwell among men. Philosophical writing, which still bore the marks of the rarity of the written word and its separation from lived experience, fell into disuse and was replaced by journalistic writing. A new literary genre, the novel, based precisely on a profusion of sensory descriptions, became the art of the masses. But the new aspirations of the press and the novel soon came into conflict with their written form. The need for a direct view of the simulated world, which had replaced the lived world, demanded the creation of a technique capable of directly recording the sensible world. At the same time, the incessant rearrangement of sentences and words brought about by the proliferation of texts made the formal dimension of writing all too apparent. Literature began to wallow in experimentation and decompose. In every intellectual sphere – law, economics, philosophy, the sciences – people began to criticise formalism. The time was ripe. It was not a technique but a society that created cinema.

17

The techniques of image capture gave birth to spectacle capitalism, which was in gestation. As at every stage of the capitalist dialectic, the previous forms are not suppressed but overcome. The sovereign state, bourgeois democracy, the law, the market, and the press are preserved and become the conditions of possibility for a new social relationship based on the image.

18

In spectacle capitalism, the image has replaced the abstract symbol as the fragmentary expression of reality and the expression of fragmentary reality. The pseudo-world, which was sought in the ordering of written signs, becomes directly perceptible and can assert itself, all the more so since it is the effective real. The splitting of the world no longer manifests itself in the opposition of the intelligible and the sensible, for it is the sensible world itself that is now split.

19

The spectators, definitively separated from the social totality, are no longer attached to it except through the contemplation of the prevailing images. Blind and completely alienated from each other, they find in these images the few crumbs of social reality that enable them to orient themselves awkwardly in life and maintain an ersatz form of communication with each other, their lives having become too poor and partial to provide them with any maxim of action.

20

All the social spheres that had become autonomous in earlier forms of capitalism – the press, the economy, the law – were materialised in images, which became the regulators of practice, relegating the old abstract symbols to the background. Audiences no longer read novels and newspapers; they watch films and television programmes. They no longer base their choices on prices but on the representations of opulence they find in advertisements; they no longer fear laws but surveillance cameras. Images have become the building blocks of separate pseudo-worlds, and the law now exists as much through cinematic representations of crime and justice as through codes and rulings. This is why lawyers scrutinise the films that depict them. They know that they owe the aura with which they are still graced and which ensures their social power to images.

21

The flow of images reconstitutes a unity from the pseudo-worlds that had become detached from the course of life. Spectacle capitalism thus first appears as a resurrection of the society of myth in fascism and Nazism. But the unification achieved in the flow of images in no way eliminates the division of labour, the separation between citizen and state, between spectator and screen, and is therefore itself the by-product of separation. The myth is not reconstituted, and the centralisation of images simply makes the bureaucratic centralisation of power that it presupposes more visible. Thus begins the era of spectacle-bureaucratic capitalism, characteristic of the 20th century.

22

The concentration of social power in images gives rulers hope that they will be able to control the whole of social practice. By taking control of images, they want to take control of society. The first forms of cinematic communication mimicked the bureaucratic relationship. At the cinema and on television, isolated spectators were unilaterally subjected to a standardised discourse to which they were unable to respond. But the exponential increase in the number of images generated by the spectacle soon revealed the narrowness of these distribution channels and gave rise to new ones all the time. At the end of the 20th century and the beginning of the 21st, screens had become sufficiently individualised to do away with spectacle-bureaucratic capitalism as such and make way for spectacle-reticular capitalism.

23

Spectacle-reticular capitalism retains the essential elements of spectacle-bureaucratic capitalism, and all the previous analyses remain generally valid. It differs, however, in two respects: one quantitative, the other qualitative. From a quantitative point of view, images have multiplied so much that they have taken over the whole of our time. Cinema and television still drew a line between individual existence lived in the physical world and social existence lived through images, a line that no longer exists today. From a qualitative point of view, the specialisation of images put an end to the collective practices they mediated. When viewers watched the same screen, the same films, the same soap operas, virtual socialisation standardised viewers' real-life practices. We borrowed our clothes, hairstyles, and dance steps from the same stars, and a community of references maintained the illusion of a common language. This illusion is dead, and the process of personalisation has swept away the last remnants of social life, which is no longer even simulated.

24

All communication is abolished. Images suffice.

25

Studying court rulings and sitting in a dark movie theatre are part of the same attraction for things that are outdated. Law and cinema, the relics of earlier forms of capitalism, show us the last traces of simulated communication, which are still just the shadow of authentic communication.

Reference List

Comizi d'amore (Directed by Pier Paolo Pasolini, Carlotta Films 1964)

Debord G and Knabb K, *Complete Cinematic Works: Scripts, Stills, Documents* (AK Press 2003)

Debord G and Nicholson-Smith D, *The Society of the Spectacle* (Zone Books 1994) <http://ebookcentral.proquest.com/lib/sciences-po/detail.action?docID=6280130> accessed 10 October 2023

Defferrard F, *La pensée juridique de Sheldon Cooper: Ou comment faire du droit avec the Big Bang Theory* (Mare & Martin 2019)

Frison-Roche M-A, 'Introduction' in E Epinous and M Flores-Lonjou (eds), *La famille au cinéma: Regards juridiques et esthétiques* (Mare & Martin 2016)

Giraudoux J, *Tiger at the Gates* (C Fry tr, 2nd Paperback edn., repr, Methuen 1971)

Hurlement En Faveur de Sade (Directed by Guy Debord, 1952)

Latour B, *The Making of Law: An Ethnography of the Conseil d'Etat* (Polity 2010)

Le Pluard Q, Marion T and Marguénaud J-P, 'Bambi' in *Du droit dans Disney : [Actes de la VIe journée d'études des doctorants juristes de l'Université de Bretagne Occidentale et de l'Université de Bretagne Sud, le 22 mars 2019]* (Mare & Martin 2020)

Le Pluard Q, Marion T and Urvoas J-J, 'Ouverture' in *Du droit dans Disney: [Actes de la VIe journée d'études des doctorants juristes de l'Université de Bretagne Occidentale et de l'Université de Bretagne Sud, le 22 mars 2019]* (Mare & Martin 2020)

Le Pluard Q and Talbot M, 'Quelques mots d'introduction' in Q Le Pluard and M Talbot (eds), *Du droit dans Disney: [Actes de la VIe journée d'études des doctorants juristes de l'Université de Bretagne Occidentale et de l'Université de Bretagne Sud, le 22 mars 2019]* (Mare & Martin 2020)

Ost F, *Si le droit m'était conté* (Dalloz 2019)

Ost F, *Nouveaux contes juridiques* (Dalloz 2021)

The Swimmer (Directed by Franck Perry, Columbia Pictures 1968)

Index

Made in the USA
Las Vegas, NV
19 September 2026

1c576198-a79a-4913-b05e-2a38a4d9dda0R01